D0987463

Spirituality and Human Nature

SUNY Series in Religious Studies
Harold Coward, Editor

Spirituality
and
Human Nature

✸ ✸ ✸

Donald Evans

State University of New York Press

BL
624
.E93
1993

Published by
State University of New York Press, Albany

© 1993 State University of New York

All rights reserved

Printed in the United States of America

No part of this book may be used or reproduced
in any manner whatsoever without written permission
except in the case of brief quotations embodied in
critical articles and reviews.

For information, address State University of New York
Press, State University Plaza, Albany, N.Y., 12246

Production by Marilyn P. Semerad
Marketing by Fran Keneston

Library of Congress Cataloging in Publication Data

Evans, Donald, 1927-
    Spirituality and human nature / Donald Evans.
        p.   cm. — (SUNY Series in religious studies)
    Includes index.
    ISBN 0-7914-1279-2 (hard). — ISBN 0-7914-1280-6 (pbk.)
    1. Spirituality.   2. Psychology, Religious.   I. Series.
BL624.E93   1993
291.4—dc20   91–44693
                                                                    CIP

10 9 8 7 6 5 4 3 2 1

JESUIT - KRAUSS - McCORMICK - LIBRARY
1100 EAST 55th STREET
CHICAGO, ILLINOIS 60615

Contents

✳

Section 4. Spirituality and Religion

Preface

"That prof going by on his bike is the one who teaches the weird courses." The remark came from a student lined up to register for courses at Victoria College, University of Toronto, where I teach. Probably the student was referring mainly to Philosophy of Mysticism, with its optional weekly workshop on the basics of meditation. But she may also have been referring to courses on human sexuality, existentialism, and the origins of good and evil in human beings, all of which include elements of spirituality, though they deal mainly with other dimensions of human nature.

These courses, like this book, are deviant not only because they include spirituality, but also because I propose a controversial conception of spirituality. In our culture, most people who write about spirituality focus on the underlying motivation and orientation we bring to whatever we experience or do. I agree with this focus, but I insist that spirituality also includes becoming aware of spiritual presences and spiritual energies, as it did for our "primitive" ancestors. It is true that spirituality involves a process of personal transformation of one's underlying motivation and orientation, but a crucial part of this process is a growing openness to spirit. And the process culminates in a mystical awareness of the soul as that which unifies the whole self (body, passions, mind and spirit) at the metaphorical place where one is united with the mysterious Source of all that exists. On the basis of my own experience I am convinced that spirit and soul are real. I cannot prove their reality, nor can I refute the skeptics who claim that spirit and soul are obviously unreal. I can, however, show that such skeptical certainty depends on blind acceptance of questionable dogmas concerning how reality claims must be substantiated. Since these dogmas pervade contemporary academic life, my approach may understandably seem "weird."

Another reason why the student spoke of "weird" courses may have been that I present ideas concerning human nature from the avowed perspective of a humanistic mystic, drawing on my own experience of various dimensions of human nature, and inviting students to articulate their own perspective and draw on their experience. This is not all that goes on, for the courses are conventionally philosophical in their emphasis on developing skills in conceptual analysis, whatever the subject matter. During my five years of graduate work at Oxford, doing analytic philosophy, I became quite good at this, and I always hope that some of this will "rub off" on my students. The courses are also conventionally academic in the sense that we do almost all of our thinking in dialogue with various thinkers (though not mainly with other philosophers, I must confess). What is unusual in the academic classroom is that sometimes our reflections are primarily reflections on our own experience. Beyond this, in the first three chapters of this book what I present is almost entirely a series of reflections on my own experiences in psychotherapy and meditation. In the next three chapters, however, the tone is largely impersonal, for I use reason to chart some of the limits of reason.

Another disconcerting feature of my thinking in the classroom and in this book is that much of it is not fashionably postmodern, or even modern, but premodern. Although I share in much of the postmodern emphasis on how our varying perspectives shape whatever we experience, I do insist that we can to some extent experience reality directly. Everything is not in the eye of the beholder. And although I concede to modernism and the Enlightenment that the intersubjective agreement made possible by impersonal reason in science and in ethics is important, I hold that an impersonal approach blinds us to what is most important, and I cite the premodern insight that "only the real can see the Real." Another way in which I am premodern is in venturing toward a tentative overview of human nature in all its dimensions, rather than confining myself to an increasingly detailed investigation of some particular facet of human nature. This involves the danger of merely coming to know less and less about more and more, but it is an important alternative to current trends in the humanities and sciences, which involve knowing more and more about less and less. Although I respect specialized, minute analysis in philosophy, I propose that some of us return to a premodern view of philosophy as comprehensive synthesis. Such a synthesis may be realizable only at some eschatological End, but we can make our own tentative contributions toward it, in dialogue with others. So I invite others not only to criticize the movement toward a synthesis that begins to emerge in this book, but also to propose one of their own.

A Preface is an occasion to provide, as I have, some background concerning the kind of thinking that led to the writing of a particular book. It is also an occasion to acknowledge those who helped in the process. So I first want to thank various publishers for their professional courtesy in granting permission to include revised versions of some work which has previously appeared in print:

- The University of Ottawa Press, Ottawa: A much briefer version of Chapter I was published in M. Faghfoury, ed., *Analytic Philosophy of Religion in Canada*, 1982, with the title, "Towards a Philosophy of Openness." A version of Chapter VIII was published in Theodore Gaeretz, ed., *University of Ottawa Quarterly* 55, No. 4, 1985 (proceedings of a conference in honor of Paul Riceour), with the title, "On the Nature and Origin of Good and Evil in Human Beings".
- University of Calgary Press, Calgary: a version of Chapter VII was published in Hugo Meynell, ed., *Religion and Irreligion*, 1985, with the title "A Mystical Humanist Perspective on Religion and Morality."
- Canadian Buddhist-Christian Dialogue, Toronto: a version of Chapter IX was published in Stanley Fefferman, ed. *Awakened Heart*, 1985, with the title, "Christian Spirituality and Social Action."

- Trinity Press, Burlington, Ontario: A version of Chapter X was published in Wesley Cragg, ed., *Challenging the Conventional—Essays in Honour of Ed Newbery,* 1989, with the title, "Christian Openness to Other Faiths."
- Oxford University Press, Oxford: A version of Chapter XI was published in L. D. Hurst and N. T. Wright eds., *The Glory of Christ in the New Testament,* 1987 (studies in Christology in memory of George Caird), with the title "Academic Scepticism, Spiritual Reality and Transfiguration."

I am very grateful to various individuals who provided very helpful criticisms of ideas in this book. They are of course not responsible for my continuing to advocate views which, in most instances, they do not accept. I think of Jim Brown, Brad Abernethy, Harold Coward, Stanley Fefferman, Peter Hess, Darlene Juschka, John McDargh, Giles Milhaven, William Nicholls, Kai Nielsen, Austin Repath, Jack Stevenson, Valerie Schweitzer, Jeffrey Wattles, Richard Weisman, and two anonymous readers for SUNY Press.

Special thanks go to June Hewitt, who with great patience and professionalism typed the manuscript through many revisions.

Finally, I wish to express my deep gratitude to my wife, Frances Smith Evans. Although some of the book was in early drafts before I met her, what I now regard as its deeper insights arose out of our life together.

Introduction

The word *spirituality* can have a great many different meanings.[1] What I mean can best be approached by a route that begins with an everyday reflection concerning one's own motives and then enlists depth psychology to uncover motives that have been unconscious. Suppose that I ask myself, "When I offered my seat to the old man on the subway train did I do this *in the right spirit*?" Such a question is an invitation to examine my motivation: "Was I being genuinely altruistic or was I showing off to my companion, or even to myself?" If I go on to probe my motivation in many other actions and if I draw on depth psychology to bring into consciousness various repressed emotions and desires that have been at work, deeper and deeper levels of motivation are revealed. At the bottom, depth psychotherapy uncovers the most fundamental motive, which influences all my emotions and desires and pervades all that I do. This is narcissism, a self-centered preoccupation with my own comparative status and power. In order to detect narcissism, however, I must have had some experience of its opposite, which is love. Indeed, love sometimes seems to be at least a part of our motivation. Sometimes we genuinely care about someone else, appreciating them or aiding them in a way which is to some extent not self-centered.

Issues of spirituality, however, include a deeper dimension than the psychology of motivation. Let us examine again the question, "Did I act in the *right spirit*?" We saw that "spirit" can be a metaphor for motive, but we can also interpret it quite literally as a reference to a spiritual energy or even a spiritual entity which is animating my action from within myself. In most human cultures, other than our own rationalistic-scientific one, many people have been aware of themselves not only as being and having a body but also as being and having a spirit and as being influenced by spiritual energies and spiritual presences which can help or hinder us in our quest for happiness. Indeed,the Greek word for *happiness* was *eudaimonia*, which originally meant "having a good demon or spirit." In most cultures other than our own, people have realized that some discarnate spirits could, by dwelling within us, help us not only in our quest for happiness but also in a deeper way. They could transform our conception of happiness or blessedness by helping us to open up to loving and radiant spiritual energies which can animate our lives. In our own culture most religious believers share a spiritless world-view with their atheistic or agnostic neighbors. Although the believers affirm the reality of *God*, few now affirm the reality of a spiritual realm that can be discerned as a dimension of themselves and of all that arises from God. Like their secular neighbors, most believers do not experience "angels and archangels and all the company of heaven" or even their own spirits. But this narcissism on a spiritual plane, separating ourselves spiritually from everyone and everything (whether embodied or disembodied or angelic) is most unacknowledged and undetected in our culture.

So a second element in spirituality, going beyond issues of psychological motivation, is a transformative process by which we stop resisting the reality of spirit. This process is accessible to people of many different religious and secular perspectives. I will call it *spiritualism*, though we will eventually see that it includes much more than that term usually suggests, for our spirit is interdependent with our bodies and our emotions and even with the body politic. The process of spiritualism enables us to uncover our "spiritual unconscious" with its repressed life energies, just as depth psychology enables us to uncover our "emotional unconscious" with its repressed desires and passions.

Depth psychology needs the resources that spiritualism provides. For example, depth psychology can reveal that love is an attitude of caring, commitment, and receptivity combined with a desire for both psychical and emotional intimacy, but through spiritual disciplines such as yoga meditation and spiritual healing we can come to see that love is also a way of being open to a channeling of *loving life energies* to another person. Moreover, this very channeling helps to dissolve some of the psychological obstacles to love that depth psychology uncovers. Our fear and rage and self-pity and possessiveness are not easily discarded by a sheer act of will, even when they have been uncovered from the emotional unconscious in a process of psychotherapy. And our self-centered preoccupation with our comparative status and power is even less easily discarded once it is uncovered; egoistic efforts to get rid of egoism are an exercise in futility. A participation in loving life energies, however, provides an alternative way of being in the world in which our psychological "dark side" can gradually be dissolved or transformed. This does not happen, however, unless the dark side is fully faced, so depth psychology and spiritualism need to work together.

Spirituality, however, has a third and deeper dimension, a mystical core. This is not an awareness of new contents of consciousness, whether psychological or spiritualistic, but a new way of being conscious of *any* contents, whether new or old. Through depth psychology I realize that narcissism is a fundamental *motive* I bring to whatever I *do*, but through mysticism I realize that narcissism is a fundamental *way of being conscious* I bring to whatever I *experience*. Narcissism is not only a secret impetus for action, it is also a hidden recoil from the divine Source of everyone and everything. Insofar as I actively, though unconsciously, separate myself from that divine Source, I separate myself from all that arises from that Source, so my motivation is bound to be self-centered. In order to be aware of narcissism in this mystical way, however, I must have at least glimpsed its mystical opposite: a letting go of my narcissism so that I am lived by the Source in all that I do and all that I experience. This contrast between self-separation and self-surrender is a contrast between two fundamental ways of being and of being conscious in the world. *This contrast is the essential core of spirituality.*

Spirituality consists primarily of a basic transformative process in which we uncover and let go of our narcissism so as to surrender into the Mystery out of which everything continually arises. In so far as such a surrender occurs, the Mystery lives as us without our resistance, and we are the Mystery expressed in human form. Mystics testify that the Mystery is unconditional Love, unlimited Compassion. A true mystic *is* this Love and Compassion, expressed in his or her whole humanity. The path *toward* this divine-human way of being presupposes a commitment to right conduct and begins with a depth-psychological exploration of "right spirit" in the sense of right motivation, for only as our motivation arises from our more generous human impulses do we become more open to being lived by the Mystery as Love and Compassion, which is the essence of spirituality.

Our motivation becomes more loving, however, insofar as we open up in a spiritualistic way to loving energies and loving presences which help us to transform the dark side of our emotional unconscious. And spiritualism is even more directly related to our ultimate surrender into the Source. In most cultures other than our own, people have realized that some discarnate spirits could, by dwelling within us, help us in our release from narcissism into the ultimate Mystery. In our own nominally Christian culture, however, many Christians share with atheists a world-view in which it is no longer intelligible that a human being could be inhabited by the risen Jesus Christ and thereby enabled to share in Jesus' surrender into God so as to be lived by God. This book is a direct challenge to such a world-view.

The first three chapters were written as direct reflections on my own experience: depth-psychological, spiritualistic, and mystical. There is a minimum of explicit dialogue with other writers. Hence my style is less academic than it is in some later chapters, and the genre of philosophy is what Kierkegaard called "edifying discourses." You, the reader, are invited to probe your own repressed motives, your own repressed contacts with spiritual reality and your own repressed origination in the divine Source.

Chapter I interweaves psychological and spiritualistic approaches so as to provide a much more detailed and concrete account of the many species of "closedness" (narcissism) in contrast with various kinds of "openness" (loving participation). I also show how our movements toward greater psychological openness and spiritual openness can lead to a mystical openness, a surrender into the Source.

Chapter II also begins with depth psychology and moves on through spiritualism to mysticism. We reflect together psychologically concerning how love for others and love for self are similar and interdependent, having contrasted both loves with the self-inflation of Narcissus and the self-deflation of Echo in the Greek myth. Then we consider how both loves can arise out of a common participation in loving life energies, either receiving these into ourselves or channeling these to others. Eventually such a participation in spiritual energies can be transformed into a mystical identification with the source of spiritual energies and of ourselves and of everyone and everything. The Source is Love, not separated from anyone or anything.

Chapter III, which focuses on human sexuality, is an example of another element in spirituality which here becomes very explicit: the inclusion of *all* dimensions of the self in the self that is surrendered into the Source. Not only myself as spirit is to be released into Love, but also myself as passion and myself as body. Moreover, if the whole self is involved in this, we need to understand and experience the interconnections between the various dimensions of the self. If the whole self is to be surrendered into the Source so as to be lived by the Source, the best setting to learn this, surprisingly, is sexual intercourse. If our approach is narrowly spiritual we are refusing to let the Source live through the whole of our humanity, which is passionate and embodied. In Chapters I and II we did include our passions, but once we focus on sex it becomes clear that we must also include our bodies. Indeed, we naturally begin our experience of sex as a bodily desire and only then do we go on to uncover the intrinsic emotional and spiritual dimensions of sex. Such an uncovering involves an *art*, for neither the emotional unconscious nor the spiritual unconscious are accessible by techniques alone. So in Chapter III, I include a discussion of the art of de-repression, beginning with the art of psychotherapy as it is usually practiced in relation to emotion, and then extending the art to include spirit. Finally, I refer once again to the mystical art of surrendering the whole self, body, emotion, and spirit, into the Source which lives us in all that we do—including sexual intercourse.

In the first three chapters I assume without argument that spiritual energies and spiritual presences are real. In the next three chapters I respond to skeptics who deny the reality of spirit. In my response I do not try to persuade skeptics to accept what I believe. Rather, I note that much skepticism depends on three unquestioned assumptions, prevalent in academia, that dogmatically rule out in advance any possibility that spirit could be real. Then I show these presuppositions are open to question, and that if they are set aside the context for discussion changes. It becomes intelligible that a reflective person could base truth claims concerning the spiritual on personal experience and that others might come to think, "Maybe there's something in it."

The first presupposition, *impersonalism*, is the dogmatic rejection of any truth claim that requires personal transformation to be adequately understood and appraised. The only possible truth is truth that can be known impersonally, through pure reason. Allegedly the only reality is whatever can be established through methods of investigation that anyone who has intelligence and training can learn. These methods may belong to science or philosophy or law, or to some other academic discipline, but they are all impersonal. Anyone's investigation of a truth claim can be replicated by someone else, regardless of differences in values, attitudes, life orientation, fundamental motivations, self-understanding, or basic way of being in the world. An impersonalist dismisses any truth claim that allegedly requires a process of personal transformation for adequate understanding and appropriate testing.

To many people impersonalism seems obviously true. It is not self-evident, however, for it is merely an assumption.

And not only does it constrict reality, it also distorts reality. When one uses only impersonal pure reason one has detached one's intellect from the rest of the self and refused to explore any of the ways in which that intellect is self-deceived as it represses awareness of other human dimensions, such as spirit, passion, freedom, and communal interdependence. Any exploration of a dimension that we have self-deceptively repressed requires a process of personal transformation, which impersonalism rules out. It is true that pure reason, as it appears in science, law, and some research within the humanities, can contribute much to human life. In our everyday functioning together it is important that *some* truths can be established for all of us impersonally, regardless of any differences in our attitudes, character, values, or personal experience. But imperialistic claims by pure reason to have jurisdiction over all the territory of human life must be resisted. Most of our human dimensions can be adequately uncovered only if we undergo a difficult process of personal change in which our self-deceptive repression of the dimension is challenged. This is especially obvious in the case of our spiritual dimension.

The second presupposition, *perspectivalism*, is the dogmatic rejection of any truth claim based on direct experience of reality; all we can study are the various human perspectives that human beings bring *to* an alleged reality, not the reality itself.

Perspectivalism as a dogma is the exaggeration of a genuine insight to the point of absurdity. The insight is that we human beings experience everything *through* a variety of perspectives, and that if we are to arrive at truth we must become aware of how these perspectives both distort and illuminate. The insight with which perspectivalism begins applies to all our knowing of things or people or spirits. The absurd dogma with which it ends is the conviction that we can never know reality itself, that we can know only the perspectives which we bring *to* reality, the various frameworks of language which shape our experience, and the various factors which shape those frameworks.

The absurdity of the dogma is threefold. First, even as we make truth claims concerning the perspectives and their origins we are assuming that we can somehow know that these are real, and that we do not merely have meta-perspectives on these perspectives, and so on in infinite regress. If we can know the reality of perspectives, why not the reality of things or people or spirits? Second, we can originally detect distortions caused by perspectives in our attempts to discern realities only if we can *contrast* such causes with veridical experiences. The reasons given in support of the universal skepticism of the skeptic presuppose that we *can* already sometimes know what is really "out there." Third, the universal skepticism of the dogmatic perspectivalist thwarts all attempts to test truth claims *pragmatically* in terms of the consequences of believing that such-and-such is true. Whatever kinds of consequences are selected to make these tests, one must assume that they are real. Otherwise one has to test truth claims concerning the consequences pragmatically, and there is another infinite regress.

Insofar as perspectivalism is applied to spiritual reality it reduces the "spiritual" to frameworks of concepts and symbols that people bring to the everyday world. There are no spiritual energies or spiritual presences existing independent of human beings, and any claim to base one's belief in spiritual reality on *experience* of spiritual reality is summarily dismissed. In all consistency a thoroughgoing perspectivalist should also dismiss any claim to base one's belief in the reality of a chair by sitting on it, but remnants of such "naive realism" are usually tolerated in relation to *material* realities as contrasted with spiritual realities.

The third presupposition, *positivism*, is a species of impersonalism introduced by Comte and Saint-Simon in the middle of the nineteenth century. Positivism or scientism is the dogmatic rejection of any truth claim that cannot be tested scientifically; scientific method is the only way to knowledge of reality.

Scientific method involves four principles: (1) *isolation* of genuine causal factors by using control groups; (2) *repeatability* of experiments by any trained person so as to establish invariant laws or statistical correlations; (3) *quantifiability* of data; and (4) *plausibility* in relation to a theoretical framework and perhaps also to some nonobservable theoretical entities. When these principles are applied to *paranormal* claims, only a small minority of such claims can be investigated: a psychic must be able, at will and repeatedly, to discern or produce a statistically significant number of publicly observable events. This requirement rules out most paranormal claims, for psychic abilities often elude control by the will, or are manifested in a person only occasionally, or pertain directly to energies or entities that are not publicly observable. At most, as in some statistical studies of apparent healing of mice by a psychic healer, psychic energies may be postulated as nonobservable theoretical entities that might explain what has happened. A psychic, however, can directly experience such energies, which are for him not merely postulates but realities. Sometimes, however, a psychic discerns a publicly observable event in a paranormal way, and this raises different issues. For example, someone may clairvoyantly "see" a relative's death occurring many miles away. I will show that, if the vision is very detailed, one is being quite rational in believing that it did not happen merely by chance, even though such a conviction is not open to scientific verification.

In Chapter VI, I contrast psychic experiences with genuinely spiritual experiences. The latter occur only when a person is committed to a particular process of personal transformation. This process involves a deepening receptivity to whatever spiritual realities help one to let go of a self-centered preoccupation with power and status and help one to become more expansively loving. As one is enabled to let go of narcissism there is a deepening surrender into spiritual energies and presences that are unconditionally loving, and this gradually facilitates a surrender into the Source of all that exists.

There are two reasons for contrasting the paranormal and the genuinely spiritual. First, we should realize that whereas the paranormal is to a limited extent open to scientific investigation, the genuinely spiritual is not. I say this in spite of the fact that some people attach much weight to the compatibility or incompatibility of the metaphysics suggested by scientific *theories* with the metaphysics implied by the genuinely spiritual. This is not a decisive consideration, however, for *the meaning of spiritual claims is closely linked with their appropriate method of verification*, which is not scientific speculation but participation in a spiritual process. A second reason for contrasting the paranormal and the genuinely spiritual is that our spiritual dimension includes both, and they are often intermingled and confused. The differences between them, and the relations between them, need to be clarified if both are to find their proper place in a complete humanity. On the one hand, a preoccupation with the paranormal can be a dangerous obstacle to genuine spiritual growth. On the other hand, for some people in our culture, paranormal experience can be a valuable entrance way into a genuine spiritual path. For example, an experience of the presence of a spirit-guide can help in opening oneself up to transformation by the indwelling presence of Jesus Christ or the Hindu saint Ramana Maharshi.

In response to the skeptical dismissal of psychical and genuinely spiritual truth claims by impersonalists, including positivists, I argue that the meaning of such truth claims is liked with their appropriate method of verification, which is not impersonal. In response to attacks from perspectivalists, I argued that some "naive-realist" insistence on direct experience of realities is plausible and is secretly presupposed by perspectivalism itself. My responses do not amount to a proof of spiritual reality, but they do clear away some intellectual obstacles.

In the third section of the book I turn from issues of epistemology or theory of knowledge to consider the implications of spirituality for *ethics*: both ethics of doing and ethics of being. Ethics of doing tries to answer the question, "What ought I to *do?*" In Chapter VII I ask whether spirituality provides any distinctive bases or directions for answering this question. Ethics of being tries to answer the question "What ought I to *be?*" which in turn raises questions concerning the nature and origin of good and evil in human beings—the topic of Chapter VIII.

In Chapter VII the mystical humanism of this book is reviewed and applied to ethics of doing. My conception of human nature is "mystical" in that it includes a spiritual dimension in each person and envisages the whole person being lived by the divine Source. It is "humanistic" in that it includes, and builds on, much of what is advocated by secular humanists. Since our moral judgments concerning what we ought to do are based on our conceptions of human nature, the addition of a spiritual dimension and a surrender to the divine Source both reinforces and revises our morality. I readily agree with secular humanists, however, that a workable minimal morality does not have to include a spiritual dimension in its basis and does not have to be derived from statements about God. Indeed, I contrast the God of much conventional religion with God as known by the mystics, and I agree with many of the secular-humanist criticisms of conventional religion made by Kai Nielsen, whose philosophy is presented and considered in the chapter. He and others provide a perceptive moral critique of most religions. On the other hand, the rise of secular humanism in the last 200 years has been deplorable in its hostility to spiritual experience. Indeed, a fully adequate morality *is* dependent on religion *as spirituality*, for only a recognition of each human being as *spirit* and a participation in Spirit can enable us to love unconditionally, and only a surrender in the divine Source eliminates the fundamental narcissism which separates each of us from everyone and everything.

In Chapter VIII, I investigate the most fundamental issue that confronts anyone who seeks wisdom concerning human life: the origin and nature of good and evil in human beings. Spirituality provides distinctive insights concerning this issue, but it raises very difficult questions. Having uncovered narcissism as self-preoccupied motivation, as resistance to loving energies, and as recoil from the divine Source which lives us, we must ask whether some degree of narcissism is inevitable, as an ineradicable tendency in human nature. Or can narcissism, in principle, not only be reduced but actually eliminated on some spiritual paths? Are we caught up in a tragically inescapable conflict between good and evil inclinations? Or is this apparent conflict only the self-deceptive product of a narcissism that can eventually be completely surrendered into God? Is there a basic human paradox exemplified in an existentialist who somehow unites, in constant conflict, two inherently opposed human tendencies? Or is there a very different basic human paradox exemplified in incarnation, each of us being both the divine Source and a particular expression of that Source? My own *hope* is for full incarnation, but the human obstacles are clearly formidable, for in addition to the narcissism of individuals there is a great deal of institutionalized evil.

In the fourth section of the book, having explored spirituality in relation to depth psychology, to skepticism, and to issues of good and evil, I relate spirituality to *religion.* Since my own religious background and central convictions are Christian, I present three issues for Christians. The issues, however, arise in analogous ways for people of other faiths. Indeed, this book arose initially as a series of reflections on a personal spiritual process in which I drew mainly on *non-*Christian resources: depth psychology, Hindu meditative yoga, spiritualism, Buddhist meditation, and Da Free John, a contemporary spiritual master. In each case there was something that I needed to learn, and in each case as a philosopher I was interested in "mapping" the journey. What I present is sufficiently *compatible* with Christian spiritual traditions for me to write in an explicitly Christian way in Section 4. What I propose, however, is both a return to Christian faith and a revision of Christian faith. The return is to a Christian confidence in the reality of the spiritual that existed before it was radically undermined, first by the impersonalism of the Enlightenment and now by the perspectivalism of postmodernist thought. The revision is in response to the spiritual depths of other faiths.

Both concerns are evident in Chapter IX, which originated as a presentation at a gathering for dialogue between Christians and Buddhists. The particular issue posed, how to link spirituality to social action, picks up a concern about institutionalized evil that arose incidentally in Chapter VIII. In my approach I draw on a mystical emphasis from Section 1, where I said that the *whole* self is to be surrendered into the divine Source to be lived by the Source, and that this whole self includes not only spirit but also body and emotion. In Chapter IX I go on to stress that the whole self also includes the *"body politic "*to which each of us belongs. This expression is appropriate because human society is like an organism in the way it connects us with other human beings institutionally. Social action is needed because many of the institutional power structures are unjust and oppressive. If we are to be lived by the Source in all dimensions of our humanity, we must be involved in action to reduce institutionalized evil.

In Chapter X, I continue to focus on issues arising in interfaith dialogue, but my question is posed to Christians: "How can Christians be open to other faiths while remaining loyal to the uniqueness of Jesus Christ?" This is a central issue for contemporary Christian spirituality. It is not an issue for people in other traditions. As I try to shed some light on it, however, I distinguish between alternative spiritualities that are also found in other traditions. I also suggest how a pooling of perspectives can be a creative response not only to religious pluralism but also to other divergent convictions concerning what it means to be human.

In Chapter XI, entitled "Spiritual Reality, Academic Skepticism, and Transfiguration," I return to the perspectivalist dogma that leads most modern people, whether religious or nonreligious, to regard all claims concerning spiritual reality as sheer superstition. In particular, perspectivalism radically distorts a modern Christian's understanding of scripture. I take as an example the story of Jesus' transfiguration. Since I am not a fundamentalist I do not rule out the possibility of some error in the account. I am confident, however, that human beings and the cosmos have a spiritual dimension, so I do not dismiss or psychologize all the spiritual elements in the story. But this is what most spiritually skeptical Christian scholars do, thereby losing most of the point of the story. In contrast with this, a spiritually open reader of scripture can see in this story the possibility of sharing in Jesus' transfiguration, identifying with him as he surrenders into the radiant Source of everyone and everything.

As you read this book I ask you to keep in mind its common theme, which is the presentation of a controversial conception of spirituality. This conception is considered in a series of diverse contexts: depth psychotherapy, academic skepticism, secular-humanist ethics, tragic existentialism, social action, interfaith dialogue, and Christian interpretation of scripture. Since the most concrete and detailed account of spirituality is in Section 1, you are advised to read it first. Some readers who like the concrete reflections of Section 1 may decide to jump to Section 4, but I suggest that you give Section 2 a try. Although it is somewhat more abstract it is completely accessible to nonphilosophers. Only later, in a few pages of Chapter VII, will the general reader perhaps encounter a little difficulty.

So begin with the "edifying discourses" of Section 1!

Section 1

Spirituality and Depth Psychology

I *** On Being Open and Closed

Some people are very open. Their faces shine with a light that radiates out from some hidden source within themselves. Their hearts, filled with warmth and well-being, overflow in a generous expansiveness, a spontaneous sharing of an inner abundance. From them a flame of life flashes forth, igniting new life in others. They care passionately about people, rejoicing in the creativity and the happiness of others, grieving over their tragedies and their self-betrayals. Their words and actions issue directly from an intense center of powerful passion. They love life.

Such people do exist. It is difficult to acknowledge this. Even if we allow ourselves to become aware of them we tend to find fault, for we feel envious. Since their very existence reminds us of the extent to which we are missing out on life, we cannot bear to see them as they are. If someone attempts to describe them we are likely to dismiss him cynically as a mere sentimentalist. Or, alternatively, we see the radiant people but elevate them to a distant pedestal that is unattainable by us and therefore not tantalizing.

Sometimes, however, we can see them realistically, as an invitation and challenge to new hope for our own lives. This is more likely to happen if we realize two things: they can give so much only because they are open to receive, and they have become open because they have acknowledged and dealt with whatever makes them closed. Their abundance is not a private possession or a proud achievement but rather the outcome of an openness to life energies available to all of us. And their openness is not just a natural endowment, but depends on an ongoing process of uncovering, and letting go of, the ways in which they have been closed to life. Indeed, as they persist in the process, ever-deeper layers of closedness emerge to resist the growth in openness. As one gets to know them, it becomes obvious that they are not always open, always radiant. Their human nature is the same as ours. They differ from us only in degree, not in kind.

All of us are both open and closed. We have inbuilt tendencies toward participation in life and defensive structures that keep us imprisoned within ourselves. The issue is whether the closed stance or the open stance will be dominant in our lives. It is true that some people start by being less closed than others, but for almost everyone there is a possibility of gradual change toward greater openness. Since each stance affects everything we say and do and feel, the choice is of momentous importance. But since the process is only partially conscious, many of the most profound decisions in our lives are made without our being more than dimly aware of them. This chapter is an attempt to become more aware of the process, bringing it more fully into the light of consciousness and understanding, available for free decision. It is not a matter of doing an inventory of one's life, listing its various contents so as to decide what is dispensable, what needs changing, and what is missing. The decision has to do with basic attitudes that pervade everything one does and thinks and feels—all the contents of one's life, whatever they are.

People differ considerably in the extent to which they are closed; that is, self-centered and self-preoccupied. In some the stance is minimal, but in others it is very blatant and extreme. There is a joke about a narcissist who talked about himself for two hours and then stopped to say, "I'm sorry, I've talked too much about me. Let's talk about you for a change. What do you think of me?" Usually, however, closedness is less obvious. Many social conventions help us to conceal it from ourselves. Sometimes it is even successfully disguised as altruism. Yet it is often fairly easy to detect in others. In the presence of a self-preoccupied person, even if she is charming and outwardly interested in me, I feel that I do not matter in myself, but only in my significance for her.

Self-centeredness is very difficult to see in oneself. The operations of my self-centeredness are mostly unconscious, and they are manifested in behavior which to others may seem self-centered but to me may seem quite natural, especially if I am not clearly aware of what it feels like to be open. A person who is not aware of any language other than English is not aware that he talks and thinks in English. Similarly if I am not aware of an alternative to a closed-up life I do not realize how constricted my present existence is. Moreover, I have a great deal invested in continuing a self-centered existence and in not becoming aware of its alternative, for self-centeredness is an unconscious strategy for psychic survival. It is a second-best mode of existence that I adopted early in my life because it seemed better than having no existence. Any challenge to this desperate compromise is alarming. So in general the more self-centered we are, the less we are aware of it. This means that if we are to uncover the ways in which we close ourselves off from participation in life, we need considerable courage and honesty, as well as a vision of what that participative life would be.

For some people an additional obstacle is the religious teaching to which they have been subjected. Often religion justifiably attacks one form of closedness, namely pride or self-inflation, but goes on to confuse and constrict human life by praising another form, a so-called humility that is really self-humiliation, a self-deflating submission that is still preoccupied with issues of comparative power and status. To make matters worse, religion often reinforces our tendency to regard any personal shortcoming as a justification for self-punishment, so the discovery of self-centeredness becomes an occasion for destructive, paralyzing self-recrimination. It is possible, however, to struggle in more creative ways toward greater personal honesty and openness. And, as we shall see, there are religious conceptions that can express and reinforce a stance of openness to abundant life.

At this point I should say something about the intellectual origins of this chapter. In 1970 I began an earlier work, *Struggle and Fulfilment*,[1] which was supposed to deal with religion and morality. At first I considered beliefs: religious beliefs concerning the attributes of God and moral beliefs concerning how we ought to behave. But as I became convinced that matters of belief are secondary in both religion and morality I began to study the attitudes on which the beliefs depend. These attitudes are pervasive stances of the whole personality which shape our responses to the universe as a whole and to each particular in it. As I investigated some of the most important attitudes, for example, basic trust, I gradually came to realize that they are both religious and moral. They are religious in that they are stances toward whatever unifying reality pervades our whole environment. They are moral in that they are virtues which radically influence the way we deal with other people. I also came to realize that they are "ego-strengths" that are crucial in the process of psychotherapy, and that they are constituents of human fulfilment. So it became clear that religion and morality and therapy can converge in stances which are central in human life as such. Openness is such a stance.

In *Struggle and Fulfilment*, however, the focus was on trust and the pervasive attitude of distrust that is its opposite. I described the struggle between these two as I experienced it in my own life and in the lives of others and as it is illuminated by religious and moral traditions. So the book arose not only from a new view of the inner dynamics of religion and morality but also from a process of personal struggle and change. When I finished it I planned to write some sequels, for the book contained brief sketches of various other struggles that are important in human life, and these sketches invited further expansion. I decided to begin with a book that would focus on issues concerning power and status. After a while I began to realize that in people generally, and me in particular, a preoccupation with comparative power and status is a central feature of a radically pervasive stance which I was only just beginning to recognize and acknowledge: closedness. Insofar as we are closed, we are preoccupied with whether we stand over or under others in power and status, and we alternate between self-inflation and self-deflation. Insofar as we are open, we can transcend this self-centered syndrome so as to share non-competitively with others in life energies that are common to all. Gradually I came to see that the closed person differs from the open person in an additional way. She is preoccupied with how she stands or falls in comparison with others because she is out of touch with what is vital for herself. Insofar as I am closed I lack a love for life—not only life within others but also life within myself. I not only cannot get outside of myself; I cannot really get inside myself. This realization came as a shock, though fortunately I am also sometimes open. The investigation of what it means to be "closed" or "open" turned out to be not only a theoretical inquiry but also a personal challenge.

The contrast between closed and open stances can be described in many different ways. Religious thinkers contrast "sin" and "faith" or "pride" and "humility"; moral philosophers contrast "vice" and "virtue" or "egoism" and "benevolence"; psychoanalysts contrast "narcissism" and "object-libido"; existentialists contrast "I-It" and "I-Thou"; metaphysicians contrast "alienation" and "participation"; contemplatives contrast "the egocentric life" and "the divine birth in the soul." I do not claim that these contrasts are all the same. Rather, I draw on elements in each of them as I write about "closed" and "open" stances. I shall write in a language that can be related to each of these different ways of thinking and that draws on insights from each of them, but that is less technical and more directly experiential.

There is a problem in the presentation. To explain what it means to be closed one must at the same time explain what it means to be open, and vice versa, for each is understood to a great extent as the opposite of the other. But each stance has its own characteristics quite apart from the contrast with its opposite. So I will paint pictures of each on its own as well as alongside the other. The overall picture will emerge only gradually as I proceed.

The most crucial characteristic of openness is difficult to describe. I call it participation in life energies. The most basic and primitive way in which this is experienced is as a physical sensation. Since some people have not had a clear contact with this, I will make a practical suggestion, although this chapter is not a "how-to-do-it" manual. It is possible to induce a brief and superficial physical awareness of life energies as vibration in a very simple way, which provided my own first clear experience of it. Rub the palms of your hands together vigorously for about five minutes with your eyes closed. Separate your hands about five inches and then bring them closer together, without touching. Move them apart again, varying the distance between them, concentrating on the space between them. Probably you will experience energy, in a quite tangible way, pulling and pulsating between your hands. A similar experience can occur, without any rubbing, in yoga-breathing meditation, though the energy will usually feel less "gross" and more "delicate." And during various disciplines such as zazen or bioenergetics or kundalini yoga there are experiences of energy "streaming" through the whole body. This happens when tensions and rigidities within the body, which ordinarily impede the flow of energy, are momentarily reduced. "Streaming" sensations also occur in genuine sexual orgasm.

In some people who are largely out of touch with their own bodies the experience of life energy is not physical and tangible in content but "mental" or "psychic" or "spiritual." Their ecstatic experiences of love or creativity or God are virtually disembodied. The physical dimension of participation is both blocked and hidden. Such a mode of contact with life energy is certainly better than none at all. But it is incomplete, just as purely physical contact is. Fortunately, however, there is a way of participation in which both body and mind are involved, for the blocks in both have been reduced. Then the whole personality is pervaded with life energies, and the participation persists rather than being fleeting and fragmented. What is then experienced is both physical (perceived in various locatable parts of the body such as the spine or the heart or the genitals or the fingers) and mental (saturating whatever one is thinking and doing and feeling at the time). Sometimes the physical aspect predominates and is in the forefront of consciousness, sometimes the mental. When both are present the state of elation and exuberance and excitement permeates the whole personality. When this happens, descriptions of participation in physical terms are both literal and metaphorical. John loves "with all his heart" because what he actually feels is a sensation in the physical organ as well as something pervading his consciousness generally. And when Mary feels "inspired," her breathing may well be similar to what occurs when someone does deep yoga breathing to open the body up to life energy, though what she is most conscious of is not the breathing but something mental that has come to her: a new musical composition, or a loving insight concerning how to help a troubled friend, or an experience of ecstatic harmony with nature, or a vision of Christ.

Often the physical dimension of participation in life energies is obscured and not recognized for what it is. Many people who are not radically split off from their bodies have been aware of energies without being clearly conscious of this. They have felt deeply "moved"—perhaps by music or drama or dance—but the vibration-sensations of moving energy have been pushed into the background of consciousness. One reason why the hand-rubbing exercise or various body-involving disciplines are useful is that a clear perception of the vibration-sensations enables us to recognize them later when they are mixed with other elements.

Participation in life energies feels like sailing or whitewater canoeing or body surfing or gliding. (Indeed, these are not merely analogies but also occasions for participation.) During a day of open participation, it is as if wild waves of water or wind invade and invigorate and impel us in all that we do and think and feel. Alert and sensitive to the broad ebb and flow of forces that surround us, in "tune" with the elements, we steer a course of our own. Empowered by forces from beyond ourselves, we enthusiastically expend and expand ourselves. Receptively relaxed and actively involved, eagerly taking in and exuberantly giving out, we rejoice in life.

Life energy is experienced not only within oneself but also outside oneself, in nature. Sometimes as I have gazed at a tree it is transfigured, as if sunlight were not only reflected from its surface but also radiated from deep within it in all directions. I feel an energy coming from the tree and I feel this stimulating my own zest for life. And, still more mysteriously, I feel that my own outpouring of energetic attention seems to be stimulating or intensifying the outpouring from the tree, though there is also a sense that the vision of transfiguration is a way of discerning what is always going on there. Indeed, the whole happening comes as a gift, a blessing, a grace. One is active in it, yet one did not bring it about. One is participating in a flow and exchange of life energies that is going on always and everywhere. According to the witness of very open people, the infrequency of our awareness is due to our own insensibility. They see that although the concentration of life energies varies considerably in intensity from context to context, and especially from person to person (a very closed person deadens life energy within and around him or her), the vision of nature as transfigured is not so much a change in nature as a change in us—like blind persons suddenly seeing.

An encounter with a tree or a flower or a stream is for many people less familiar and intelligible than an encounter with a person. This is often the paradigm experience of participation in life energies. When two people who are very open in both body and mind meet together, life energy radiates out from each one to the other. Each is already "turned on" within and also "turns on" the other still more. Each is a creative catalyst for the other's creativity. Each experiences a rise in the level of life energy. The encounter is not like two people feeding each other, where each person's stock of food is depleted by the other. It is more like a dialogue where each person's words stimulate new ideas in the other and the ideas come as gifts. Neither person is depleted. Each is renewed and refreshed.

The mutual heightening of life energy that occurs in encounters is sometimes even more intense in a group where most or all of the people are open. It is as if the level rises in geometric proportion as additional people join in. The room becomes charged with a life energy that is partly tangible. It swirls around people and within them. It is poured upon them and by them in a lavish and electrifying way. This can happen in many different contexts: a service of worship, a therapy group, a work project, a dance party, a symphonic concert. As I write this I vividly remember occasions of each kind. For example, when Rostropovitch conducted the Toronto Symphony Orchestra in 1977 his charismatic generosity of spirit galvanized both orchestra and audience in an ecstatically life-affirming way.

Sometimes a group can facilitate not only a momentary "lift" but an ongoing "high" as a mode of life. Some communities of people living together and committed to openness enjoy a fairly continuous and lively participation in life energy. This is typically expressed in a generous spirit of sharing and cooperation, giving and receiving in a mutual interdependence that liberates new creativity in each individual and that enables the community to create a physical and personal environment that affirms life. The sense of an abundance of life energy encourages people to be generous rather than self-protective, expansive rather than self-constrictive. The lived-out openness in dealing with one another makes possible a still higher participation in life energies, and this in turn fosters still greater openness to others. Most people require such a community if they are to grow in openness.

Openness to life energies involves openness not only to nature and other people but also to oneself. Each of us in our closedness has a secret yearning for a life that is full and rich and expansive. In most of us this yearning is heavily repressed and held down because such fulfilment has come to seem impossible. So we close down real aspirations and preoccupy ourselves with our comparative power and status. I find that participation in life energies shakes me out of this misguided self-preoccupation. Instead, I begin to enjoy being me. It feels marvelous to be alive as I am now. I can readily accept my limited power and status for I am actually drawing deeply on my capacities for creativity in relation to myself and nature and other people. These capacities become my own unique way of focusing and expressing life energies that I receive, channel, and give back in a new form. At times when I am open I rejoice in being me, and I rejoice in others as they offer their own creative expression of the fundamental gift in which we all share.

Openness brings joy. One feels expansive, happy, loving. Anxiety and despair recede into the background. There is a feeling of fulfilment. But the new cherishing of life in oneself and others brings a new sensitivity to whatever undermines that life. Openness brings a new realization that oppressive life-denying tendencies are at work within oneself and others. Along with joy, openness also brings a sober sense of sin. Along with a hope based on present participation in life energies, openness also brings sadness and indignation—how skimpy and perverse most human life is. Openness brings an acute awareness of just how destructive closedness is when it is dominant.

So we will now turn our attention for a while from openness to closedness. But before we do so I should issue a warning. It is important that as we try to be honest concerning our own closedness, we examine ourselves from a perspective of as much openness as possible. Otherwise the new insights will be merely oppressive, reinforcing our self-preoccupation and self-imprisonment. Later I will describe how one element in closedness is a self-deflation or self-rejection in reaction to the discovery that I am not perfect. This self-rejection is intensified by a scrupulous self-scouring for sins if the context makes openness a remote ideal of perfection. One essential element in openness is acceptance and forgiveness, not only of others, but also of ourselves. This is possible insofar as we receive acceptance and forgiveness into our lives just as we receive the gift of life itself, and insofar as we are resisting our closedness as well as we can at the moment—which may not be very well. In a context of self-acceptance and realistic hope for change, new insights concerning our closedness can be opportunities for growth.

As we look at some of the varieties of closedness we will in each case also consider the corresponding variety of openness. The first contrast is between *closed self-inflation* and *open self-inclusion*.

One manifestation of closedness is a preoccupation with how my power and status compare competitively with the power and status of others. In one extreme form it is a hope or delusion that I am as all-powerful and all-important as God. This fantasy occasionally emerges explicitly into consciousness. I remember an incident I once witnessed in a therapy group. A young man with a long beard had been very withdrawn and self-effacing, always on the periphery of the group. One evening, however, he moved to a chair in the center of the room and as the rest of us sat below him on the floor he revealed his fantasies: "I am God. I look at each of you in turn and I make you disappear and reappear at will. Whatever I imagine and want happens. . . . Now I am alone, the center of the universe. I need no one. I am invulnerable, completely self-sufficient. I am free to become whatever I choose to become. I am all-powerful."

Such megalomania is not a rare psychotic aberration. The young man was not crazy. His daily life would be regarded by most people as "normal," and though he was troubled he was no more troubled than many. Even as he spoke he knew that what he was saying was false. Indeed, he was uncovering a fantasy so that in his daily life he would be less subject to its sly influence. He had become conscious of a secret self-image that is common to us all and that provides an important motive in all our lives. It varies greatly in strength from person to person. In some people it is not dominant and in a few it is firmly subordinated. But in all of us it is at work, though its influence is largely hidden from us. Only gradually and painfully do I become aware of what goes on in my unconscious imagination, where I want to be the center of everything, unlimited in power and status. Instead of being dependent on anything or anyone for my existence and my significance I want somehow to create myself entirely by my own efforts.

The self-inflating fantasy of divinity is usually repressed, but it is manifested in the way we each engage ourselves in various projects. We each want to stand out from others, display a recognizable superiority, make a special imprint on the universe. For example, I sometimes detect in myself and others a form of closedness which can be called *tunnel vision*. In this state, the only thing of importance going on in the world right now is my project, my movement toward achieving the goal I have set ahead for myself—whatever that is at the moment. The projects of other human beings feel like distractions that must be resisted, encroachments on my time and energy. Other people are important only insofar as they contribute (or fail to contribute) to my project. Often the project is not a selfish one; it is intended to bring good not only to me but also to others. But the project is self-centered; the crucial feeling about it is that it is *mine.* It is as if the tunnel down which I gaze were full of mirrors, so that whatever I see at the end is mixed with reflections of myself. Such a stance sometimes brings a concentration and intensity and single mindedness that results in considerable achievement. The price, however, is that one becomes increasingly alone in the world and precarious in one's existence, for any setback to the project constitutes a threat to the significance of life itself. When nothing else matters, nothing else can help.

Sometimes tunnel vision is characteristic of a group. The closedness of individuals is expressed in the closedness of a couple or a family or a commune or a nation. What happens is that one's individual egoism is disguised by being experienced as a group egoism: "*We* are the center of the universe, and *I* am part of this 'we'." Instead of focusing in a tunnel-vision way on *my* project as the most important thing going on in the universe, I identify myself with the group and I focus in the same way on *our* project. No other group or individual really matters. The competitive comparison and conflict is then between *us* and *them.* We are the special people, and they are either utterly insignificant or significant only in relation to us—as a mission field or as our enemies. Such group self-inflation can move a religious community or a nation either to an imperialistic encompassing of the globe or to a protective withdrawal from the contaminations of the world.

Insofar as a person is open, she does not need to narrow her perspective to a tunnel vision, whether this be individual or collective. She can devote herself with great concentration an intensity to a project, feeling that it is immensely important and worthwhile, without thinking that other persons' projects are less so. Comparisons seem irrelevant. Indeed, she can be genuinely encouraging, rejoicing in the progress of others as she does in her own; and she can be supportive in times of failure. She has a special relation to her project in that it is what *she* is committed to and responsible for, but this does not set her apart from others. Such a stance is also possible for a group: "Our project is very significant, and specially significant to us because of our special relation to it, but it is not in itself more significant than those of other groups. If another group whose project is similar to ours is more creative, this is not a humiliation but an inspiration."

How is it possible to have such a strong sense of individual or group zeal without being comparative or competitive? It happens in my own experience when I feel that wherever there is genuine creativity we are all participating in an abundance of life energies that come as a gift. Each individual and each group can respond to this gift in a unique way. What I express is my own personal way of receiving and shaping this gift; it is my own distinctive contribution and self-offering. I can enjoy a sense of being special without being set apart from others, for we receive and exchange and express the same life energies. Instead of depending ultimately only on myself, I am interdependent with others in a shared life. Instead of regarding others as either useful or intrusive, I open myself to give and receive at a deep level. The relation between us becomes crucial to my creativity, and to theirs. Indeed we can consciously try in practical ways to build together a physical-social context that stimulates individual and communal creativity.

Openness brings a broadened vision, a vast vista, for my own projects and my group's projects are ways of expressing a participation in life energies that are given to all humanity and that pervade the whole cosmos. I can participate in something grand: a universal stream of life energy. This vision is not a grandiose fantasy, a self-inflation. It is a self-inclusion. I am not the center of the universe, but only a part of it. Yet as a part I am important. I have my own unique self-offering to make in response to the ongoing outpouring of life, my own melody to contribute to the symphony of life.

For some people such an open vision may seem like a romantic dream, but for me it is sometimes an experienced reality. Often, however, it is blurred by closedness, and sometimes, when tunnel vision takes over, it is obliterated. When this happens life seems heavily serious and I am moved by anxious strivings. Occasionally a sense of humor can outwit this closedness and open me to openness. When I am caught up in closedness I cannot bear having someone laugh at me,[2] but I may be able to laugh at myself. I may manage to see that my tunnel vision is so pretentious as to be ludicrous. I am like a clown suspended by a large helium balloon, performing intently on the tightrope as if I really knew how to do it. When I see this, what matters is how I laugh. I may gently deflate the balloon so as to let myself down gently. When I land I can then stand erect on the earth, affirming myself as a limited being who has been a bit silly but is still worthy of respect. Or I may suddenly and savagely puncture the balloon in a self-shaming, self-sadistic way. Then I plummet to the ground and can only grovel there, painfully shattered. This severe self-deflation is also manifested in someone who chronically mocks himself, constantly putting himself down in his own jokes. For all his attempts at humor, he is still taking himself too seriously, obsessively comparing himself adversely with some inflated figure. It is a different matter to see my self-inflating strivings as an elaborate, pompous game—a comedy of errors posing as a momentous melodrama. But perhaps this perspective on tunnel vision as a funny foible is possible only if one has already had a contrasting experience of participation in real life as a basis for recognizing human dignity. Otherwise the self-mockery is likely to be scornful and cynical rather than affectionate and life affirming.

We make fun of pretentious people in either of these two ways. But some of the harshest ridicule is directed, not at self-inflation, but at *openness.* This is because we tend to *fear* openness. The move from closedness to greater openness is very frightening. Instead of enjoying the relative security of a secretly self-sufficient way of life, I begin to expose to myself and others not only my strengths but also my radical neediness and vulnerability. This feels like a plunge into total dependence. I will be overwhelmed, swamped, engulfed, taken over. This is because insofar as I am closed I feel that if I am not controlling others, I am under their control—and clearly I am not controlling them if I am being receptive to them. Interdependence seems at first like helpless dependency. I am so used to running my own show in isolation that it feels as if pooling my energies with others will result in everything being taken over by others, and then taken away.

One reason for our fear of letting others into our lives is that we project on to them our own inordinate longings. Insofar as I am closed I want so much for myself—the whole world, no less—and I assume that others want this too. Instead of wanting a mutual relation, I want to possess, absorb, and devour, incorporating into myself whatever I can lay my hands on. When I project this craving onto others, it seems as if any opening up to their influence would mean that I would disappear. What could be more terrifying? So I must remain, at some inaccessible level deep within me, independent and aloof. People can penetrate only so far and no further; then they are turned back by my protective armoring. Insofar as I am closed, I *am* my armoring, like a nation whose entire budget is expended on defense. Thus in my fear of dependence I am very dependent, for my life is dictated from outside and I have no really free life of my own. The mighty bastions I construct are monuments to my own vulnerability, and the aggressive excursions I make into an alien world are diversions from my own dread of helplessness.

Insofar as we are closed we tend to swing between two fantasies, both of which prevent us from drawing on the life energies that are freely available and from seeing significance in our finite focusing of these energies. I am either god or infant, all-powerful or powerless, self-sufficient or totally dependent, everything or nothing, full or empty. I am either haughty on a throne or humiliated in a gutter, proudly defiant or cringingly submissive, arrogantly exhibitionistic or shamefacedly shy. I am either adored by all at the center of the universe or scorned (or even worse, ignored) by all in outer darkness. Each extreme stimulates the opposite. If first one feels the vulnerability of an infant, one flees from this by somehow imagining that one is an invulnerable god. But then the awareness that this is a ludicrously unrealizable fantasy sneaks into the back of one's mind, the pretension is pricked, and the self is deflated. But as emptiness and helplessness return to some corner of consciousness one becomes so afraid of littleness and lowliness that one must return to delusions of divine grandeur.

Those alterations, mostly unconscious, are not restricted to people who seem to be obviously "disturbed." The dynamics are powerfully at work in many impressively successful celebrities. It is as if the person unconsciously says to herself, "I'll pretend to be glorious and grandiose so that no one, not even myself, can realize that I am tiny and trivial." But although one may fool others, it is difficult to fool oneself completely. The blurred outline of a humiliating self-image hovers in the background of consciousness where it is like a constant inner critic, mocking all one's attempts to be important. The person's life feels like a hollow stage performance. She acts out various magnificent roles in showy costumes, but all the while she is vaguely aware that underneath it all she is a naked nobody.[3] Others may respect her, but they are merely being taken in by an impressive display, for inside she has an obscure but powerful feeling of insignificance and emptiness. This pervasive sense of inner unreality can prevent her from seeing her own quite genuine achievements with an eye to their real worth, for all her actions seem to be mere play-acting and whatever she produces seems tainted with inauthenticity. Even if she is a creative genius she may be so plagued by self-humiliation that her finest work seems to her to be merely a fraudulent pretense.

Sometimes an artist is so caught up in this secret self-depreciation that she can never finish a painting. Her unconscious reasoning is that she and her work seem worthless, but as long as the painting is still in process it is conceivable that it might turn out to be perfect and thus refute the verdict of worthlessness; and only a perfect picture could do this.

Such an addiction to perfection arises from a fear of total imperfection. In some people, however, the latter fear is dealt with by confronting it in an addiction to degradation. Instead of trying at all costs to avoid being put down, a person knocks himself down. Before anyone can hurl insults at him he insults himself, thus retaining some initiative, though in a perversely self-destructive form.[4] Instead of steering clear of shameful situations, he sets them up. The strain of striving to be a somebody can be eliminated if he gives up and goes on a binge that makes him a nobody. The binge is an alcoholic stupor or some other form of self-inflicted degradation that puts him where in fantasy he already lives: on the periphery of society, scorned or ignored. When he goes on the binge there is at least a feeling of tenuous dignity in that he is the one who is doing himself in. Instead of dreading his drab destiny and perhaps eventually succumbing to it, he is actively concurring in it. Thus self-destructiveness can seem positive. Sometimes even its final form, suicide, can seem comparatively creative. Such is the perverse power of our delusions, not of grandeur, but of shame.

But of course the two delusions are complementary. If one is operative, so is the other, though indirectly and not so prominently. Even when self-deflation seems to swamp the whole personality, as in a masochistic binge, the shame of being small comes partly from the frustration of a secret aspiration to be the greatest, and the sense of worthlessness comes from the reluctant realization that one cannot be perfect. And, conversely, when self-inflation is dominant, the hidden motive is a fear of being a nobody. Thus, for example, a self-inflating tunnel vision may be secretly fueled by a self-deflation concerning one's life project. At a time when I was becoming aware of my own tunnel vision I had a dream in which I was a little boy digging a tunnel in a sandcastle with a spoon, while all around me mighty men were operating giant bulldozers and cranes to erect a skyscraper. No one noticed me in the midst of all this noisy and impressive work. To them it was as if I did not exist.

Although such a self-humiliating way of viewing one's project is obviously the opposite of a grandiose tunnel vision, both stances have two features in common: self-isolation and self-preoccupation concerning comparative status and power. One cannot make these two ways of being closed disappear merely by deciding to eliminate them. Rather, they can gradually be *eroded* as one becomes more open to a flow of abundant life energies that come as a gift and that pervade everyone and everything. Then one's project still matters, but it does so within an inclusive vision in which other people's projects as well as one's own can be appreciated as an interconnected part of a larger, cosmic project.

Religious writers have often stressed the dangers of self-inflation, pride, wilful self-assertion, and so forth but have often ignored the other side of closedness, the shameful self-deflation, the self-humiliating surrender of the will. There is of course a sense in which openness involves a "surrender of the will"—the self-inflating will which tries to control everything. But openness means that such a will is replaced, not by an infantile passivity which is its foil and fuel, but by a stance which transcends both. Openness has two aspects: an active receptivity to life energies that enables us to be nonwilfully creative, and a humble acceptance of our general and individual limitations as human beings. Closedness acts out fantasies of illusory expansiveness and illusory constriction, but openness deals with real expansiveness and real constriction. The open person really is magnificent and flawed, cosmic and frail. The divine treasure is in earthen vessels.

We have seen that one manifestation of self-inflation, of illusory expansiveness, is tunnel vision. Another manifestation is the kind of altruism that is always helping others and never letting others help oneself. So we will now consider *altruism as a form of closedness*, contrasting it eventually—and paradoxically—with a *"solitude" that is necessary for openness*.

One way I can effectively disguise my closedness and hide it from myself is by being altruistic. Sometimes altruism is an expression of openness, but often it is not. The difference depends on whether the real focus of interest is on the people and their needs or on *me* being helpful to them. Sometimes as I am helping someone I notice the self-centered feeling, "What a fine thing *I am doing.*" Fortunately it is possible then to switch my attention. Indeed, such shifts can be a matter of daily discipline in everyday life, not harsh or judgmental toward oneself, but firm. Sometimes no such shifts are needed, for I am continuously present to the other person. At those times being open comes quite naturally and unreflectively. Often, however, I am not even aware of my closedness and so I cannot begin to challenge it. Then I need other people who can detect it and point it out to me. More than that, even when I have become aware of it, I sometimes need a powerful presence from them to stir me out of it.

All this is relatively obvious. "What-a-good-boy-am-I" altruism is self-centered. Other kinds of altruism express closedness in more subtle ways. For example, there are many people who have a life-style in which they alternate between devoted service to others and private self-absorption. The service is typically of a kind that involves taking on a great deal of responsibility for others, whom the server allows to draw on his or her own energies. The server becomes a supportive crutch rather than a spur who stimulates others into activities that draw on their own energies. After a while the server feels drained. Other people's needs or requests seem like insatiable demands. The server feels beleaguered and resentful. It seems necessary to withdraw into privacy, cutting off connections with other people. The energy system then becomes self-enclosed, like a baby sucking its thumb. The inner monologue is, "What matters now is my own feelings, my own needs, not theirs; I cannot give out any more energy; I must conserve it, holding it within myself. My resources are depleted and scarce. Instead of saying 'Yes' to every demand, I will say 'No' for a while." But after a while the person returns to the phase of altruistic service, and the cycle continues.

What needs to be seen here is that the altruistic phase is also a form of closedness. Both phases have a continuing basis: an attempt at *self-sufficiency*. As a helper of others, I do not feel dependent on them. Insofar as I take responsibility for their lives, I prevent them from intruding into mine. In extreme cases, taking responsibility for others becomes an attempt to control them, completely negating their freedom. In less extreme cases, it is a matter of not encouraging them to take their own initiatives. But in all cases I thereby exclude them from real contact with my own life. I remain aloof and independent. Closedness makes me afraid to reveal my own neediness and vulnerability lest I plunge into a state of total dependence. But I can feel secure as the voluntary servant of someone else. I can even devote myself to that person to the extent that he or she becomes for a time the center of the universe. I feel safe because I retain ultimate control of the situation. I can return at will to my own position of inaccessible preeminence, like a "Lady Bountiful" who delivers food hampers among the poor for several days, all the while knowing that she can at any time return to her mansion on top of the hill outside of town. (This is very different from the New Testament idea of divine "kenosis" or self-emptying, where Christ actually relinquishes his power and status, and ends up crucified on a hill outside the town.)

Insofar as I am closed, my altruism moves me to do unto others as I would have them do unto me. I yearn to be loved and cared for, but instead of letting others in on my needs so that they can help me, I help them; then I withdraw so as to cope with my own needs as best I can myself. Even the commandment that I love my neighbor as myself can be understood in this way: help others and then help myself, but do not let others help me. At all costs I must remain self-sufficient, and this means being always a giver (to others, to myself) and never a receiver.

Many people in service professions structure their daily lives in accordance with a pattern of service and withdrawal which expresses an underlying drive for emotional independence. During their work life they serve others and during their private life they recuperate by serving themselves. This pattern can sometimes persist unchallenged for many years. There is some safety in being alone and aloof, and one need not allow oneself to feel the need for a less meager mode of existence. There is an implicit contract with one's clients at work: "I do not expect to receive anything from you and you are not expected to give anything to me." This self-sacrificing way of helping people helps oneself to feel virtuous and worthwhile. Difficulties arise, however, if one tries to treat a spouse or friend or colleague as a client when he or she wants a genuine mutuality of giving and receiving. One's defensive self-distancing is not then so easily hidden in the role-relationship of patron and client. One is being challenged to acknowledge one's own need to receive from others. But then the problem is how to do this without merely reversing roles with the other as distant donor and oneself as passive beneficiary.

An open person deals with neediness—other people's and his own—in a different way. He can be like a good parent to needy people, responding to their voracious emotional and spiritual appetites so as to encourage their own initiative toward a richer life and enable them to find freedom from helpless dependency on himself or others. And when he himself feels needy, as everyone does from time to time, he can receive similar "parenting" from others, for he has uncovered and largely overcome his own fear that any receptivity means helpless dependency and passivity. What this "parenting" means in terms of life energy is that sometimes he is channeling it more toward others and sometimes others are channeling it more towards him. Since he encourages an active participation in life energies by others he is not letting himself be drained, and since he is responsive to similar encouragement from others he is not draining them. Sometimes, of course, he and another person come together when neither is feeling needy, but each is full to overflowing with life energy, pouring it forth on the other. Such giving differs from self-centered altruism in that what one gives is not one's own controlled possession but rather a gift one is continuously receiving. And one receives not so much *from* the other as *via* the other (as well as *via* oneself). As the encounter grows deeper in dynamic intimacy, the distinction between giver and receiver disappears. Both together receive and channel life energy, and both together radiate it in all directions. This is most obvious when two open people are in love and have just made love.

Thus an open person can parent or be parented or meet in full mutuality and communion. Metaphorically speaking he can prime another's pump or respond to another's priming or unite with another to form one living spring. For such encounters to happen he must sometimes participate in life energy when he is not involved in encounters. Otherwise he could not bring an overflow, or at least a responsiveness, to the encounter. Each of us needs to be able to prime our own well, to cultivate a contact with life energies in solitude. This is not like the withdrawal into private self-serving that the closed person devises in his attempt at psychic self-sufficiency. Solitude is privacy for participation. It reinforces a sense of natural and communal interdependence in a cosmos sustained and saturated by life energies. One withdraws from the world to be more deeply and widely present in it.

Participatory solitude has two main forms—the way of expansiveness and the way of inwardness. I have already given some indication of the first way. One starts with a partly physical awareness of life energies within oneself. Sometimes this happens spontaneously, but often it is stimulated by one of the disciplines of expansive solitude: one breathes deeply into the whole body or moves to music or recalls previous occasions when one felt very much alive. Then one's awareness expands outward to respond to things and people as they really are—transfigured. (This can happen even though the people are not physically present.) The outward movement continues until eventually everything is included: a grand vista of cosmic transfiguration, a whole universe teeming with radiant beings. Intense emotions surge up from within the body and flood the consciousness: exuberant happiness, passionate love of life, fervent gratitude to whatever is the marvelously generous source of all this magnificent life. The heart quickens, the whole body throbs with excitement and one wants to shout and sing for joy.

Inwardness is very different. Instead of movement there is stillness and instead of loudness, silence. Instead of passionate participation in the life energies of a transfigured world there is a contemplative contact with a soul center in an inner realm purged of matter, sensation, and thought. Instead of harmony with the outer world and gratitude to the source of its life energy, there is peace at the point of coincidence of the self and its infinite ground. Instead of the end of Beethoven's Choral Symphony, the final chorus of Faure's Requiem.

My own experience of inwardness has been limited and rare. Occasionally there has been a foretaste of it during meditation and once while listening to the Requiem, which expresses and evokes an inward state of calm assurance and blissful serenity. As I listened I felt that the turbulence and anxiety of my life had been temporarily transcended and my longings for mother and for God as limitless comforter had been transformed and satisfied, for I was aware of a silent center of certainty and reality—not as a private resource and resting place, but as an eternal ground which is at the depth of everyone and everything. I have had only fleeting glimpses of this still center, but whenever I do I have a sense of having found what I have been longing for all my life. When I was still a boy I was stirred to tears by a song in a romantic musical, "Ah, sweet mystery of life at last I've found you!" And since then I have always assumed that the mystery would be, as in the musical, another person: and I have also somehow associated it with a god who is out there beyond me in the distance. But the inner reality of inwardness surpasses the most fantastic fulfilment that I have imagined coming to me from outside. It is an awareness of divinity within myself. When it happens I can also discern the same in others. So I can discern in others what I have been longing for because I have already found it within myself. What this inwardness means is that each of us can bring to our encounters an unassailable dignity and a quiet strength. A profound respect for the other replaces a search for someone to satisfy me.

I have had fleeting foretastes of all this, and it does not permeate my life. But some people are very different. They are in fairly constant contact with the point of coincidence between the self and its ultimate ground. Their oneness with the ground of all beings is expressed in a supportive concern for all beings. Their openness to the divine center is lived out in an openness to the divine dimension in everyone and everything. The path to such a state of being is arduous, for it involves not only disciplines of inward attentiveness but also a gradual overcoming of one's self-centeredness, which does not surrender easily. Indeed the very pursuit of inwardness can be twisted by self-centeredness into the most devious and pretentious of all our self-inflating quests for power and status. Self-deception in these matters is easy, for although true inwardness is the enemy of self-centeredness, it can seem paradoxically similar. One moves beyond self-preoccupation by focusing on one's inner self. One moves out of narcissism by gazing at one's inner self mirrored in the depths of the ultimate—or by seeing the ultimate reflected in the depths of one's inner self. One moves toward a realized kinship with all external beings by withdrawing attention from them and turning inward.

The paradox is only apparent, of course. Although I find that I am rooted in the infinite in my own unique way, I find that the same is true of all other finite beings. Although I am in a sense divine, so is everyone else. We all participate in the same reality that grounds and pervades the depths of the whole world. We are all like plants sustained by the same earth. Indeed, our connection is more intimate. We are all like branches of the same tree. We are united with other beings in the most fundamental way possible, without losing our distinctiveness. And we have a special closeness to other beings who, like us, can become *conscious* of our common divine ground.

Inwardness gives us new insight into the origins of self-inflating closedness. Self-inflation is partly a distortion of something that is actually true at every moment in our lives: there *is* a godlike center, a soul, in each of us. We inflate ourselves with fantasies of divinity and because we want to realize this somehow in our lives. Closedness is a perversion of a secret awareness and aspiration. Much as sexual perversions distort a longing for a state of mutual love, closedness distorts a longing for a state in which I discover the infinite ground within myself. And like any perversion, closedness becomes a major obstacle in the path toward its own hidden goal. Insofar as I am closed I have a perverted notion of what it means to be divine. It seems as if I must compete for divinity: either I am the center of the universe and everything else is peripheral or I am not the center of the universe and I am peripheral. I aspire to be divine in contrast with others, excluding them from my own preeminent position. Inwardness, however, reveals a divine reality which is both the center of everything and every thing's individual center. Like the open person who is the closest analogy, the divine reality includes and shares. So my attempt to be "Number One" in the universe is mistaken, but I do have a dignity far beyond any such status. What I see is not a complete illusion, like a mirage in the desert. I have a perverse perspective on something which is really there. I long to possess for myself a gleaming gold crown which I seem to see on a distant hill, but actually I am standing unawares, with everyone else, on streets paved with gold.

This is an inadequate metaphor, for the "gold" of ultimate reality is within us, not outside us. Yet it is within us as the "ground" of our existence. And to become aware of it we need to be physically well grounded, in touch with the life energies within our bodies as these connect us not only with the sun in the sky but also the earth on which we stand. Although in inwardness such awareness recedes into the background of consciousness, it is an indispensable precondition. (Indeed the typical postures for inward meditation encourage a close contact with the earth: slow walking, the lotus, zazen kneeling, etc.) A physically ungrounded inwardness can be twisted into a form of closedness which I call *angelism*: a flight from body and earth to be an unlimited spirit. This is a spiritual self-inflation accompanied by a physical self-deflation. Here I merely note it as a danger which can be largely avoided if the path of inwardness is complemented by the path of expansiveness, with its participation in life energies—especially the physical dimension of this participation.

In presenting a solitude that is open and altruism that is closed I have perhaps gone against certain preconceptions concerning what it means to be "open" and "closed." But openness does involve engaging oneself with other people, and closedness is often more obviously self-centered. This is obvious in the contrast which we will now consider between *open responsiveness* and two forms of *closedness: subjectivism* and *objectivism*.

Subjectivism is a form of closedness in which the world becomes my experience of the world. I am preoccupied and fascinated with my own feelings, so that when I have feelings concerning a person or a sunset or a work of art what matters is not these other realities but my feelings concerning them. If I am religious, subjectivism means that what matters to me is not God but my piety toward God. In general, everything outside of me has significance only in relation to *me*; what concerns me is not this or that reality but *my experience* of it. Even if someone is so important to me that I idolize him, I am engrossed in his importance *to me*. Subjectivizing the world is like incorporating it all into myself, inflating myself so that I expand to the size of the cosmos.

If I subjectivize another person I devour her and drain her. I try to control her in a way similar to the way in which I control my own body and mind—total domination and possession. Others exist, not for themselves, but for me, to confirm my sense of my own central significance and power. I cannot receive real love, but only a dependent, fascinated attraction to me which enables me to control and possess the other. I cannot give real love to anyone, but only an identification with a person whom I can regard as an extension of myself—a child or a disciple. Or I can become fascinated with someone in whom I can see my own mirror image, either because of a real resemblance or because I project my own characteristics on to her. My fascination with her is merely a continuation of my fascination with myself.

Fortunately there are less extreme forms of subjectivism, with which I am more familiar. When these occur, I acknowledge the independent existence of the other person as a separate person, but my absorption in my own feelings prevents accurate empathy. The eminent psychoanalyst, Heinz Kohut[5] notes that the empathy of a narcissistic mother for her infant may be defective in three different ways. Faulty empathy means that she projects and dumps her own moods and tensions on to the infant. Selective empathy means that she responds only to those moods and tensions in the infant that correspond to her own; and she adds hers to his. Blocked empathy means that she simply does not respond to the moods and tensions of the infant because she is so self-absorbed that she does not notice them. These three kinds of defective empathy are not restricted to mothers who subjectivize infants. They are fairly common in human relations generally. The first two involve an identification with the other person in which he becomes me. The identification is of such a kind that although I am preoccupied with my own feelings I do not acknowledge them as my own and take responsibility for them, but put them out there on another person—where they do not exist or where I exaggerate and aggravate what does exist. Then I feel some relief from my own anxieties and the other person feels worse. Genuine empathy is very different, for I acknowledge and distinguish my own feelings and that these feelings are his, as mine are mine. More generally his life is his, though insofar as I subjectivize him I put pressures on him to become me, with my perspectives and values and goals.

Subjectivism is one form of self-inflating closedness. There is another form that is opposite to it and yet closely connected with it: objectivism. This means setting the world at a distance from me, viewing it as a system of external objects. Having detached myself from my feelings, I look out on people and things as a dispassionate observer, a disembodied intellect. I impose a structure on the world so that

I can master it with my mind and manipulate it with my will. As a spectator of life, even my own life, I dwell in a realm where I am safe from any intrusions into my own innerness—even *I* do not intrude. In fantasy, objectivizing the world is like becoming an electronic observatory in a spacecraft flying up to the top edge of the universe so that from there I can peer down on everything with the all-seeing, all-powerful eyes of a divine computer.

The fantasies of subjectivism and objectivism are very different. On the one hand the world is my experience of the world, like a movie projected on to the inside of a cinesphere; the sphere is my consciousness and I am the projector. On the other hand, the world—including my own body and my own experiences—is entirely outside of me and I exist solely as the external onlooker, the imperturbable perceiver and remote controller. But whether I include everything or exclude everything I am like a god in my aloneness, my self-sufficiency, and my domination of the universe. In the one case I dominate by devouring and assimilating into my experience. In the other case I dominate by subjecting to my intellect and will.

The fantasies are of course mostly unconscious. What I am most conscious of is the fact that at times in everyday life I am unable or unwilling to relate to other people in reciprocal encounter. Instead of being open to another person's distinctive reality, allowing this to register deeply within me I see her only in her significance for me. Instead of moving out toward her with my whole self, I fend her off by being reserved and distant. Subjectivism and objectivism are alternative ways of not letting other people into our lives as independent equals with whom I may become interdependent, in dynamic mutual involvement. When such an involvement occurs there is a mutual exchange of energy. Sometimes I can actually experience this not only within my body but also on or near its surfaces. In contrast with this, when I am closed I sometimes feel as if my skin and eyes were covered with a thin film of cellophane so that no energy can escape. This trapped energy moves sluggishly in some parts of my body, or on occasion it feverously agitates me, but it cannot radiate. I am wrapped up in myself. One apt image of this closed energy system (and also one of its origins) is an infant sucking his thumb and refusing to relate to his mother. Another image, literally true in many cases, is a cold countenance. We have all met people whose face gives out no warmth and almost arrogantly proclaims an aloof self-sufficiency, a cool control of self and surroundings. Such people, like Narcissus in the myth that we will consider later, may be mysteriously attractive and fascinating to many others. They seem to have "arrived." Underneath the mask, however, is a desperate fear of emptiness and helplessness and dependency. The face has the facade of a gleaming marble fortress, but inside are meager rations, anxiously hoarded and defended, and a vulnerable power source which may be cut at any time.

Subjectivism and objectivism complement each other. They are alternative strategies that I can use on different occasions when I am closed and seek to ward off people. If one does not work, I can try the other. Some individuals, however, rely almost exclusively on one and others on the other. So we have the types which are sometimes called "Romantic-Dionysian" and "Technological-Apollonian." The contrast between these types has seemed very stark in North America since the 1960s. But few social commentators have noticed the fundamental similarity between the two.[6] Whether the focus is on my own feelings as I assimilate and incorporate John Doe or on my intellect and will as I categorize and manipulate John Doe, the same self-centered power drives are at work and the same resistance to genuine involvement with others.

What is needed is not a mean between the two extremes. It is no use just diluting subjectivism and objectivism with each other, so that devouring is modified by distancing and vice versa. John Doe would still be reduced to a combination of my experiencing of him and my categorizing of him. The subjectivism and objectivism need to be transcended and transformed. What is needed is an encounter with John Doe in which I open up my whole self to him in mutual giving and receiving. Openness changes the two closed stances into a sensitive and realistic *responsiveness*. John Doe stops being merely a screen on which to project my feelings, for he is seen realistically as a distinct and separate person with feelings of his own. Yet my own feelings as I respond to him are important—not primarily as *my* feelings but as my feelings about *him*. Openness means that my "subjective" feelings are no longer self-centered, for they help me to respond to him as he really is and to respond with my whole self. Openness also transforms my self-centered objectivism, for I use my mind to be realistic in my understanding of him, but I do so in a context where I see him not as a distanced object but as a separate other whom I allow to impinge on my whole self. I still have private experience and I still apply categories, but these are subordinate to what happens in the mutual encounter as I respond in openness.

Subjectivism and objectivism are each one-sided self-inflations: of experience and feeling, or of intellect and will. The inflation is deplorable and must be resisted, but that which is inflated and thereby distorted is an essential ingredient in the open self as it enters into encounters with others. Openness to life energies brings an inner abundance that radically reduces the need for any kind of self-inflation, for one is not defending meager rations or a precarious private power source. Within the context of a mutual exchange of energy that comes as a gift, all of one's faculties can be used creatively.

In practice, of course, openness does not permanently overcome closedness. There are breakthroughs, but there are also setbacks. Nevertheless there can be gradual growth. One condition of growth is introspective alertness. I cannot successfully resist my closedness unless I am aware of it, and this involves a private-eye investigation into my own privacy, an uncovering of hidden motives, feelings, and self-images—usually in some process of religious, moral, or psychological self-examination. Eventually, when I am well into openness, I will not be conscious of myself being open, for I will only be conscious of that *to which* I am open. Nevertheless the initial shift toward openness often requires a conscious decision deep within myself. There is then a danger that all this initial introspection may reinforce rather than reduce my own subjectivism. I may become fascinated by my psyche, with its clever strategies of closedness and its (at times) self-conscious strivings toward openness. I may become proud of both my pride and my humility—what fine specimens they are! My inner struggle with all its private intensity may be inflated into being the central happening in the universe.

Some religious, moral, and therapeutic paths encourage this and are rightly criticized for doing so. The critics, however, tend to advocate a swing to altruistic or objectivistic life-styles that are also self-inflating. And they tend to dismiss all introspective paths, not realizing that the best ones advocate an introspective alertness that is acutely aware of the danger of self-inflation through introspection. Nor are these paths apologetic about emphasizing what goes on within each individual. It is true that my personal process is only one of the important things going on in the universe, for other people have their own struggles that are just as important, and the whole universe as perceived in openness is full of transfigured realities. But I am responsible for my own process. Insofar as its outcome depends on anyone it depends on me, not on anyone else. I can refuse to be open. The process, however, is only a means to an end. The end is the actual participation in life that openness makes possible.

A subjectivistic perversion of the process can be partially prevented by a constant encouragement of *extraspection* alongside the introspection. The most effective challenge to one's closedness is often an insistence on what is really going on "out there" rather than a further uncovering of the inner closedness which impedes my attempts to look out there. So as a matter of practical policy it is important to have work therapy alongside primal therapy, group therapy alongside individual therapy, meaningful labor alongside monastic meditation, service to others alongside moral self-probing. Insofar as we are closed we are unable or unwilling to enter into genuinely reciprocal relations with the world. Insofar as we are open we move out of this self-isolation to participate in life. This moving out is partly a matter of behavior, and an accompanying focus of attention outside ourselves. We have seen, however, that closedness as a matter of psychological motivation is not remedied simply by behavior. Unselfish service of others, for example, may have a hidden self-centered motivation.

A preoccupation with uncovering the forms of one's own closedness is, nevertheless, a form of closedness, and some remedy for this needs to be found. Behavior that focuses attention outward can help, but a much better remedy is a focus on life energies, whether these be outside or within oneself. When we experience the loving expansiveness of life energies this provides us with the *contrast* by which we can clearly *discern* the self-enclosing barriers we have built against Life and Love. And with the *help* of life energies we can *discard* the very barriers that impede their flow. This is perhaps the most important experiential discovery that anyone can make through elementary meditation practices. When we breathe light in—or love or healing energies or spirit—we can detect the physical tensions and emotional constrictions and mental rigidities that oppose the flow, and we can breathe these out into the flow, which either carries them away or transforms them into its own likeness. Even rage and terror can be dissolved, or transformed into love, if we let go *into* the love we are experiencing.

Even more deeply, one can learn to let go of one's clinging to *everything*, not only to barriers against life energies, but also to the life energies themselves. In inwardness one sinks downward into the dark mystery of one's soul center, where the self arises out of its infinite ground. For closedness is not only a self-centered psychological motivation and a resistance to spiritual life energies. It is, most fundamentally, a *self-separation from the Source* of all that is, a fear of being lived by God. This closedness as self-separation is detected as one begins to surrender mystically into the Source, and gradually this closedness is discarded as one is lived more and more by the Source in every dimension of oneself.

Most of us are remote from a mystical understanding of closedness as contrasted with mystical openness or surrender. We can begin, nevertheless, where we are, with a commitment to openness as we now understand it, perhaps mostly in psychological terms, enriched by some spiritual experience. When we weaken our closedness on one level—physical and behavioral, psychological, spiritual, or mystical—we weaken it on all the others. What matters is our ongoing opting for openness and our not clinging to any stage of self-understanding until we let go of ourselves completely into God.

II ✳ ✳ ✳ On Loving Oneself Well

Narcissism is to be avoided and self-love is to be cultivated, but often the two are confused. One reason for the confusion is our first impressions of the story of Narcissus.[1] At first it seems to be a simple fable concerning the folly of self-love. Instead of loving anyone else, Narcissus falls in love with himself. So there seem to be only two alternatives: love yourself or love others.

Ovid tells us that, when Narcissus was sixteen, many lads and many girls fell in love with him. He relished the fascination and longing he evoked in them and he toyed with their affections while proudly refusing to let anyone touch him. Thus he remained in control of others. One day he fell in love with his own reflection in the pool, and he spent the rest of his life admiring that image. So narcissism is apparently a self-inflating refusal to love others and a decision to love only oneself.

But the story is not that simple. In the first place, the story of Narcissus is so closely interwoven with the story of a maiden called "Echo" that the two stories are actually one story. Narcissus inflates himself and Echo deflates herself and together they symbolize the two narcissistic tendencies in all of us. If I were interested in coining new words, which I am not, I would suggest that we replace the word *narcissism* by *narcissechoism*. The story of Narcissus and Echo depicts two interconnected ways in which we isolate ourselves from other people, and each way is equally disastrous. Moreover not only Echo but also Narcissus lacks self-love. Instead of loving themselves they are in love with fantasies, and they are caught up in a form of narcissism which is the archenemy of self-love: masochism.

Echo was one of the maidens who fell in love with Narcissus. She had been cursed by the goddess Juno who became enraged by Echo's manipulative chattering. Juno decreed that henceforth Echo could never speak first herself, but could only repeat the last words of what others said. When she tried to embrace Narcissus, he said, "Away with these embraces! I would die before I would have you touch me!" She answered, "I would have you touch me!" but he scorned her, and she hid herself in the woods, wasting away from unrequited love until only her bones were left. When even those bones had turned to stone, only her voice remained, and her life consisted solely of echoing whatever she heard. And that was her only way of relating to other people—echoing their words.

Echo is the ultimate conformist, devoid of initiative toward others, able only to imitate them, finding her whole life in their lives. She longs to be loved, but she is able to bring nothing of herself to a relationship, only a reinforcement of the other by reiteration. And since the way of idolatry leads to a loss of everything individual in oneself, Echo's body wastes away and disappears, leaving only the voice, which is merely a set of sounds mimicking the words of real people expressing real thoughts. Echo is completely controlled by others and eventually she *is* what others say: the ultimate conformist.

Narcissus is the opposite, the epitome of self-inflation and self-sufficiency. He must always be in control. First he is in control of others by having them fall in love with him while being untouched by this love. Then he seems to be in control by falling in love with his image in the pool, for his image is completely dominated by him. His image is a visual echo, imitating absolutely everything he does: a perfectly obedient slave. But there is no real other to whom Narcissus can relate. There is no real love in return from the image, which is like an ungiving mother in this respect. The image also resembles Narcissus himself in his refusal to respond to love from others. Yet the image differs from both an ungiving mother and an aloof Narcissus. It has all the *semblance* of love, all the gestures that express the desired response. Herein lies its special fascination. The response, however, is empty, insubstantial. Narcissus cannot give to himself what must be given by another. But he goes on trying, fascinated by his own image. He cannot allow anyone else to give to him, for such receptivity would mean that he is no longer the self-sufficient center of the universe.

Indeed, what Narcissus craves cannot be given to him by anyone. Like Echo he is not genuinely loving, but "in love." He is in love with himself, and she is in love with him. Each has an ardent, insatiable longing to be filled up by the whole world, like an infant whose every want is immediately satisfied. Each has fallen in love with a fiction that fits this fantastic hope. To Echo the self-sufficient, all-attracting Narcissus seems like a god who could fulfil her wildest dreams. To Narcissus his own image in the pool seems similarly capable of fulfilling his heart's desire. Echo does not love Narcissus, but an image of Narcissus. Narcissus does not love Narcissus, but an image of Narcissus. Before either of them can love a real person, each must renounce the unfulfillable infantile cravings that are involved in "being in love"; and each must initiate some true self-love. If Narcissus really loved himself he would wrench himself away from his obsessive gazing at the image in the pool so as to get on with his own life; that would be at least a beginning. And if Echo really loved herself she would stop letting her body waste away and start lobbying the gods for an opportunity to develop a voice of her own. And Echo could stop pining for Narcissus and get on with her own life.

Instead, each falls into one of the most destructive forms of narcissism: masochism. Each is attracted and ensnarled by the strangely pleasurable pain of being scorned by an unattainable loved one. When Echo's approach to Narcissus was rebuffed, Ovid says, "She concealed herself in the woods, hiding her shamed face in the shelter of the leaves, and ever since that day she dwells in lonely caves. Yet still her love remained firmly rooted in her heart, and was increased by the pain of having been rejected."[2] The masochism of Narcissus took a different form. He endlessly went on trying to kiss the face and to grasp the neck of the image in the pool. Naturally, he became more and more miserable in his self-frustration. If he really wanted to be rid of his agony all he had to do was shift his gaze elsewhere. Instead, he relished his agony, glorying in it and making it an occasion for a self-inflating comparison as he addressed the woods: "You who have lived so many centuries, do you remember anyone, in all your long years, who has pined away as I do? I am in love, and see my loved one, but the form which I see and love, I cannot reach."[3]

Narcissus addressed the woods, indeed, the universe, but his words are not a form of communication. He is really talking only to himself, enjoying the fact that his exquisite self-torture gives him a unique status in his own eyes. Just as he sees only himself, he talks only to himself. Echo, too, says nothing to anyone; she merely repeats what others say. In contrast with Narcissus, she has no status or significance in her own eyes, and her unrequited love expresses and increases her self-deflation. She has nothing to say because she is nothing, though she enjoys the special status of being nothing. So neither the self-inflater nor the self-deflater speaks forth to others. No real communication is possible between them. Each, however, can reinforce the closed state of the other. Narcissus' self-sufficiency reinforces Echo's dependency, and vice versa.

Narcissus and Echo are symbols of extremes that do not exist in pure form, though in some people Narcissus predominates and in others, Echo. In all of us there is a bit of both, for each tendency provides feed and foil for the other. In particular, self-inflation, which people sometimes mistakenly think of as self-love, arises partly from fear of our own tendencies to self-deflation, which is very obviously not self-love. Pride is spurred by fear of shame. Secretly I despise myself, so I try to idolize myself. Secretly I put myself down, so I try to rise higher than others. Secretly I fear dependency and yet feel drawn to it, so I try to be self-sufficient and to control others. Secretly I am partly an Echo, so I try to be a Narcissus.

Or if I am more obviously an Echo, I am secretly a Narcissus. Secretly I want everyone to fall in love with me. When I realize this cannot be, I fall forlornly in love with someone who seems to have such power. Then I feel important by being vicariously identified with my all-powerful beloved. Or, as in the myth, I feel important at least in my anguish, which gains center stage in the cosmos. In the myth of Narcissus and Echo both compete for center stage to present their self-pity as the supreme sign of cosmic injustice. Both cling to the context that gives rise to all the pain, so that they can rage against it rather than turn away from it. This is masochism, the archenemy of healthy self-love. And healthy self-love is the archenemy of masochism.

Mashochism is a subtle combination of self-deflation and self-inflation, the two poles of narcissism. As I explore it more fully my account is drawn both from my own experience and from the illuminating studies by an original psychoanalyst, Edmund Bergler.[4] Narcissism begins with the inevitable rupture in an infant's state of primal unity, bliss, power, and perfection—in very early infancy and perhaps also at birth. When the infant begins to feel to a slight extent distinct from, and separate from, the mother, two mental constructs simultaneously begin to develop: the grandiose self and the grandiose other. Both are idealized, and have a grandiosity that is carried on from the primal state—an unlimited perfection and power and pervasiveness. As a grandiose self, I *am* the world, and all else, including mother, is part of me. As a grandiose other, mother *is* the world, and all else (namely, me) is part of her; as part of her, identified with her, I too am grandiose.

Bergler points out that when the infant's grandiose self is traumatically challenged and the infant suddenly feels powerless instead of all-powerful, the response is furious rage. Instead of mother being a part of himself, to control and possess, she is controlling and possessing him. Indeed, she is refusing and denying him his grandiose self and—before that—the primal unity and bliss. He cannot express his fury to his mother, however. In addition to being the arbitrary depriver, she is still powerful, though now clearly imperfect along with her aura of perfection. Because of his fear he represses his anger, turning it back against himself so as to *constrict* the grandiose self; and he feels some compensating activity or life in doing this, for he is doing something to himself rather than simply being the passive subject of it. His anger at Bad Mother also takes the form of blame and bitterness toward her; a grave injustice has been perpetrated on him. Instead of being everything, he is nothing. Where can he find any enjoyment, any pleasure in all this? He finds it in a self-inflating way: he has a sense of having been singled out for denial and humiliation. God or the cosmos has a special interest in making his life miserable, and this uniquely terrible treatment justifies a secretly pleasurable resentment.

In later life, though the original experiences that precipitated the masochistic pattern have been repressed, he reenacts the pattern, taking the initiative in this because he can thereby unconsciously feel that he is in charge. He creates situations, or misuses situations, so that someone can be seen as Bad Mother, denying him what he wants and needs. And instead of letting himself become conscious of his wish to be rejected, instead of letting himself become conscious of his own initiative in setting up or perpetuating situations of rejection, he is conscious only of self-pity and injustice (how unfair that this should happen to me!). Unconsciously he outwits the punishing conscience (the rage against mother now turned against himself) by unconsciously savoring his resentment concerning his plight. An extreme form of this is Kierkegaard's despairing self, which has pretensions of being an all-powerful, self-creating god, but cannot evade various tormenting reminders of flawed finitude:

"Revolting against the whole of existence, (the self) thinks it has hold of a proof against it, against its goodness. This proof the despairer thinks he himself is, and that is what he wills to be, therefore he wills to be himself, himself with his torment, in order with this torment to protest against the whole of existence."[5]

The pleasures of grandiose resentment are usually unconscious, and masochism cannot be recognized and dealt with until these pleasures become conscious. We strongly resist becoming aware of the fact that we are making ourselves miserable because we enjoy the resentment that we can then feel. The realization comes as a shock. If it occurs while reading one of Bergler's books we can almost hear him saying, "Gotcha!" for he seems to take an almost sadistic pleasure in *exposing* masochism! He is not much help in *replacing* masochism by healthy self-love. Such therapy may stir one to do something about one's masochism, but it is likely to stir up one's neurotic conscience to punish oneself with further self-humiliation: "How could I be so destructive, enjoying being destructive?" Bergler's therapy is in essence a puncturing of the self-inflated "balloon" of grandiosity hidden in one's resentment at not being god. At best he challenges us to live more mindfully and responsibly, not acting out our masochism in daily life. At worst he so radically deflates us that we must find another secret way to inflate ourselves in order to survive psychically. Even at best his approach does not liberate us from the self-centeredness of Narcissus and Echo. Nor can such liberation come from following Freudian advice to let go of masochistic pleasure by *finding more pleasure elsewhere*, though this can sometimes be a step in the right direction, the direction toward participation in Life. Bergler's shock-tactic approach can be helpful initially, but it needs to be supplemented and corrected by psychotherapies that are gentler in dealing with our grandiosity.[6] Later in this chapter I will propose two spiritual ways to replace the masochism of Narcissus and Echo by healthy self-love. The two ways are an openness to cosmic life energy and mystical surrender into the Source.

First, however, we need to get a clearer conception of what healthy self-love would be in everyday life, and why it is important. I will try to show that love for others and love for self are really very similar. I also will try to show that self-love is necessary if we are to give or receive love in our encounters with others. Nobody can come up with a final definition of love, but I will describe six elements in love. The kind of love I have in mind here is love between equals, not love where one party is very dependent on the other, as in the case of the love between parent and child. Love between equals, friendship-love, provides the best analogy for self-love. In my book, *Struggle and Fulfillment*,[7] I set forth six elements in friendship-love. When you think further about friendship-love you may come up with a different list. But here is mine, for your consideration.

Friendship-love first of all involves *confirmation* of the other person. Martin Buber wrote eloquently about this:

> I become aware of him, aware that he is different, essentially different from myself, in the definite, unique way which is peculiar to him, and I accept whom I thus see, so that in full earnestness I can direct what I say to him as the person he is. Perhaps from time to time I must offer strict opposition to his view about the subject of our conversation. But I accept this person, the personal bearer of a conviction, in his definite being out of which his conviction has grown . . . I *affirm* the person I struggle with; I struggle with him as his partner, I *confirm* him.[8]

If I confirm you, you feel firm on the ground, your own ground. As you stand before me, you feel that I am *with* you, *for* you. I am not going to pull the rug from under your feet. I am not going to invade your territory or draw you into mine against your will.

How is this possible? I can only affirm your existence in your own space and your own style if I already affirm my own existence in my own space and my own style. Only if I have a strong sense of who I am can I reinforce your sense of who you are. If I do not feel firm on the ground, if I feel shaky and insecure and threatened, I am likely to try to undermine you. Moreover, if you are not already to some extent confirming yourself, I cannot effectively confirm you. My confirming friendship-love must latch onto some confirming self-love in you to draw it forth or to reinforce it. I cannot create it ex nihilo, out of nothing. If you rely solely on me for your sense of having a basis and a right to exist, I am not confirming you at all; I am merely making you dependent on me.

So I cannot confirm you unless I am confirming myself, and you cannot receive my confirmation unless you are confirming yourself. More generally, I cannot love you unless I love myself and you cannot receive my love into your life unless you love yourself. And these truths apply to all the elements of friendship-love, not just confirmation, as we shall see.

A second element in friendship-love is *confrontation*. Someone who confronts me stands temporarily in my way, challenging me to acknowledge that I am being destructive towards myself or others. She says, in effect, "Before you go on, let me put in a word." She challenges me to be more honest about my motives, more realistic about the consequences of my actions, more faithful to my better self. She does not simply point out a life-denying tendency within me, though she may do that. She also calls on me to draw upon the life-affirming resources within me and around me. She asks me to face my weaknesses as she also sets before me my strengths.

Let us suppose that I am in the midst of a bout of masochism, prickly as a porcupine in my resentment and wallowing like a pig in my self-pity. Not an attractive human specimen at the moment! My friend speaks to me with great concern and respect and forthrightness, pointing out what is going on and calling forth my capacity for love and gratitude. I think to myself, "My God, she cares more about me at this moment than I do myself!" How is such loving confrontation possible? One condition is that she has cared enough about herself to face her own masochism. One exceptionless rule in therapy and life generally is that one cannot lovingly confront someone else about anything unless one has confronted it in oneself. Of course I can attack and condemn a vice in others that I have not honestly dealt with in myself. Indeed, that is the main source of destructive denunciation, self-righteous indignation. But caring confrontation of another person presupposes caring confrontation of oneself: no other-love without self-love.

And I cannot respond positively to confrontation unless I use it as a stimulus to confront myself. Maybe at this moment she cares more about me than I do about myself, but her words must spark my own self-caring or they will have failed in their purpose. So here again self-love is required at both ends of the friendship: in the confronter and in the person being confronted, in the person giving love and in the person receiving it.

A third element in friendship-love is *celebration*. Confirmation, confrontation, celebration—these three; but the greatest of these is celebration. If I look on someone as a close friend, I celebrate his very existence. His unique way of expressing the life and creativity which are given to us all evokes feelings of praise and thanksgiving in me. His breakthroughs toward a life of even greater creativity and happiness are occasions of great rejoicing.

How is such celebration possible? It is impossible if I do not celebrate my own existence, rejoice in my own strengths, feel grateful for my own unique way of expressing the life and creativity given to us all. If I cannot celebrate myself I will envy him. I will resent his light because it accentuates my darkness. At worst I will try to destroy it. Or if I am not envious, I will be a parasite, feeding on his strengths. Instead of appreciating him for his own sake, I will devour him.

But he cannot receive my celebration unless he celebrates himself. If he is chronically putting himself down I cannot get through to him with my celebrative friendship-love. There is a joke of Groucho Marx, taken up by Woody Allen, which goes something like this: "I wouldn't want to be a member of the Club de Rome; I wouldn't want to be in any club that would let in a slob like me." Some people's self-contempt is so strong that they feel contempt for anyone who would be so stupid and self-degraded as to love them. Indeed, if you still need to be convinced that self-love is a good thing, think for a moment about how frustrating it is to try to love someone who lacks self-love. "Only a slob or a fool would love a slob like me"—that is the message one receives. We have to somehow crash through this self-deflating defense and find some spark of self-love to blow on so it can become a cleansing fire.

If a person is caught up in self-*inflation* the resistance to being generously celebrated is more subtle. On the surface, a vain person seems very open to receive praise; endlessly, without limit. Secretly, however, the vain person can not be nourished by any praise, for no amount of it can saturate the inner emptiness that motivates the self-inflation. Celebration by others slides off such a person, as it were, for there is no inner self-celebration for it to reinforce.

It is important to distinguish celebration of a friend's "specialness" from narcissistic attachment to a "special" person. Celebration is an appreciation of the friend for his or her own sake, and it involves a realistic perception of hidden strengths and potentialities. Narcissistic attachment is focused on what the person means for me in fulfilling my own needs and longings, and it involves a projecting of fantasies on the person. When we fall in love and someone becomes very special, gaining an irreplaceable place in our life and heart, there is typically a mixture of celebrative appreciation and narcissistic attachment. Similarly our sense of our *own* specialness is typically a mixture of these two elements. And it is crucial for us to learn to distinguish them, nurturing our celebration of our own existence and letting go of Narcissus and Echo as we uncover them within ourselves. I am special, but so is everyone else. Specialness is not a matter of comparative status and power. My specialness is not truly discerned by seeing myself as "Number One" or as "the worst of sinners." Specialness consists in a unique way of expressing a life energy that is common to us all.

We will consider this participation in life energy later on, but here we should return from my digression on "specialness" to explore the fourth element in friendship-love: *commitment.* I commit myself to care for my friend. Friendship-love is not just a momentary "I-Thou" encounter. Implicitly I make a vow that I will be loyal and consistent in my caring through all kinds of unfavorable circumstances: "for better, for worse, for richer or poorer, in sickness and in health"—perhaps even "till death do us part." At times, if my friend seems to be disappearing into a destructive self-isolation (which is very different from a creative retreat for revitalizing reflection), I will pursue him both for his own sake and for the sake of our friendship.

Such commitment to my friend is possible only if I am also committed to myself: loyal and consistent in my active concern for my own well-being, not giving up on myself in adverse circumstances or during times of self-betrayal, determined to be true to myself and to fulfil my vocation, my reason for being on this planet. And if my commitment to my friend is to be efficacious it must reinforce his own commitment to himself, his sustained endeavor to be true to himself and his calling.

A fifth element in friendship-love is *respect*, which has two aspects, *patience* and *permission*. Respect as patience is not a matter of standing to one side, passively waiting for the other person to start moving. It means being actively present to her while granting her her own time in which to grow, her own space in which to think and feel, her own room in which to find herself, her own rhythms in which to change. Indeed, I do not "grant" her these things, for they are already her own. I help her to find them and to claim them. Patience is not only a matter of reticence, not rushing in where angels fear to tread. It also means actively helping the friend to discover and create her own path in life.

Obviously I will have no sense of what love as patience could be unless I have already learned to love myself in a patient way, respecting my own inner rhythms rather than imposing alien patterns, finding my own flow rather than manipulating my faculties to bring about preconceived products. And my own patient love for my friend will not work unless it stirs a patient self-love that is already there to some extent.

The second aspect of respect, permission, is closely related to patience. It is respect for the other's freedom, his right to make his own decisions, his responsibility for his own life. Even the ultimate choice between life and death is his alone, not mine. So are the penultimate choices, and the trivial ones as well. I must accept his freedom as the context in which I confirm and confront and celebrate him and commit myself to him—even if it be the freedom to turn away from me or the freedom to destroy himself.

Here there is a subtle difference between love for others and love for oneself. When I love someone else by respecting his freedom, two freedoms are involved: mine and his. When I love myself by respecting my own freedom, there is only one freedom: mine. Self-love here means taking *responsibility* for my own choices, whether ultimate, penultimate, or trivial, rather than handing my life over to fate or to other people. Obviously if I do not acknowledge my own freedom I cannot authentically respect and encourage yours. And obviously my respect for your freedom will not be effective unless it reinforces a sense of responsibility for your own life which you already have.

The sixth element in friendship-love is *affection*, which is the desire for physical and emotional closeness or intimacy with one's friend. The physical component is important even if the friendship is not that of lovers who have sexual intercourse. Affection is embodied. I feel it in my body and I want to express it through my body. I want to see and hear and touch and embrace. And affection means that I want emotional closeness too, feeling whatever he is feeling, enjoying intense pleasure in the intimacy as such. I enjoy being close to him. I like him.

But what if the friend has little affection for himself? What if he dislikes himself, cannot stand his own body, and abhors his own feelings? My affection will be thwarted by his self-disgust. I may give him affection, but he cannot receive it. And I can only give him affection if I enjoy being close to myself, if I like myself, accepting my body as I am aware of it through all my senses, and accepting my feelings, whatever they are. The ways and the extent to which I can be affectionate toward others are restricted by the ways and the extent to which I can be affectionate toward myself.

We have considered six elements in friendship-love: confirmation, confrontation, celebration, commitment, respect (patience and permission), and affection. In each case it is clear that what is required in friendship-love for another person is also required in friendship-love for oneself. Other analyses of friendship-love might propose a different map. For example, "honesty" might replace "confrontation" and "trust" might replace "patience." But the similarities and the interdependence between love for others and love for self would still remain.

Jesus, drawing on his Jewish heritage, quoted scripture: "Thou shalt love thy neighbor as thyself." I think this can be interpreted to mean, "Love your neighbor in the same way you love yourself, and love yourself in the same way as you love your neighbor." The two loves are interdependent. Not only do I need to love myself if I am to be able to love my neighbor and to receive love from my neighbor, *I need to love my neighbor if I am to be able to love myself.* If, for example, I am not confirming others, I cannot confirm myself. Why is this so?

The answer to this new question helps us to understand why I cannot confirm others unless I am confirming myself, and more generally why self-love and neighbor-love are so radically interdependent and so remarkably similar. The answer is that *both loves are actually the same love.* Love is a cosmic force, a flow of life-energies, a spiritual current, in which we participate as *channels, not as originators.* The emotions and attitudes and actions which we usually call *love* are very important, not because they themselves are love, but because they are the human occasions and conditions in which love, the presence as power which pervades everyone and everything, can flow. Whether I love myself or love my neighbor, I am not the originator of the transfiguring power at work. I am the facilitator and the expression of that loving life energy.

Perhaps a metaphor of the self as musical instrument will help here. When the damper on a piano string is withdrawn, the string will vibrate in resonance with any sound of the same pitch. When I love I remove the damper of my narcissism so that I can resonate with the vibrations of cosmic love and sing forth that love from my very being. I love, yet not I but cosmic love loves through me. And both I and that which I love are transformed and transfigured. My love for myself and my love for the neighbor—that is, my confirmation, confrontation, celebration, commitment, respect, and affection as attitudes toward self and neighbor—facilitate and express the flow of cosmic love or healing life energy within me and through me to the neighbor. Love as a human attitude brings openness to life energy.

Let us consider another metaphor. Imagine a water pipe that is closed with corrosion at both ends and clogged with corrosion inside. It is lying in a stream of water and currents surge past it on all sides but it is impervious to its self-enclosure, its narcissism. But through *self-love* it opens up one end to let water in. The water cleans up the inside of the pipe so as to reduce the corrosion that resists the flow. Neighbor-love means opening up the other end of the pipe to allow the water to flow out wherever it is most needed. The flow itself will gradually remove the corrosion in the water pipe if the water pipe lets go of its attachment to that corrosion; for example, its masochistic pleasure in resenting being such a poor pipe.

Of course the metaphor is imperfect. I am not a thing, a water pipe, and I am free to choose whether or not to remain closed and clogged. Moreover the flow does not only cleanse me of narcissism, it *transfigures* me. As in the metaphor of the piano string, I resonate with the cosmic love and become an expression of it.

But both metaphors are inadequate in a more fundamental way. Each depicts me as a separate entity (a pipe or a string). Others, presumably, are also separate entities. We are separate entities connected by a cosmic current of love. In reality, however, we are all being lived by the same divine Source of those energies and the divine Source of me and my neighbor.

Openness and *surrender* are different. In my own experience it is one thing—a marvelous thing, but relatively easy for all of us to experience—to be sufficiently *open* to the cosmic life energies that one can feel them coming in through the heart and going out through the hands to heal another person. But it is something else to shift beyond this, though perhaps including this, to surrender one's whole self into the living God who is living me. Then one is not only a *channel* of love, one *is* love, divine love. I live, yet not I, but God lives me. This is not an experience, a particular content of consciousness. It is a way of being conscious. Insofar as it can be linked with breathing, one breathes out the old narcissistic self and one breathes in God. And instead of being self-consciously aware of oneself as a channel of loving life energies one is not aware of oneself at all, but only of God, the hidden esoteric meaning of the prayer, "Thy will, not mine, be done." As Meister Eckhart explained, one no longer has a separate will with which one tries to fulfill God's (separate) will,[9] but one is "*empty* both of his own will and of God's will,"[10] and these are no longer experienced as distinct. "Let your own 'being you' sink and flow away into God's 'being God.' . . . God must simply become me and I must become God—so completely that this 'he' and this 'I' share one 'is' and in this 'isness' do one work."[11] This "work" is Love. There is only God. There is only Love.

Such surrender dissolves our boundaries as separate entities, even if these entities are linked by love energies. The primary awareness is an awareness of the God who lives us all, though God lives each of us in a unique and special way. Beyond love as a human attitude of openness and beyond love as a cosmic life energy there is Love as the Source of all that is, including human beings and cosmic life energy.

Openness, however, can help us to move toward surrender. And even if we do not fully surrender, openness is intrinsically valuable in the process of learning how to love ourselves and others well. But the process of becoming more open to loving life energies involves a radical overhaul of personality and life-style. The self is like a car. It has been fueled by the narcissistic energies of anxiety, fear, resentment, and competition. Now it needs a new engine if it is to be fueled by loving life energies. The overhaul is like changing from gasoline to solar power. But the simile breaks down, for even now we can make limited use of the new energy. We can begin to resonate with cosmic love, receiving it and channeling it to others, thereby learning how to *love ourselves and others well.* And beyond this we may begin to surrender into God, learning how to *be Love.*

We began this chapter by examining narcissism. Now, at the end, we see that narcissism can first be understood and experienced in purely psychological terms, as a Narcissus-Echo complex of self-centered human attitudes and motivations that prevent an individual from entering into reciprocal and mutually creative relationships with other individuals. In psychological terms, the opposite of narcissism is love, where love is understood and experienced as a complex of non-self-centered human attitudes that facilitate such relationships. Second, we saw that narcissism as a psychological complex can be more deeply understood and experienced in spiritual terms, as a self-separating resistance to loving life energies. In spiritual terms, the opposite of such narcissism is love, where love as a psychological complex is understood and experienced also as an openness to loving life energies. Finally, narcissism as a psychological-spiritual complex can be even more deeply understood and experienced in mystical terms as a self-separating resistance against union with God. In mystical terms the opposite of such narcissism is love, where love as a psychological-spiritual complex has become surrender into God as Love. If such surrender is complete and continuous, all the levels of narcissism have disappeared.

Meanwhile we can all learn better how to love ourselves well, whatever our current depth of understanding and experience may be, even if this is superficially psychological, with no clear awareness of spiritual or mystical reality. We can begin where we are.

III ✱ ✱ ✱ Sexuality, Spirituality, and the Art of Therapy

If we want to come to understand ourselves better not only emotionally but also spiritually many of us can be helped by a psychotherapist who realizes that therapy is an art and who practices this art in a way that is open to both the emotional unconscious and the spiritual unconscious, especially in relation to sexuality. The purpose of this chapter is to explore the relation between the emotional and spiritual dimensions of sex, but first I want to consider, very briefly, the art of therapy.

Therapy is an art, for it goes beyond the application of techniques. A technique is a procedure that connects a specified kind of means to a specified kind of end. It requires only some skill in manipulating the means so as to produce the end result, and it can be repeated again and again in many different situations. An art goes beyond techniques, though it may involve techniques in a subordinated way. As an art, therapy transcends techniques in four different ways.

First, *personal characteristics of the therapist are important.* The success of the therapy depends mainly on the therapist's empathy, presence, caring, hope, and insight. A technique, in contrast with an art, can abstract from such variable personal elements, for it can be used impersonally, by anyone who has the appropriate skill. A therapist's main "tool," however, is himself or herself, and this tool varies from therapist to therapist. Each therapist is different.

Second, a therapist's work is to help uncover not only the client's destructive patterns but also his or her *creative possibilities.* Indeed, a client cannot face the weaknesses unless some hidden strengths are discerned and drawn out by the therapist. Since the creative strengths of each individual are unique, a therapist cannot rely on techniques. What is needed is an appreciative love for the client, like the love of a friend for a friend, celebrating the client's distinctive creativity. There may be more scope for techniques in dealing with the client's destructive patterns, for these often resemble those of other people. In theory, there might be a technique for each kind of pattern, each neurosis or psychosis. Indeed, some therapists who employ only drugs and behavioral conditioning attempt to approximate this, as if therapy could be simply an applied science. But in real life our destructive patterns not only have a different and complicated mix in each one of us, but also include much that is unconscious. And the deeper the "layer" of the unconscious, the more all-pervasive the destructive pattern, and the more impervious it is to techniques. There are no simple recipes for removing narcissism and masochism, as perhaps there may be for symptomatic problems such as agoraphobia.

A third way in which therapy is an art, transcending technique, is the reliance on *judgment* and *intuition* in diagnosing a client's difficulties and, even more, in deciding when to say what and how to say it. Timing and voice timber are crucial. Each moment in a client's life, indeed each moment in a session, is different in its therapeutic possibilities. Insights concerning problems are a dime a dozen, especially if a therapist has psychic abilities. The therapist as artist, however, knows how to communicate through the client's resistances in just the right way and at just the right time.

Fourth, *the client's own commitment and determination are crucial* at every stage of the therapy. The therapist tries to spark the client's own initiative, not only respecting the client's own freedom, but fostering it. No technique can bring about the free act of another human being. Indeed, the freedom of the client is a factor that distinguishes the art of therapy from other arts. A sculptor takes a piece of marble and shapes it according to his or her own vision. The medium used by an artist, in this case the slab of marble, does limit what the artist can do. Indeed, the medium challenges the artist' s creativity. In contrast with this, however, the client is not the therapist's medium, but a free agent. A responsible therapist does not even try to shape the client according to the therapist's own vision.

Once we recognize how therapy differs from other arts, however, we can see that it is a special kind of art, a teaching art. It is *the art of teaching an art*. It is like being a *coach* to a budding sculptor or singer or composer. The client's raw material is simply himself or herself. The client is learning how to shape that material into a new form. The therapist helps the client to learn how to uncover flaws and limits and destructive tendencies, shedding some of them, changing and incorporating others; and also how to uncover and draw on hidden strengths and creative possibilities. A good therapist is essentially someone who is in the process of personally learning how to do this and who has made sufficient progress to be able to help someone else who has less understanding of the process. And as the client learns the art and applies it to himself or herself, the analogy with other arts returns, for the client's own vision is applied to a "medium," which is the client's self. Scars in the self, like flaws in marble, are limits that challenge the creativity of the self-therapist as artist.

Since the process of uncovering hidden flaws and hidden creativity is always most difficult in one's own case, a therapist may well consult another therapist about personal problems, while regarding him or her as equal in this area. But, in general, therapy is an art one eventually learns to do with oneself *by* oneself—"with a little help from my friends," like the Beatles.

Therapy is an art that one learns for oneself from another person. Rare, and brave indeed, are those who learn solely by themselves: a Freud or a Kierkegaard. For therapy is not merely a matter of counseling. Unlike a counselor, a therapist has a special competence and interest in the *unconscious*. Where a counselor deals with what a client is conscious of concerning himself or herself, and with what is easily brought into consciousness because it has merely been forgotten, a therapist also helps the client to uncover the unconscious, that is, aspects of the self of which we are unaware because we *resist* being aware of them. The unconscious dimension involves *self-deception*, a lie to oneself.

The notion of self-deception is paradoxical. How can I refuse to be aware of something? If I refuse to be aware of X, surely I must be in some way aware of X; otherwise I would be merely ignorant of X. How can I be both aware and not aware of X? How can I ignore X and yet be ignorant of X? How can I be both unwilling and unable to be aware of X?

Some thinkers try to resolve the conceptual muddles here by seeing the unconscious as the *barely* conscious. Suppose that I am unconsciously angry. If the unconscious is the barely conscious, then my anger is in the background rather than the foreground of consciousness. It is like the hum of my typewriter as I am typing. My attention is focused elsewhere, so the hum is obscure rather than clear; it is implicit rather than explicitly identified in consciousness. Consider another analogy. I am at a cocktail party in a crowded room and I do not notice that Joe Brown has entered the room, even though I have glanced in his direction. I am not ignoring him, willfully refusing him my attention. If I do become more clearly aware of his presence, I have not had to overcome any resistance. Somebody at the party—analogous to a counselor—has merely to say, "There's Joe Brown," and I shift my attention easily to Joe, clearly recognizing him.

A closer analogy is provided, however, if Mary Ann is at the threshold of the room, if she is somewhat difficult to discern in any case, and if I have had painful experiences of her and do not want to encounter her again, ever. While I am talking to my current companion I glance at the threshold, but I do not allow myself to recognize her. I *ignore* her. Such an analogy, as we will see, is useful in understanding one aspect of the unconscious, but it does not reckon with the fact that much of the unconscious is completely inaccessible to consciousness at a given moment, like a person in a totally different room from the cocktail party, a person whom I do not know is there and whom I only met once, years ago, and whom I never want to meet again. I am not willfully ignoring *that* person.

So some theorists of the unconscious try to explain the paradox of self-deceptive resistance by insisting that the unconscious is *completely* unconscious. Then they have to postulate a hidden unconscious self that is doing the resisting, and a problem arises: How can the conscious self be responsible in any way for the activities of this hidden entity? In such a theory it is not *I* who is resisting awareness of the repressed emotion, it is the super ego inside me—or some other postulated entity. This account makes the conscious self too ignorant of resistance: not willful enough, a helpless victim.

These conceptual difficulties can be *partly* remedied once we recognize that the unconscious has "layers," some of which are utterly remote from consciousness, some very close, and some in between. In terms of the cocktail party analogy, some unwelcome persons are in a very remote room, some are at the threshold of the doorway of the room which I am in, and some are just outside in the corridor, awaiting their turn at the threshold. At some time or other in the past we refused to remain aware of *all* of these, relegating them to the well-defended realm of the unconscious, from which they nevertheless still influence what we feel. (How do they do this? In the analogy I could postulate a secret psychic influence which the rejected persons exert on us, but this does not illuminate the way in which the unconscious goes on influencing us.) Some items in the unconscious are at the moment completely inaccessible (like people in a remote room) but other items are accessible on the fringes of consciousness (like a person at the threshold). The accessible items are being willfully ignored, actively resisted. We do not allow our attention to focus on them, though we are obscurely aware of them. We are neither totally ignorant, nor are we clearly aware. Here is the locus of self-deception.

Any current therapeutic work can be focused on this "threshold" material. Attempts to bludgeon below this borderline are dangerous, so therapy is a very gradual process of uncovering repressed material and then reshaping one's daily life in relation to what has thus been revealed. As each item crosses the threshold and is dealt with, another item, previously inaccessible, moves into place at the threshold. Sometimes an uninvited guest will "crash the cocktail party," but usually the "host" has to give permission by deliberately focusing attention on the threshold, reluctantly admitting whoever is there. Sometimes, after a conversation with the visitor from the past, the host asks him or her to leave. Sometimes, however, the visitor is changed during the conversation and remains to become "the life of the party." This very happy outcome *can* occur even if the visitor had inflicted much harm on the host in the past. It is even more likely if the visitor had attempted to help. Sometimes, for example, we were too frightened as children to let in love, because it had become too closely associated with being controlled or with eventually being rejected. Now we can dare to welcome love.

What does the unconscious include? Freud has shown how infantile sexual material has been buried there, profoundly influencing our emotions ever since. This is very important. But what I have said about the unconscious applies not only to the *emotional* unconscious but also to the *spiritual* unconscious. Some aspects of spirit are at present inaccessible to most people, like old acquaintances who are in a remote room. Other aspects of spirit are at the threshold of consciousness, but are being ignored. Here the attitudes of a therapist are often crucial for a client.

Each therapist brings his or her own *permissions* and *prohibitions* into the therapy. These are communicated unconsciously as well as consciously. Most therapists realize how true this is with regard to, say, anger or sexual desire. If the therapist is still repressing these, the clients will find it difficult to let their own angers or sexual desires come to the surface in the presence of the therapist. The same dynamic is at work in the domain of the *spiritual*. Many therapists unconsciously resist spirit, and thus reinforce their client's resistance to spirit.

Indeed, sometimes resistance against spirit seems necessary so as to uncover sex, for example when a person is trying to overcome the antisexual conditioning of a puritan religious background. And on the other hand sometimes resistance against sex may seem to be necessary so as to uncover spirit; sex can be a drug that makes us oblivious to spirit. So either of these strategies may be appropriate for a particular client at a particular stage in his or her life. But they should be conscious strategies for particular situations, not *unconscious* prohibitions and permissions that the therapist brings to *every* client. As universal strategies they are both radically inadequate. In reality sex and spirit are interconnected expressions of the same self. To repress the spiritual aspect of sex or the sexual aspect of spirit is to split ourselves as human beings and to acknowledge only part of the truth about ourselves.

It is time that we looked at what people usually mean by *sex* and *spirit*. I am going to start with two definitions which reflect our common understanding of both and which see them as obviously opposed.

Sex is nothing but the desire for pleasurable sensations of physical intimacy with others, usually humans. These sensations are obtainable by oneself in masturbation by combining touch with fantasy. Sex is like hunger or thirst, which we share with other animals.

Spirit is the desire for nonphysical ecstatic intimacy with others: with the nonphysical aspect of other persons, works of art and nature, and with pure Spirit or God. Spirit enables us to transcend the physical world.

Given these definitions it is not difficult to see why some people would deny sex to uncover spirit or deny spirit to uncover sex. Yet both sexual desire and spiritual desire are part of our human nature, and both must be acknowledged if we are to be honest with ourselves. Sex as bodily pleasure and spirit as ecstatic or transcendent intimacy are both realities. In isolation, however, they are distortions. It is false to say that sex is *nothing but* a desire for bodily pleasure and that spirit is *nothing but* a desire for transcendent intimacy.

Reductionist or "nothing-but" views of sex and spirit, however, can be found in contemporary therapy. Some sex therapists focus almost exclusively on enabling a client to enjoy sexual pleasure. Some transpersonal therapists focus almost exclusively on enabling a client to attain a disembodied "higher consciousness." Both therapies are narrow, yet both deal with a universal tendency in human beings. Each kind of tendency is real, and each needs to be experienced as part of us. In all human beings there is a tendency toward sexual hedonism and a tendency toward spiritual hedonism. In many people both desires are repressed, hidden from consciousness. We resist becoming aware of animal lust and angelic longing. We need therapeutic help in uncovering these split-off, unconscious desires. Insofar as we do not uncover, acknowledge, and integrate these desires, our lives are deeply influenced by them in many destructive ways. As Wilhelm Reich[1] has shown, repressed sex leads to hatred of life; and as Carl Jung[2] has shown, repressed spirit leads to meaningless life.

But once I realize that I want to be an animal, satisfying myself sexually in the same way I satisfy my hunger or thirst, and once I realize that I want to be an angel, living out of my body in realms of nonphysical pleasure, what do I do about these desires? From an enlightened mystical perspective, neither one is superior to the other, and both are narcissistic, both are ways of resisting God. Later in this chapter I will explain this mystical claim more fully, but here I want to show how both animal lust and angelic longing can be transformed and reinterpreted when we properly understand *who we are.* I will speak in the first person singular concerning who we are, though I believe that what I say about myself is true of all human beings.

I am conscious of myself in a threefold way: as bodily desire, as passion, and as life energy. I am body, passion, and "aura," all three, in intricate interdependence.

Suppose, for example, that I am aware of bitter resentment in me. I am aware of it in three ways. First, there is a constriction in the front of my chest and between my shoulder blades. Second, there is an emotion located in that chest region, an emotion directed toward a particular person or toward the cosmos in general or toward the very source of my existence, God. And third, I am aware of bitter resentment as a constriction, a holding-in, of the life energies of my aura in the same chest area. The resentment can be uncovered and released by *physical* therapy (massage, yoga, osteopathy, etc.), by *psychotherapy* which deals directly with the emotions, or by *spiritual healing*, which deals directly with the aura, or by all three together. Any change in body, passion, or aura affects the other two. So in replacing resentment by gratitude or love, a postural corrective for opening up the chest may be, in a particular instance, more important than primal therapy, which uncovers a resentment that began in infancy. Alternatively, a spiritual healing of my life energies in the chest area may be more important than work on my body or work on my emotional unconscious.

Sex involves all three dimensions: body, passions, and aura. Sex is not only a bodily desire. It is also a bundle of passions and a state of the aura. I will talk about the aura later. First, sex and passions.

Many contemporary psychotherapies stress the close link between bodily intimacy and emotional intimacy in infancy, and they explore the ways in which adults transfer infantile passions toward their sexual partners. When people observe infants without censoring what they see, and when people reexperience their own infancy, it becomes evident that sex, as an intense longing for bodily and emotional intimacy, begins then. Each of us as an infant felt not only a passionate longing for intimacy but also a fear of intimacy: a terror that I may be overwhelmed and made totally dependent. So there was not only a movement toward affectionate tenderness, expressed in mutual caresses. There was also a contrary recoil in terror, a flight from feeling utterly vulnerable and helpless. And since the longing for intimacy was not satisfied, there was also agonizing grief and bitter rage. Why was the longing not satisfied? There are three main reasons. First, as I have already indicated, the infant is ambivalent towards intimacy, both desiring it and fearing it. Second, the parents bring to the infant their own impediments to loving intimacy, impediments that began for them in early infancy. These vary greatly from person to person, and some parents are less closed than others, but no parents are perfect. All have some impediments, especially some narcissism. Third, even if the parents were ideal, the infant has a tendency to narcissism: "The world must revolve around me to satisfy me." This makes infantile desires insatiable, limitless, and impossible to fulfill. Frustration and disappointment are unavoidable.

Infants differ considerably in the "strategy" they adopt to deal with frustration of sexual passion as a longing for bodily and emotional intimacy. In *Struggle and Fulfillment*[3] I distinguish five common strategies: anxiety or chronic agitation and inner pressure; hostile and resentful wariness; idolatrous addiction to substitute satisfactions; masochistic despair that gets pleasure out of pain; and stoic detachment that self-deceitfully says, "I didn't want it anyway." The turbulent passions and distrustful strategies to which sexual desire gives rise in infancy do not disappear, but are buried in the unconscious where they continue to operate secretly as the child becomes an adult. They are stirred toward the surface of consciousness when once again—this time in sexual intercourse—flesh touches flesh all over. In addition to infantile longing and infantile tendencies there are also conflicting feelings directed toward the sexual partner: terror and rage and grief and fear of rejection. There are also narcissistic demands that the sexual partner exist entirely for oneself, and a bitter resentment because he or she does not: "You won't love me enough, so I can't love you; and I hate you for it." And we deal with the sexual partner in accordance with one or other of the strategies that began in infancy: anxiety or wariness or addiction or masochism or dispassionate detachment. If detachment dominates, one may succeed in repressing almost all the unconscious emotions that sex has carried with it in the body's nervous system since infancy. Thus one can treat sex solely as a physical pleasure disassociated from passion. But this is a colossal self-deception. Sex is intrinsically a longing for emotional and bodily intimacy, a longing present in every human being, and the sexual gestures of tender caressing and bodily intimacy are inherently linked with affection. Moreover, sex is also unavoidably associated with the passions and strategies that I have indicated. All these elements are infantile in origin and character. They can be largely replaced by mature love, but this transformation requires a psychological discipline that exposes the perpetual conflict between insatiable longings for intimacy and self-created barriers against intimacy. Contemporary psychotherapy at its best provides such a discipline, and nothing else does it as effectively. Although elements in it were discerned in many cultures prior to Freud, he and his successors[4] have provided an essentially new approach in human self-understanding, especially concerning sex. Loving sex is rare, not because sex is merely an animal appetite that is inherently unloving, but because for humans sex is largely an ambivalent emotional attachment that began in infancy.

Psychotherapy can also reveal that we transfer passions and strategies from infancy not only to our sexual partners but also toward God. The passions and strategies are pervasive in scope, for they began when mother was the whole world and they continue toward the whole world, and especially toward whatever underlying reality unites that world; that is, toward what we unconsciously view as God. Whether or not we consciously believe in God, we have unconscious feelings and atittudes toward God. In *Struggle and Fulfillment* I showed how five distrustful infantile strategies are directed toward the world and God, and how these undermine five forms of cosmic trust that also begin in infancy. In general sexual distrust and cosmic distrust are very closely related dimensions of the emotional unconscious.

It is possible to repress the emotional unconscious and to treat sex as simply a physical pleasure, but this is a self-deception. If I deny that I desire such pleasure, I am deceiving myself, but I am also deceiving myself if I ignore the emotional components of sex. Indeed, any strong physical desire has unconscious emotional associations. Some people say, "Sex is just a physical desire like hunger," but this ignores the fact that hunger has deep emotional reverberations that go back to our infancy. Hunger is never simply hunger, and lust is never simply lust. We have an emotional unconscious.

It has become obvious to many people that sex as bodily desire and sex as passion are closely linked. The *spiritual unconscious*, however, is largely unexplored territory for most of us, including psychotherapists. It seems that only therapists influenced by either Wilhelm Reich[5] or tantric yoga[6] see that sexual desire and sexual passion are also linked with a spiritual urge: the desire to merge one's aura with that of another human being and thereby move into an altered state of consciousness, a union not only with the other person but also with the cosmos. This aspect of sex is not easily understood and is not likely to be acknowledged unless one has experienced one's own life energy system and its connection with the body and the passions. For many people, the spiritual unconscious is as strange a realm as the emotional unconscious once was for almost everyone. Each of these repressed realms have to be *experienced* to be adequately understood.

I am aware of four main kinds of path by which anyone can become to some degree aware of life energy: not necessarily seeing it, but definitely feeling it. First, there is one or other of the various therapies in the Reichian tradition, of which Alexander Lowen's bioenergetics[7] is perhaps the best known. Another kind of path is through meditative yoga, especially where this encourages spontaneous bodily movements in response to the energies. A third approach is through shamanic practices in which one learns to resonate with the life energies of other animals. Fourth, we can learn spiritual healing and the art of contacting discarnate spirits from teachers in such traditions as the Spiritualist Church. (This fourth path, however, tends to be less embodied and passionate than the others, so the connections with body and emotion are not made as clear to consciousness.)

What is the aura, the pattern of life energy? All of us have at one time or another experienced life energy in some form or other, perhaps not recognizing it as such: in the high that immediately follows sexual orgasm; in a religious ecstasy at a charismatic or pentecostal rally; while responding in a bodily passionate way to music; while running, suddenly finding oneself switched into "overdrive"; sensing something happening between self and friend during an intimate "I-Thou" encounter; or enjoying the glow of glorious excitement that surges through the whole body when, in therapy, some previously repressed feelings (perhaps very painful ones) have just been fully released.

The aura, as a personal pattern of life energies, is constantly changing. It pervades the physical body and it extends beyond it. Some people can see other people's auras, but most frequently it is felt as vibration, pulsation, tingling, or streaming. When my aura is relatively open or flowing I feel very alive and energized,and this is one reason for calling what I perceive *life energies.* Hindus call it *prana* or *shakti* or *kundalini.* Jews and Christians in their scriptures call it *spirit.* And both prana and spirit are linked with breath. Receiving and giving out life energy is very much like inhaling and exhaling and can be closely linked with inhaling and exhaling during meditation.

Life energies are experienced not only within the body but also beyond the skin at various distances from the body. My consciousness travels, as it were, *within* life energies not only inside my body but also beyond it. In meditation I become clearly aware that as aura I am larger than my physical body. The external edges of the aura are blurred, for its vibrations radiate outward indefinitely, like ripples on a lake. Also I can become aware of other people's auras, especially when they are pulsating positively or negatively in relation to my own aura as our "ripples" meet. Often such aura consciousness can be evoked by practicing meditation for only a few hours in a group with a skilled leader, even if people have not previously had any such awareness.

Special sensitivity to auras is often accompanied by psychic abilities that are very important in the work of some therapists, who may see images of a dream that the client has not yet told, or images of a childhood memory that the client is not yet aware of. An intuitive therapist may know that a client is raging with resentment on the way to the session today, or that the client has a pain in the right knee and in the head above the ears. Even emotions of terror and anguish that are still deeply buried in a client's unconscious may be felt in empathy by such a therapist. Since a person's aura spreads out in subtle ways in all directions, other people can tune into it, even at a considerable distance, using their psychic abilities like a radio that tunes into a radio wave. During sleep a therapist's "receiver" is involuntarily "turned on," so a client may sometimes psychically invade the therapist with conscious or unconscious emotional messages. Whether voluntarily or involuntarily, a therapist can discern a great variety of physical or emotional items associated with the client's aura, whether the items are conscious or unconscious for the client. The more a therapist is open to his or her own life energies, the more such intuitive powers develop. The other prerequisite is an attitude of love, concern, and caring toward the client, a generous attitude that fosters, and is fostered by, an expansive, healing aura. With the client's implicit permission, such an aura can move into the client's aura in a nonintrusive way.

Intuitive powers can, of course, be used in ways that are intrusive and manipulative. Some people "psyche into" other people's conscious and unconscious minds for their own egocentric purposes. That is part of what so-called black magic is all about. Like nuclear technology, understanding of auras can be used for good or ill. Fortunately deliberate and conscious black magic is fairly rare. *Unconscious* psychic influence, however, whether destructive or creative, is very common. Indeed, it is what a great deal of therapy, whether individual or in groups, is all about. And where a therapist's own aura is hopeful, caring, and expansive, it can spark hope and initiative in the client. Such subtle influence is the essence of therapy, whatever else may be going on. It can be happening, of course, even when the therapist is not aware of auras. Awareness simply intensifies and clarifies the interaction between therapist and client.

We have been considering the relation between human auras and psychic intuition in therapy. That was a digression, for our main interest is the aura itself as a context for bringing together what we usually distinguish as "sex" and "spirit." In my own experience of meditative yoga there are seven "chakras" or major energy centers in the aura. Each chakra has its own distinctive characteristics.[8]

First, at the bottom of the spine, there is a chakra which, when open, *grounds* me. It is like feeling the pull of gravity on the whole body at a particular spot in the body. Maybe the experience *is*, in part, an experience of gravity. From the bottom chakra I can sometimes feel energies streaming down my legs into the earth. Focus on this chakra is aided by moving spontaneously to "primitive" music, stomping one's feet on the ground.

Second is the *sexual* chakra, a little higher on the spine and forward into the genital areas. The life energies are experienced here as an exquisitely pleasurable sensual streaming through the whole reproductive area, the lower part of the lower abdomen. Even without focusing on the area, people sometimes feel this during meditation: at the end of an exhalation, during a pause before inhaling. It is not the same thing as sexual arousal, though once one becomes aware of it, it typically accompanies sexual arousal. Almost everyone can feel sexual arousal. Most people, however, have "frozen" this chakra.

The third chakra is in the area of the navel and solar plexus and backward to the spine. (Actually, the first five chakras are mainly on the spine, but occupy a space into the front of the body as well. Initially it is often easier to become aware of them in the front area.) The third chakra has to do with *power* and *assertiveness*. This is the main focus in martial arts, which use life energies to augment the physical forces of the body. One way to become aware of it is by rapid expulsive diaphragm breathing, panting like a dog.

The fourth chakra is located from between the shoulder blades to the center of the chest beside the heart. This *heart* chakra is the seat of love—as longing, as tenderness, as joyful appreciation. Postures that open up the chest and bring together the shoulder blades help to focus attention on this chakra. So does music that expresses longing or tenderness or appreciation. The heart chakra and the navel center together are associated with a wide range of emotions, both life affirming and life destructive. When either kind of emotion is repressed from consciousness the navel and heart areas are tense and constricted. When either kind is acknowledged, there is a release of life energies. When a negative emotion, for example, resentment, is acknowledged and expressed, we can let go of it, and only the positive emotion, in this case gratitude, remains.

But expression of emotion includes using the voice, making a *sound*. The life energies need to move up from the navel and the heart through the throat. And the fifth chakra is centered in the *throat*, though it includes much of the lower part of the face and head, including the mouth. The opening up of the throat chakra is associated with *creativity* and *communication* in general, and not only with giving vent to our emotions. One way to become initially aware of the chakra is by making a buzzing noise like a bee: "ZZZZZZZ."

The sixth chakra is perhaps the best known by the general public. It is the so-called *third eye*, located between the eyebrows or a little higher on the forehead. It has to do with insight and intuition and psychic power, and when it is specially powerful there may also be a compelling force emanating from the two physical eyes. Great artists and great intellectuals as well as psychics often have intense third-eye chakras. If people are on a spiritual path the opening up of this chakra is often manifested in visions of white light or blue light.

The seventh chakra is located on the top of the head, where Jewish men wear a skull-cap. If you become aware of this center it feels as if one's hair is being gently pulled upward in that area, each one individually, as if there were a thousand mini-magnets just above the head, which is no doubt the origin of the halo as painted in conventionalized art. The experiences associated with this chakra are ethereal, blissful, paradisal. One seems to be dwelling in a heavenly realm that transcends the physical earth. An intense experience of this chakra is the ultimate spiritual "high," yet what is discerned thereby is not God as such, but heavenly realities.

With practice one can focus on any one of the chakras, or be aware of the life energies flowing freely up and down the spine and brain. The pleasure in each chakra is different, but in each case it far exceeds any purely bodily pleasure.

Some people have an out-of-body experience (OBE) at a time of near death, or perhaps during meditation, or even quite spontaneously. Then the aura or astral body leaves the physical body, and as the aura travels one's consciousness travels with it. In an OBE one can observe one's own physical body and other physical objects from a distance, perhaps from the ceiling of an operating room where one's body has stopped breathing. Or the aura may travel in some nonphysical realms of spirit. Such out-of-body experiences make it easy to conceive what life after death could be: the aura continuing in existence, carrying with it the center of consciousness and the emotional-dispositional character, but having left the physical body. Death need not be the end of personal existence. Unfortunately this personal existence may perpetuate the same largely narcissistic character that one has now. In the myth of Narcissus, he continued even after death to gaze on his own reflection, this time not in a pool but in the river Styx.

While we are alive as physically embodied beings, however, sex fortunately can *combine* bodily pleasure and the pleasures of the aura of astral body. And more generally, while we are physically embodied beings it is important that we acknowledge that we *are* bodies. We do not merely *inhabit* bodies. During a discussion with Alexander Lowen, the founder of bioenergetics, I rashly said, "I *am* my aura, my energy field." He was vigorous in correcting me. Such a conception of the self splits us off from our physical bodies. It is then too easy to lose our links with the earth and physical sex and touch and passion, imagining that we are pure spirits, living as if we had no bodies, as if ideally our life should be one continuous OBE.

This is how spirit tends to be experienced by many religious people, who do not consciously connect spiritual experience with the physical body at all. Typically they experience creativity or insight or bliss, for their top three chakras have been partially opened up, though without any conscious connection with the throat, "third-eye" area, or crown. And since the heart chakra is specially full of deeply *embodied* passions, it is typically opened somewhat less. Moreover, in such religious people the creativity, insight, and bliss are typically split off from sex and from all that is associated with the three lower chakras: the earth, sensuality, and assertiveness. And their emotions, which are largely disembodied rather than full blooded, tend to be thin, though perhaps quite intense. Indeed, they expend much energy in repressing any awareness of both the life energies of the lower chakras and the passions of the Freudian unconscious.

My impression of spiritual therapy, Jungian therapy, and transpersonal therapy is that they tend to err in the direction of merely reinforcing this flight of spirit from sex, the "whoosh" of energy up through the top of the head. Bioenergetics, on the contrary, tends to err in the direction of reinforcing the flight of sex from spirit, that is, expending energy in keeping the flow of energy moving down from the crown to the ground, depleting the higher centers at the expense of the lower. Of course, generalizations are risky, and there are many exceptions, but as a broad statement of generalized tendencies I think I am not being unfair.

But whether or not my generalizations are fair, the main point here is that all of us need to recognize our own tendency. Which is it, the flight of spirit from sex or the flight of sex from spirit? Then we can counteract that tendency. One person may need to find ways to ground the body; another person may need to find ways to glimpse paradise; and another person may need to find both.

When I first defined sex and spirit the opposition between them was obvious and absolute: sex as desire for bodily pleasure, spirit as desire for disembodied pleasure. At this stage in my presentation, bringing in some awareness of passion and of the aura, there is still a split. *Sex* is broadly associated with the lower three chakras, that is, with grounding in the earth, with sensual streamings, and with elemental assertive power. *Spirit* is broadly associated with the upper three chakras, that is, with articulate creativity, with intuitive insight, and with heavenly soarings. Can sex and spirit be linked together. Can there be a spiritualized sexuality and a sexualized spirituality?

There can be, in the heart chakra. This chakra is the mediator between the chakras which lie below the heart and those above it. An initial opening of the heart chakra is possible by using a technique employed by both religious revivalists and bioenergetics therapists (A reader who has lower-back problems, heart problems, or breathing problems should not try out what I am about to describe. Also, anyone who tries it out and starts feeling light-headed from too much oxygen should stop immediately.) One stands with feet comfortably apart. Tuck in your buttocks and lean back, arching your lower back and raising your hands and arms high in the air, palms forward, so that your shoulder blades are comfortably together and your chest area is very open. Your head should be comfortably back, but not too far, for this can cut off circulation. Now breath deeply in the diaphragm area, making a loud "Huh" sound with each exhalation. Continue for several minutes or until, spontaneously, something else replaces the deliberate exercise.

This "something else" could be a hint of spiritual ecstasy, a glimpse of heavenly realms evoked by an opening of the higher chakras. Or it could be the beginning of bodily vibrations in legs and pelvis that could lead to what Wilhelm Reich called the "orgasmic reflex," a total bodily sexual convulsion. The variations in response depend on differences in temperaments, in expectations, and in contexts. (Orgasmic stirrings would be very embarrassing at a pentecostal revival!) The main point is that a temporary opening up of the heart chakra, assisted by the neighboring chakras in navel and throat, can release some constrictions in the higher chakras or in the lower chakras. A more profound opening of the heart chakra can help to open up *all* the other chakras and to unite their energies together in a love that is both "sexual" and "spiritual."

The blocks to a spiritualized sexuality and a sexualized spirituality are within ourselves, not only in the heart (the physical heart, passions of the heart, heart chakra) but in other areas. There can eventually be a free flow of life energies between all the chakras, but this requires work on body blocks and emotional blocks and aura blocks that have been with us since infancy. This work is long and arduous and complex, sometimes focusing on bodily rigidities, sometimes on emotional conflicts, sometimes on life energy imbalances. But as an encouragement along the way, there are occasional brief experiences of unity, when blocks are temporarily swept aside. Life energies flow unimpeded from feet to crown and from crown to feet, and one realizes that basically the *same* life energies are being changed: from the dense, fiery vibrations in the genitals to the refined, delicate pulsations in the crown, and vice versa. And sometimes one can experience loving life energies entering the heart, spreading down to the genitals and up to the eyes, and then flowing outward through genitals and heart and eyes to a beloved partner as one makes love.

Indeed,the best place in which to realize that there can be a sexualized spirituality and a spiritualized sexuality is in sexual intercourse. This requires two people who already are relatively in touch with all the chakras and who are open to the possibility that what happens in sexual intercourse is a *merging of the two auras*. The physical and emotional intimacy also matter, for all three aspects are connected causally. But the deepest longing is for a merger of auras, and the most fantastic pleasure occurs when this happens. It happens not only, or even mainly, at the moment of orgasm. It may occur before orgasm or after orgasm or without orgasm, and it can go on for long periods of time. It is not only a merging with the aura of the other but, also since the combined auras expand indefinitely into the cosmos, it is a merging with the aura of the cosmos.

The realization may then come that I am not, as aura, separate from anyone or anything in the world. I am like a wave in the vast ocean of life energy. Everything is transfigured, radiating a marvelous light from within. This is cosmic consciousness, and sexual intercourse can be the occasion for it—not the only occasion or even the necessary occasion (here Wilhelm Reich was mistaken)[9] but *an* occasion. Indeed it is the occasion least likely to involve a flight from body and passion. When cosmic consciousness occurs apart from sexual intercourse it may involve the whole person—body, passion, and aura—in a similar way, but this is less likely. Of course cosmic consciousness may occur with one's sexual partner when there is no sexual intercourse going on, though the encounter has a strongly sexual element in it. Perhaps the lovers are merely holding hands or looking at each other's eyes. And it can occur with a person who is not one's lover, or with a tree or an animal or a work of art. The merging of auras and the indefinite expansion into the cosmos can occur in many settings. In all this, however, since one's body and emotions are felt as distinct from others, the merger is experienced only as a merger of the auras, not of the whole self. This is more evident the more remote the occasion is from sexual intercourse. But even in sexual intercourse the union is actually only a union of auras. Bodily and emotional intimacy remain as intimacy, not union, as Martin Buber[10] rightly pointed out in his criticisms of sex-mysticism. So sex (body and emotion) and spirit (aura) are still not brought together, even at this stage of cosmic consciousness. Indeed, each person's mode of consciousness may still be self-centered, narcissistic.

What is needed is a mystical transformation that goes beyond anything I have thus far considered in terms of "aura" or "spirit." This transformation is not a matter of new contents of consciousness, but rather of a new, non-narcissistic way of being conscious. It can begin at any stage in one's life, for it is a surrender of self into God, whatever one experiences the self to be at the moment. Thus far in this chapter I have been describing stages in self-understanding. I began with a narrow conception of the self and conscious physical body. Beyond this, one's self-understanding can become more inclusive, involving not only body and consciousness but also passions. Then one may add an aura or spirit that is capable of merging with the cosmos. But the focus is still on *me*, having and enjoying experiences, whether of pleasurable genital stimulation or of cosmic consciousness. I am still the center of my universe, a self absorbed in itself, a narcissistic self. I once read an account of an extreme example of this. A man got stoned on hash (which can, I hear, sometimes evoke an awareness of life energies) and expanded his consciousness of self so as to fill the cosmos. He masturbated and felt that he was, as he said, "fucking the universe." Meditative sexual intercourse with a partner is not as grossly narcissistic as this, but it can be quite narcissistic. The focus may be solely on *me* having the experience: "Wow! Here I am, enjoying cosmic consciousness!"

It is important to distinguish between two major issues in personal life. The first issue is whether I experience and understand and live the full range of who I am as a human being. This includes not only body and consciousness, passion and aura, but many other dimensions of human life that we are not considering in this chapter: artistic-creative, historical-communal, ecological, intellectual, and so on. We need to move toward completeness as human beings, excluding no significant dimension of human life from the self-understanding out of which we live. We need to ask "Who am I?" and to answer this question in as all-inclusive a way as we can. The issue of self-understanding is a crucial issue.

There is a second issue, however, which is even more important: whether at any moment, whatever I now understand myself to be, I am letting go of myself into God, the source of all my existence, being aware of myself as being lived by God, along with everyone else and everything else. The alternative to this, at any moment in time and at any stage in my self-understanding, is some form of narcissism, a defiant self-separation from the divine Source which lives me. Narcissism may be selfish or altruistic, psychopathic or conscientious, self-deflating or self-inflating, grossly hedonistic or sublimely hedonistic. The differences among these forms of narcissism are important, but they are not ultimately important. What is common to all of them is that deep down I see my life as being lived by me alone, shaped by me, with myself as my raw materials, in isolation from my Source.

Profound self-explorations, whether they be existential-ist[11] or psychoanalytic[12] or contemplative,[13] tend to coincide in what they uncover as the most basic motivation: a syndrome of megalomania and masochism. Megalomania is the desire to be god, where god is the self-creating center of everything. Closely associated with this is a resentment because one is not god, but essentially dependent, vulnerable, and helpless, like an infant. Masochism is the perverse enjoyment of my rage at the humiliation and injustice of being born as an embodied mortal.

Some thinkers claim there is no alternative to this narcissistic syndrome, though some strategies for living narcissistically may seem to be more successful or socially beneficial than others.[14] For mystics, however, the basic alternative is a surrender of the self-separating self, letting go into its Source. The Source is then experienced as a creative void which is most immediately expressed as Love. As I have already hinted, a surrender to the Source as Love takes place primarily in the heart chakra,[15] whether one is living mainly from the lower chakras or mainly from the higher ones, in sensual sex or ethereal bliss. And surrender is surrender of the whole self, including body and passions. These too are being lived by God. They are transformed and transfigured in the process of ongoing surrender, but they are not transcended. The attempt to transcend body and passion is an attempt to resist being lived by God as one actually is being lived: as a human being, not a disembodied, passionless spirit.

The divine Source of the whole self, including the aura, expresses itself as Love in a fundamental vibration. One can learn to resonate with Love so that Love is expressed through the whole person, including body, emotions, and spirit. Surrender is like removing the damper from a piano string so it is free to resonate with a given sound. As I let go of my narcissism the divine Love can sound through me. Instead of transcending or resenting the body with its passions, I can celebrate its being a medium for God, resonating with the vibrations of divine Love, *being* that Love in my passionate body.

Surrender is at the core of all genuine religion. Religion is too often confused with all sorts of narcissistic games such as the flight from hedonistic sex to hedonistic spiritual states. In true mystical religion we can enjoy sensual pleasure and we can enjoy spiritual states, but we are not *attached* to them. Whatever happens, pleasure or pain, one is being lived by God, by cosmic Love.

Through mystical surrender I realize that I *am* that which lives me and which lives all people and all things. There is no longer any *urge* to merge with others as auras, for there is a more basic way in which I am not separated from them: I am the God who lives them and they are the God who lives me. In surrendered sexual intercourse this unity is sublimely realized, for two *whole selves* are surrendered into the same loving Source of all there is.

This surrendered form of sexualized spirituality and spiritualized sexuality should be distinguished from two narcissistic forms. In one of these, the urge to merge as auras with another human being is primarily infantile: one is seeking an undifferentiated union with Mother, using one's partner as the contemporary substitute for Mother. This quest is very common among people who are psychic and immaturely spiritual, for they intuit the way in which a bonding of auras could be more intimate than anything that is possible in a bodily-emotional way. Sometimes such people may totally avoid sexual intercourse, because of the dangers which they associate with bodily-emotional intimacy, dangers that have encouraged them to flee from sex to spirit. But where bodily-emotional intimacy is somewhat less frightening, sexual intercourse can be used as an especially powerful context for merging with a Mother substitute on a psychic-spiritual plane. In such a "strategy" one focuses one's consciousness mainly on a merging of auras rather than on the sensual and emotional aspects of intercourse. Such a "spiritualized" sexuality is very different from what happens when a merging of auras occurs because each person has a generous overflowing of expansive, loving energies and is willing to receive these from the other, while still retaining a sense of one's own individuality. When the whole, individual self, not merely the aura, is surrendered into God, the distinct sexual partners must radically realize their non-separation, for each person is being lived by the same God.

Another narcissistic form of spiritualized sexuality occurs when sexual energy from the lower chakras is used as a "rocket-fuel" for experiences in the higher chakras. Here sexual intercourse is used to help the individual zoom into ever higher states of consciousness, traveling astrally into marvelous heavenly realms. Where a spiritual state of consciousness—or any state of consciousness—is the *goal*, narcissism is still at work, for one's way of being conscious is still self-centered. In contrast with this, astral travel sometimes also occurs when two people who are more surrendered than narcissistic meet in sexual intercourse. Here, however, astral travel is not the goal. It is a gift that can be enjoyed; indeed, the pleasure may exceed anything on the physical and emotional planes of sexual experience and anything known in the most exotically beautiful travel on earth. But it is received as a gift; one is not attached to it. Similarly sexual intercourse between two relatively surrendered persons may also be experienced on occasion as a fantastically intense sensual pleasure, with minimal awareness of auras or astral travel; here, as well, the pleasure is a gift to be enjoyed, but not to cling to.

Insofar as we are caught up in narcissism, we cling to whatever is pleasurable, not only because it is pleasurable, but because it *distracts* us from an intolerable terror and anguish that lurks at the threshold of consciousness because we have separated ourselves from our divine Source. Indeed, even our megalomania and our painful masochism, which seem so fundamental, are distractions from a layer of the unconscious that is too raw to touch. At all costs we must distract ourselves from *the despair and horror of self-isolation, the hell in the heart.* So we try to focus our attention elsewhere, especially on something that can so preoccupy us that we are captivated, obsessed, fascinated. One fascinating focus is sex as lust, the indiscriminate longing for physical-sensual intimacy. In humans this is not just an occasional animal urge; we are potentially in heat all the time, every moment, and whether this is so depends on the focus of our attention. We can be stirred sexually by almost anyone or anything if we want to, though after a while the wanting feels compulsive, as if our attention could not be elsewhere. Another fascinating focus is spirit, the whole realm of the psychic and the so-called paranormal. We may have an indiscriminate and insatiable longing for the disembodied, ecstatic experiences. Since the pleasures of these can exceed those of lust, we can become "hooked" on them even more powerfully, whether we take drugs or go to prayer meetings or meditate on the aura. And if we combine sex and spirit in a spiritualized sexuality that combines both kinds of pleasure in mutually enhancing ways, we can distract ourselves very effectively indeed.

All these forms of hedonism are narcissistic solutions to a problem that arises from narcissism.[16] They help to distract us from the pain of our self-isolation, the pain of the constricted heart. When we shift to surrender, however, the bodily and spiritual pleasures remain, but we are no longer attached to them. We no longer desparately need them to distract us from the hell in the heart, for the surrender has brought happiness in the heart. The terror and anguish of living without a Source is replaced by assurance and peace.

How is surrender possible? Paradoxically, I must first take responsibility for my own life, acknowledging my own freedom to *choose* its basic motivations. The message of surrender to God, received prematurely in a person's life, is almost certain to be understood in a misleading and destructive way. It is confused with passivity, conformity, resignation, or submission to this or that person, group, or book. First I must uncover the most fundamental motives and ways of being in the world that pervade my life and acknowledge that I am *choosing* them. What is eventually uncovered in every case, below the many varying scripts, dramas, games, neurotic tendencies (whatever you call them) is a form of narcissism, a mix of megalomania and masochistic resentment. Only when I can acknowledge that narcissism is my way of being in the world am I in a position to decide whether to continue in it or let go of it. Letting go involves a dark night of the soul, a death of one's self as previously lived and understood. One needs a guide who has been through this process.

How does one move toward this ultimate choice? In two ways. On a practical day-to-day level, I can encourage whatever opens up the heart chakra, replacing resentment, recoil, and contraction by gratitude, love, and expansiveness. Even this opening is open to corruption by narcissism, for I can focus on me being loving rather than on Love living me. But an opening in the heart is an indispensable preparation for surrender into the Source. Indeed, there may be many isolated but genuine moments of surrender even though one has not uncovered all of one's narcissism and let it die.

The second route is through a therapy or spiritual path which uncovers the connections between one's fundamental attitudes toward one's sexual partner, Mother, and God. We can focus on any one of these and it will help us to uncover attitudes toward the other two, for the attitudes are similar and they are interdependent. For example, if I realize that I have resentment toward God for forcing me into the world with all the limitations of embodied life, I may also realize that I have resentment toward Mother for the same reason. Perhaps, however, I uncover the latter resentment first and then realize that I have resentment toward God. In either case I may then realize that insofar as I project God or Mother onto my sexual partner, she too receives my resentment. Another set of connections may be discerned if I start with a realization concerning my dealings with my sexual partner, for example, that I am trying desperately to bond with her in a psychic-spiritual way, and that this is a megalomanic pressure which is causing many problems in the relationship. This realization can lead to the realization that I once sought or enjoyed such bonding with Mother when I was an infant. I may also realize that much of my urge toward "union with God" is quite infantile.

Such realizations are less likely to arise if one is not sexually involved. A person who is celibate *may* uncover his or her most primitive passions toward Mother and God without connecting them with passions evoked by a sexual partner; but this is less likely. Celibacy may well be an appropriate vocation for some people, but it should not be regarded as the paradigm path for surrender of the *whole* self into God. Of course, merely being sexually involved is not by itself an adequate alternative path. If sexual involvement takes the form of uncommitted promiscuity, such a lifestyle does not enable one to learn much about oneself, and it requires no fundamental changes within oneself. One of the many merits of marriage or long-range sexual commitment is that it can be a school of surrender to God—indeed, the best school. Casual sex, however much it may be spiritualized, involves no challenge to our narcissism, or even to our neuroses.

Earlier I said that one needs a *guide* who has been through the process of letting go of self-preoccupation so as to surrender into the Source. For some people this guide is an indwelling spiritual presence such as the risen Christ or a deceased spiritual Master. As one opens oneself to this presence one gradually learns how to surrender from someone who has already surrendered.

In Chapter VI the significance of such an indwelling for human transformation will be explored more fully. Here, however, I should conclude by returning to the theme with which I began, the meaning of the art of therapy. I am not proposing that therapists should become gurus, but that some of them could and should enlarge their perspectives on sexuality in two spiritual ways. First, they might begin to be more open to new contents of consciousness, specifically, the human aura—especially its higher chakras. This "spiritual" dimension of sex can be, and should be, closely associated with sex as bodily pleasure and sex as passion. Therapy needs to help clients to uncover their spiritual unconscious and relate this to their physical bodies and to their emotional unconscious.

Second, a few therapists might begin to be more open to a mystical perspective on sex. Such a perspective has to do, not with new contents of consciousness, but with a new way of being conscious and a new way of being in the world.

There needs to be a surrender of the whole self, including body, passions, and aura, into the Source which is divine Love. The opposite of such surrender, narcissistic megalomania and resentment, emerges most clearly in relation to one's parents and one's sexual partner and has to be worked through there as well as in relation to God. And where each sexual partner has surrendered his or her whole self into God, each is being lived by the same divine Love. Each person is distinct, but each person is no longer fundamentally separate from the other person, or from anyone or anything.

Such mysticism is, of course, remote from most psychotherapy in our society today.[17] But if, as Erich Fromm has said, therapy is "essentially an attempt to help the patient gain or regain his capacity for love,"[18] and if love is physical, emotional, spiritual, and mystical, then therapists should be willing to work at all four levels. Such a comprehensive approach is especially needed in the healing of *sexuality* as love. It is true that therapists who help people to love physically and emotionally are doing something important in itself and necessary for human healing and fulfilment. By itself, however, such therapy is bound to be inadequate, for we human beings are also spiritual; and, deep down, we are divine.

Section 2

Spirituality and Skepticism

IV * * * Two Dogmas of Skepticism Concerning Spiritual Reality

Throughout Section 1 I talked about many paranormal and spiritual phenomena as if they were real: telepathy, psychic intrusion, out-of-body observations, astral travel, the human aura or spirit, cosmic life energies, indwelling discarnate spirits. I also talked about a mystical surrender of the whole self into the Source. For me the phenomena, in general, are real, and the Source is ultimate reality. For many people in our society, however, my confident talk about them seems bizarre and superstitious. Nor did I in Section 1 provide any justification for such claims except for testimony based on personal experience, whether this be my own or other people's. Why should people who are skeptical concerning the reality of the spiritual believe any of this? Indeed, how can I believe any of this, if I claim to be at all rational?

A necessary condition, though not a sufficient condition, for such belief is that we set aside three presuppositions that pervade our culture and rule out in advance any possibility that spirit could be real. If a person holds any of these presuppositions no truth claims concerning spiritual reality can be validated. The three presuppositions are impersonalism, perspectivalism, and positivism. We will consider impersonalism and perspectivalism in this chapter and positivism in the following two chapters, but here I will define all three:

- *Impersonalism* is the dogmatic rejection of any truth claim that requires personal transformation to be adequately understood and appraised; the only truth possible is truth that can be known impersonally.
- *Perspectivalism* is the dogmatic rejection of any truth claim based on direct experience of reality; all we can study are the various human perspectives that human

beings bring *to* an alleged reality, not the reality itself.

• *Positivism*, a species of impersonalism, is the dogmatic rejection of any truth claim that cannot be tested scientifically; scientific method is the only way to knowledge of reality.

I cannot demonstrate that any of these presuppositions is false, for a skeptic can hold them dogmatically, as unfalsifiable beliefs that are immune to any counter argument or counter evidence. But I can present arguments which might lead some people to question the presuppositions; that is, to realize that they are not self-evident. Yet even if someone not only questions the presuppositions, but goes on to set them aside, this by itself will not provide the experiential basis for believing in the reality of spirit. My hope is that some skeptical readers of Section 2 will be persuaded to say to themselves, "Maybe, after all, there *is* something in what I've been dismissing as superstition." And I may also make intelligible how and why it is not irrational for some people to believe in the reality of spirit.

Some nonskeptical readers may be dismayed by the sudden switch from presentation to defense, from inspiring visions to plodding analysis, but the contemporary worldview that I will be challenging is to some extent in *all* of us. It is part of the largely unconscious mind-set of our culture. Even readers who are personally very open to spiritual and mystical claims, even readers who have tested these claims in their own experience, can find it helpful to bring the skeptical presuppositions into the foreground of consciousness where they can be examined. Moreover, the prevailing world-view is not merely a mistake and an enemy of the human spirit. Impersonalism, perspectivalism, and positivism each *begin* with insights that are important, though they go on to exaggerate the insights in an imperialistic way. If these insights are confined to their legitimate scope, they are important for all of us as human beings, whether our world-view rejects or embraces the reality of the spiritual.

Challenging Impersonalism

Impersonalism is typically linked with a reliance on pure reason;[1] that is, on methods of investigation that anyone who has intelligence and diligence can learn. These methods may belong to science or philosophy or law or to some other academic discipline, but they are all impersonal. Anyone's investigation of a truth claim can be replicated by someone else, regardless of differences in values, attitudes, life orientation, basic motivations, self-understanding, or basic way of being in the world. In short, a person's character is irrelevant to his or her understanding and testing a truth claim. So if a truth claim allegedly requires a process of personal transformation for adequate understanding and appropriate testing, and thus in principle cannot be settled in an impersonal way, the impersonalist dismisses it as unworthy of serious consideration.

Suppose that a mystic talks about love as a spiritual energy and about the self being lived by the Source. Suppose that the mystic then says to the critic, "You are in no position to appraise what I say, or even to think that you begin to understand it, unless you begin to acknowledge and surrender the narcissism which distorts your discernment." Such a personal challenge to the critic defies impersonalist dogma. To an impersonalist, the mystic's requirement of personal change shows that the mystical claims cannot have anything to do with reality. Indeed, his focus on a personal flaw of his critic is seen as a fallacious *ad hominem* argument: instead of pointing out flaws in an opponent's reasoning one attacks the opponent's character.

Although I side with the mystic I must concede that *ad hominem* arguments are often quite irrelevant. If what is at issue is a matter of fact that can be settled in an impersonal way—for example, the claim that imported cars require fewer repairs than domestic models—it would be fallacious for a domestic dealer to dismiss evidence presented by a foreign dealer solely on the ground that the latter's self-interest is affected by the outcome. Many claims concerning matters of fact are simply true, regardless of whether the claims are made by a saint or a scoundrel. And the claims are equally intelligible to the saint and the scoundrel.

If, however, we were to insist that an *ad hominem* argument is *always* irrelevant and fallacious, we would be committing another fallacy, the fallacy of begging the question. That is, we would be assuming, rather than showing, that there is only one answer to the question, "Must all truths be adequately understood and reliably appraised in an impersonal way?" If the answer is "No," since some truths have personal prerequisites for understanding and testing, then a reference to the inadequate character of the critic who dismisses such truths may be quite relevant. Indeed, great spiritual teachers in many religious traditions have issued *ad hominem* challenges to people generally, explicitly rejecting an impersonal approach to the basic truths which they proclaim. When Jesus proclaimed the "Kingdom of God" he told Nicodemus that he could only "see" it, that is, experientially understand it, if he were "born again," undergoing a spiritual transformation. Jesus and other great teachers have insisted that we all need to uncover a fundamental self-deception that pervades our way of being in the world and distorts our discernment. Although they have described this self-deception in differing ways, the core of it is usually a preoccupation with one's separate existence—separate from everything else and separate from the mystery out of which everything continually arises. The spiritual teachers challenge all of us to relinquish our hidden but active self-separation in favor of a different way of being, which brings with it new contents of consciousness that were previously not accessible. Also, and more radically, the new way of being brings a new way of being conscious, whatever the contents that may arise, whether old or new.

Such spiritual teachings concerning the new spiritual contents and concerning the radically different mode of consciousness cannot be understood and tested unless the new way of being has begun. If we presume that we can already understand and test a spiritual teaching without beginning the radical personal change which the teacher says is required for such understanding and testing we are thereby rejecting the teaching as a unified whole. The teaching as a whole combines a "what" and a "how": what is true is linked with how to come to know this truth. The meaning of spiritual and mystical assertions is linked with their method of verification, and this method is not an impersonal technique but a process of personal change. So if we refuse to begin uncovering and surrendering the narcissism which, according to a spiritual teacher, distorts our discernment, we are rejecting what the teacher says. This is so even if we concede, intellectually, "Maybe there's something in what you say."

The intellectual shift expressed by "Maybe there's something in it" is, nevertheless, quite important. It opens up a mind that previously was totally closed to further investigation of spirit. Such a shift toward intellectual openness is necessary if personal openness is to begin at all. And we should notice how the shift can be facilitated if a person has already undergone a conversion to some *non*spiritual perspective and has thereby come to realize that there can be exceptions to impersonalism. If such-and-such a nonspiritual dimension of human nature can only be adequately understood and appraised by someone who undergoes a radical personal change, this may also be the case for the spiritual dimension. For example, let us suppose that a mystic approaches a person who has undergone deep psychotherapy and thereby come to understand and appraise various truth claims of depth psychology. The mystic's invitation to undergo a personal transformation and thereby come to understand and appraise talk about spirit need not be dismissed because of its violation of impersonalism, for impersonalism has turned out to be inadequate in investigating depth psychology, so it may also be inadequate in investigating mystical claims. Once we realize that our way of being in the world can distort our discernment of the world in one respect we may become open to the possibility that this is the case in other respects. This does not always happen, of course. The new convert may cling to the new insight and even use it to assimilate other perspectives into itself, impervious to their challenge. But even if, for example, a convert to psychotherapy imperialistically reduces mysticism to psychology, thereby rejecting the reality of spirit, the convert's reason for doing this is not impersonalism but fanaticism.

In general, although various nonspiritual perspectives may become rivals with each other and with a spiritual perspective, all of them together as allies can provide a formidable critique of impersonalism. As each in turn insists on a radical personal change as a prerequisite for understanding and appraising its claims, each in turn undermines the impersonalist dogma. Let us consider a few examples. *Existentialist freedom* is intelligible and verifiable for a person only to the extent that he or she uncovers the tendency to deceive oneself concerning our freedom to choose our basic way of being in the world and accepts responsibility for exercising that freedom.[2] This "existentializing" process involves a profound change, for one no longer simply continues in a rut of convention, and one no longer blames others for one's own attitudes and responses. Another example is how one comes to understand *radical-political* claims concerning the self-deceptiveness of ideologies.[3] Every group that enjoys institutionalized power and privilege over other groups (men over women, whites over blacks, masters over slaves, citizens over new immigrants, factory owners over workers, commissars over workers) tends to construct an ideology that justifies and sanctions the continuation of the existing structures of domination. Not only the oppressor but to a great extent the oppressed tend to see this ideology as self-evident. It is specially difficult for an oppressor to see through the ideology and realize that it is merely a rationalization. If one's own group interest is at stake the self-deceptivenss of ideologies becomes obvious only if one undergoes a radical change in consciousness. A purely impersonal approach is not likely to uncover the truth. For example, for centuries it has seemed obvious to "reasonable men" that women should be subordinate to men!

Impersonalism is perhaps most deeply undermined when we consider the question, "Does unconditional love exist?" It seems clear to me that I cannot recognize unconditional love at work in anyone, but will necessarily see it as something lesser, with hidden conditions, unless I have actually experienced it myself, however fleetingly, as a recipient or as a channel. An experience of *receiving* unconditional love has as its personal prerequisite a capacity for unconditional trust, and an experience of *channeling* unconditional love has as its personal prerequisite a capacity to let go of narcissism. We can begin to understand what unconditional love is and to verify its reality only to the extent that we fulfill personal prerequisites of trust and surrender. Here, too, as in the list of examples drawn from nonspiritual perspectives, impersonalism is obviously inadequate. Intelligent and diligent application of technique is not enough in any of these cases. Impersonalism, as a dogma which restricts reality to whatever can be investigated impersonally, must be rejected.

The Value of Impersonal Methods

When I insist that impersonal methods of investigation are not always required I am not implying that they are *never* appropriate. On the contrary, pure reason with its essentially impersonal approach is often relevant and significant. When we consider positivism I will be explaining when and why we should apply impersonalist methods if we are investigating the paranormal hinterlands of spirituality and mysticism. Here, however, I simply want to remind us in a general way concerning the merits of pure reason. When we rely on it we can test truth claims by reference to criteria that are in principle comprehensible and acceptable for any intelligent human being. Thus we can replace a chaos of conflicting subjective opinions by a procedure for establishing what is objectively true. And we can do this regardless of differences among us in attitudes, values, motives, character, and so forth. My way of being in the world can differ from yours in many ways, but there can be intersubjective agreement between us—and in principle between all human beings—if together we rely on some form of pure reason. This is important in both our everyday functioning together as citizens in society and our theoretical investigations of humankind and nature. The issue is not whether impersonal pure-reason methods are often appropriate and sometimes even necessary. They are. Impersonalists insist, however, that the methods are *always* necessary. Someone who is strongly committed to impersonal methods of inquiry is not an impersonalist unless he or she insists that *only* such methods are acceptable.

I am not denying that impersonal methods have at least a preliminary relevance in appraising alleged spiritual and mystical truths. Since I have taught courses concerning these matters in an academic setting, where impersonal methods are rightly prominent, I have pondered their relevance. It has seemed to me important, however, to point out to students that spiritual writers stress the need for personal changes if spiritual claims are to be adequately understood and appraised. But if so, how can I expect any reader to adequately understand and appraise what I have presented in Section 1 if they have not already undergone whatever personal changes are needed? On the other hand, if a person is already seriously involved in a spiritual process of personal change, how can academic study of spirituality and mysticism be of any help? Why bother with it at all, if what really matters is the process of personal transformation?

For those who are already involved extensively in a spiritual process, an academic study can provide, at the very least, some helpful "maps" of the territory one is exploring. For others, it can offer two things. First, some intellectual roadblocks against entering a process of personal change can be removed. This happens when a reader begins to acknowledge intellectually that a personal change may well be necessary to remove distortions of discernment and to develop new capacities of awareness. As I have noted, the intellectual shift expressed by "Maybe there's something in it" can be very important.

Academic study can, second, be relevant to anyone because most people already have or can easily acquire an initial understanding of the spiritual dimension of human nature. This initial understanding is of three kinds: linguistic, experiential, and unconscious. *First*, many people already have, or can acquire in an impersonal way, a purely linguistic competence in using the language of a perspective according to its implicit rules. Thus in an academic study of Freud or Eckhart one can learn what can and what cannot be said about Freud's "Id" or Eckhart's "soul." *Second*, most people have some conscious experience, however limited, of the human dimension being considered. For example, concerning the emotional unconscious, most people have had the experience of coming to realize that on a particular occasion they were deceiving themselves concerning how they really felt: "I wouldn't let myself experience how angry (sad, lonely, jealous) I felt." And concerning our spiritual dimension most people have had at least rudimentary experiences of spiritual energy: while moving to music or making love or contemplating a sunrise or giving birth or running a distance. Often in our culture people dismiss such experiences of spiritual energy when they occur, viewing them as merely subjective sensations. Nevertheless such experiences do provide a basis for understanding what spiritual writers are talking about. *Third*, all people have had at least an unconscious contact with the spiritual dimension, for it is part of who we are. This contact has been repressed to varying degrees, but it does provide an obscure sense of what is happening within the dimension, a vague preunderstanding that can facilitate recognition. Some unconscious material is so deeply buried at a particular time that it cannot be raised into consciousness, but the closer any material is to the surface of consciousness the more accessible it is. Sometimes all that is needed for material to emerge into consciousness is for someone else to articulate it. Therefore in Section 1, I could not only expect that all readers could usually follow my linguistic "moves" and I could not only rely on some prior experiential understanding in most readers, I could also hope that sometimes, perhaps, I might evoke a clearer consciousness of something that a reader already unconsciously grasped. Thus for some readers Section 1 may have been evocative.

This section, however, is already quite argumentative. I am presenting an argument against an impersonalist dogma which rules out the reality of spirit. The basic form of the argument is a reminder of challenges to impersonalism made by great spiritual teachers, existentialist philosophers, depth psychotherapists, and radical-communal critics of ideology. Since these challenges do not appeal to impersonalism on its own terms they are merely challenges, not refutations. Yet reflections concerning these challenges do involve a use of pure or impersonal reason in a special form: as meta-reason, or thinking about thinking. Meta-reason stands *above* the impersonal investigations of pure reason, viewing these mental activities alongside other mental activities (in this case, the personalized reflections of spiritual teachers, psychotherapists, and so on). From the lofty vantage point of meta-reason, pure reason can be regarded as merely one perspective alongside others. One may then see that pure reason merely provides one perspective on reality, and that perhaps much of reality may be accessible only from perspectives that require profound personal transformation.

Meta-reason provides an impersonal way of thinking about all perspectives, viewing them alongside each other from a remote vantage point which is different from any of them. The use of meta-reason can be a useful exercise, which helps us to realize that there are many different perspectives which may be in conflict, but it may bring delusions of grandeur to intellectuals like myself, especially if we are philosophers. We may presume that our meta-reason can adjudicate the rival claims of competing perspectives and can discern the unity which is out there in the world. The findings from the impersonal adjudications of meta-reason, however, are very limited, and the only unity it can claim is within itself as abstract reflection. Nevertheless the sense of being an Ideal Observer, in godlike, lofty detachment from all the human perspectives that one surveys, is seductively self-inflating. One may be tempted to cling to this sense of self and identify oneself with it. Indeed this temptation also arises in relation to pure reason generally and not only in relation to the species of pure reason known as meta-reason.

The temptation to cling to pure reason is an obstacle to mystical surrender, for pure reason can seem to be a *substitute* for mysticism, a pseudo-version of the real thing. The delusion arises because the kind of detachment required by pure reason, especially in the extreme form of meta-reason, may seem to be similar to mystical detachment. Pure reason's impersonal methods involve setting aside all nonintellectual dimensions of the self so as not to be influenced by them. That is what makes pure reason pure! In contrast with impersonal detachment, however, mystical detachment is a surrender of *all* attachments, including attachment to the intellectual dimension of the self. If someone doubts that a commitment to pure reason can involve a secret zeal similar to that of some religious fundamentalists, I should mention a dream that a scholar of Kant once told me. (Kant, of course, was the supreme practitioner of meta-reason.) In the dream the scholar was ecstatic, for he had won $5 million and could achieve his lifelong ambition: to place a copy of Kant's *Critique of Pure Reason* in every hotel and motel bedroom in the nation!

Another way in which pure reason can become a roadblock against mysticism is by becoming a reinforcing expression of human narcissism. An intellectual who *identifies* himself or herself as pure reason tends to replace the Source by this godlike intellect-self and to separate the intellect-self from all the rest of the self and from all there is in the universe. Descartes's slogan, "I think, therefore I am" can become "I think like a god and that is all that I really am, and nothing else is clearly real." To the extent that I identify myself as pure reason I replace the Source by a portion of my self, ignoring all the rest of my self. In stark contrast with this, mysticism involves a surrender of the whole self into the Source so as to include the whole self in what is lived by the Source.

Since the whole self includes pure reason, this means that pure reason is surrendered into the Source to be lived by the Source. So pure reason can eventually have a place within a mystical life, when one no longer identifies oneself as "the thinker" but instead as the whole self unified at the soul and surrendered into the Source. With such a self-identification pervading all activities of the self, it is sometimes possible, however, for pure reason to operate autonomously, temporarily setting aside all nonintellectual dimensions of the self, for this is experienced merely as the application of a method, a useful strategy for particular purposes. At other times the intellectual dimension will be very open to influence from other dimensions such as passion or spirit and will not be operating as *pure* reason but as passionate reason or inspired reason. As Gabriel Marcel has wisely insisted, impersonal reason (he calls it *primary reflection*) is not the only kind of reason. There are also various forms of what he calls *secondary reflection*, where personal involvement is necessary if truth is to emerge. What I am proposing is a dialogue among many perspectives, a dialogue between pure reason and passionate reason and inspired reason and radical-political reason, and so forth. As reflections from various perspectives complement and correct one another, truth concerning the ongoing discovery-creation of human nature can gradually emerge. Pure reason has a very significant role in this dialogue, but it is not the sole arbiter of disputes between perspectives. And it is not, as impersonalists would claim, the sole avenue to truth, eliminating all the others.

We have seen that meta-reason can be very useful. Indeed, my critique of impersonalism is partly an exercise of meta-reason. But meta-reason is not ultimate unless we accept the dogma of perspectivalism, which we will soon be considering. Without that dogma, meta-reason is merely a useful way to *map* what we have *already* come to know in ways that do not involve meta-reason. When backed by perspectivalism, however, the pretensions of meta-reason become difficult to challenge. For a perspectivalist no direct experience of reality is possible, so that we can never see real things. We can only, as it were, see photographs of them. Then a master photograph which arranges all the others in an overall pattern would have much claim to supremacy. As a master perspective on perspectives, meta-reason would provide the best version of the only kind of truth available to human beings. If, however, direct experience of reality is possible, then meta-reason as a perspective on perspectives is twice removed from reality. It is still important, but in *indirect relation to experience* rather than in self-sufficient isolation from experience. So we turn to the dogma of perspectivalism, considering it first in general, then in relation to spiritual reality, and then in relation to mysticism.

Challenging Perspectivalism

Perspectivalism as a dogma is the exaggeration of a genuine insight to the point of absurdity. The insight is that we human beings experience everything through a variety of perspectives, and that if we are to arrive at truth we must become aware of how these perspectives both distort and illuminate. The absurd dogma is that we can never know things in themselves, assured by direct experience that they exist independently of us with their own structure, for all we can know is our own perspectives on reality.

The absurdity of this dogma lies in refusing to acknowledge that the reasons given for such universal skepticism presuppose that we *can* know reality. For example, errors in sense perception, such as seeing a bend in a straight stick that is inserted into water, are *known* to be errors because we can *contrast* them with veridical sense perceptions; for example, when we see and feel the straightness of the stick out of the water. Let us also consider how we come to realize that our emotional unconscious distorts our awareness of other people, moving us to project onto them various characteristics which as infants we experienced in our parents. The distortion can only be recognized as such if sometimes we do see other people's characteristics accurately. And, to consider yet another perspective, the errors of ideology which are exposed when someone undergoes a radical-political conversion can only be recognized as such if there is some non-ideological way of perceiving what is true concerning the power structures of society, and so on. In general, any uncovering of a pervasive self-deception concerning reality presupposes a reference to some way of knowing reality. Otherwise there would be no basis for claiming that there has been self-deception.[4] If the veridical way of knowing is not to be merely a perspective that happens, unknown to us, to "fit" reality, it must consist not only of a perspective but also of some direct access to reality.

The absurdity of perspectivalism arises in a second way, when perspectivalists, observing human behavior, make truth claims concerning what perspectives people actually have. Indeed, the basic insight of perspectivalism is that we *can* detect perspectives and can often find out their origins. When we do claim to detect a perspective, however, we must somehow know, by experience, that the perspective itself is real. Let us consider an analogy. Observing a perspective is like observing a camera and observing a photograph taken by the camera. The camera is like the form-imposing activity of the perspective, and the photograph is like a content of the perspective. Suppose that we see only a camera and a photograph of, say, a chair, so that we cannot be sure of the reality of the *chair.* We are at least sure of the reality of the camera and the photograph. It is not that we only have a *photograph* of the camera and the photograph. Similarly when post-Kantians claim to detect a perspective, they assume that they have more than a perspective on that perspective. But if we can know, by experience, that a perspective is real, why can we allegedly never know that a chair or a spirit is real? And if we cannot know that a perspective is real, are we not committed to an infinite regress of perspectives on perspectives on perspectives, so that perspectivalism itself has no basis?

A third kind of absurdity arises for some perspectivalists when they try to escape total relativism and nihilism by appealing to *pragmatic* criteria as a basis for choosing between beliefs. That is, they propose that we test truth claims by looking at the consequences of one's believing that the claim is true. The problem that arises is that whatever kinds of consequences are selected to make these tests, we must be able to experience these consequences to be real.[5] If we have only perspectives on the consequences, we then would have to test any truth claims concerning the consequences pragmatically in terms of the further consequences of believing in their reality, and so we would be launched into another infinite regress. Pragmatism as a remedy to the problems of perspectivalism is workable only if we can sometimes experience realities. In our culture these realities are typically material realities. Indeed, it is difficult in everyday living not to be certain that one is experiencing the reality of some things, for example, the chair on which one is sitting. The main reason why perspectivalism is rarely all-inclusive as an academic theory and even more rarely all-inclusive as a way of living is that people do in fact have experiences of material reality. I see my chair and I feel it supporting my weight. I do not doubt its existence even if I have read Descartes! What philosophers call *naive realism* need not remain unsophisticated. It may well be modified in very complex ways once we reflect not only on our occasional errors but also on the interpretative perspectives we bring to our experiences of material reality. But any theorizing that totally rejects the element of basic, direct knowing in this experience is bound to seem implausible to most human beings. What I sit on does exist independent of my experiencing it and "corresponds" in a rough but basic way to what I feel and see concerning it. It is true that what counts as a chair depends on the concept of chair which we bring to the object on which we are sitting. It is also true that I might mistake a flat tree stump for a chair if I sit down outside in the dark and do not lean back. But I do know directly, as I sit on it, that the object really exists independently, and that its firmness is part-cause of my sensations of firm support.

When perspectivalism is applied pragmatically to spiritual beliefs, the most plausible approach for most contemporary thinkers is to evaluate the beliefs in terms of the *non*spiritual real consequences of living in accordance with them. Allegedly nobody can know experientially that there really is a spiritual dimension to human beings and the cosmos or that God as Supreme Spirit or mystical Source actually exists. A thoroughly consistent perspectivalist would, of course, be a skeptic concerning all *non*spiritual reality as well. Then not only can one not know that Jesus Christ is alive by spiritually encountering him, one also cannot know that a chair is real by sitting on it. We have seen that such an all-inclusive agnosticism is difficult to maintain, both because of the three logical difficulties that I noted, but also because everyday living involves an implicit naive realism concerning the material world. Most people, if asked "Do the chairs and trees and people whom we see and feel and touch really exist, and do we mostly experience them as they really are?" would answer, "Of course, obviously."

Throughout most of human history many people have also had a comparable naive-realist confidence in their experiential awareness of *spiritual* reality. This is true not only of shamans, but also of many others who had convincing experiences of spiritual reality that might differ from the shaman's in frequency or intensity or sublimity. In our culture, however, impressive experiences of spiritual reality may be less frequent than they have been in most cultures, and even when they occur, they are less likely to be taken seriously even by the recipient of the experience. Since in our culture convincing experiences of material reality occur much more frequently than convincing experiences of spiritual reality, perspectivalism is understandably more plausible when applied to the latter. But on the other hand, perspectivalism, with its insistence that no experience of spiritual reality *can* occur, helps to prevent the occurrence of the impressive experiences that would undermine it.

Dogmatic perspectivalism, as applied to both material and spiritual realities, is mostly a matter of "footnotes to Kant." Although it draws to some extent on the arguments of ancient skeptics, it draws mainly on a movement of thought that Kant initiated and post-Kantians extended and revised. Kant, devising and applying his own kind of meta-reason, convinced himself that all we can know is how the human mind *must* shape sense experience. All we can know is how the human mind imposes on sense experience the forms of space and time and the very general concepts and categories such as cause and substance. What we impose gives to sense experience an intelligible structure, but what is really out there we cannot know. We can only know reality on our own terms, and what these terms are we can deduce in a "transcendental" way, using a kind of meta-reason. After Kant's time many diverse thinkers have followed him in emphasizing what the human mind brings *to* our awareness of the world, but differed from him in focusing, not on what we transcendentally *must* bring to this awareness, but on what we observably *do* bring. What we do bring varies from person to person and group to group, so our alleged knowing is relative to this. The variations in what we bring to our awareness of the world depend on a variety of factors, any one of which can be selected for emphasis. Some theories of knowledge stress sociological influences, others select psychological influences or cultural-historical influences. And some theories following Wittgenstein depict our knowing as shaped by linguistic practices within a social "form of life." What all these approaches have in common is the dogma of perspectivalism. There is allegedly no direct way of knowing reality. All we can study is the various interpretative frameworks that human beings bring *to* reality.

But both material reality and spiritual reality have structures that human beings can discern. One can discern the colors of the rainbow and the spiritual energies in the chakras. In each case the structure has shaped our human language and concepts, though these in turn have developed independent of the structure in varying degrees, shaping our awareness of material and spiritual reality in ways that may clarify or distort. It is true that people of different traditions see colors differently because of the different color language they have learned, and that people of different traditions discern discarnate spirits differently because of the different spirit language they have learned. But it is not the case that our linguistic distinctions can never be tested or justified by reference to direct, nonlinguistic experience.

Many people will concede that we do have direct experience of different *colors.* Some thinkers may even concede that there is an element of direct experience in the process of exploring *human* reality from a *non*spiritual perspective, whether this be psychotherapeutic or existential or interpersonal. But when a person claims to be exploring *spiritual* reality, the perspectivalist dogma typically triumphs. For example, when social scientists ask why some people believe in spirits they give all sorts of relevant explanations—psychological, sociological, historical, cultural—but they totally ignore the possibility that sometimes part of the answer is, "Because this person has actually experienced the presence of a spirit." This would be only part of the answer, for the experience is interpreted by the person in ways that are open to *non*spiritual explanations. For example, if someone has a vision of the Virgin Mary, her appearance and clothing will be influenced by cultural conditioning, and her characteristics may even be somewhat distorted by unconscious projections (as in the case of seeing an embodied person). But if there really are spirits, the person may have had an experience of a spirit. The experience will involve much more interpretative overlay than does the experience of the color orange, and much of it may be distorted, but the core of the experience may be true.

Before anyone dismisses as illusory the experiences of millions of people in most societies within human history, one should consider the possibility that here too, as in other aspects of human life, there is a mixture of reality and illusion. So if a person claims to have had a vision of Jesus Christ, or to have been inwardly counseled by an ancestral spirit, it is possible that this is what actually happened, even if many features of the experience can and should be explained in nonspiritual ways. In the next two chapters I will be considering, in some detail, the methods of verification which are appropriate to such claims. Here I am merely challenging the assumption that all such claims can and should be totally explained in nonspiritual ways. I am questioning the unquestioned skepticism which shapes most contemporary academic investigations of spiritual reality. (This skepticism is very common even among theologians, as we will see in Chapter XI.)

Establishing Truth by Dialogue between Perspectives

One alternative to perspectivalism is impersonalism, which proposes pure reason as a way—indeed, the *only* way—to establish truth claims concerning reality. We have seen, however, that this approach to truth is inadequate, for it refuses to acknowledge the genuine insight on which perspectivalism is based. As we realize that we see the world *through* various perspectives we come to realize that pure reason at its best is merely one perspective, though a very important perspective, alongside others. Indeed, we realize that often what purports to be pure reason is not pure at all, but is the slave of a pervasive self-deception. Although pure reason has an important role in establishing truth, it needs to be supplemented and corrected by insights from other perspectives. Through such dialogue truth can gradually emerge.

There are three kinds of dialogue, of which a dialogue among perspectives is the third. The first dialogue goes on within the individual. It is *intra*personal. Some progress toward truth is possible because there is some experiential access to reality within the process of investigation as we apply a perspective. The understanding and testing which experience facilitates is not final or complete, and we are always (except in mystical surrender) perceiving reality to some extent *through* a conceptual grid that we bring to it. Our progress in knowledge is not simply a matter of directly experiencing what is real. Rather, we gradually uncover and correct distortions of discernment through a process of inner dialogue between our interpretative perspective and direct experience, each correcting and complementing the other.

The second kind of dialogue is an outer dialogue among people who belong to the same perspectival community, for example, a philosophical association, a religious group or a community of Jungian psychotherapists. The perspectives and experiences of individuals differ somewhat for each individual, so in dialogue they can correct and complement each other's claims to truth.

In addition to the process of self-correction which each perspective can undergo within individuals and within its community, there is also the possibility of a correction by an external critique from other perspectives. Since this critique typically comes at least as much from other people as it does from oneself, the search for truth is very much a communal project. Indeed, one can hope that more and more of

humankind will gradually become involved in mutual dialogue, correcting and complementing each other's perspectives in a process that involves both the uncovering and the
creation of our human nature.

What I am proposing differs from perspectivalism in two
respects. First, I am insisting that there is some experiential
access to reality that can be a part of the dialogue within
perspectives and between perspectives. Second, I am insisting on an important role for pure reason because it provides
the best prospect for achieving *some* intersubjective agreement among most human beings. As we will see in Chapter
VIII, this is especially significant in our attempts to establish
a minimal moral code recognizable by all humankind. And
pure reason as science is also obviously very important in
our investigations of material reality.

Within the contemporary university most academics tend
to alternate between impersonalism and perspectivalism,
though usually with more emphasis on one than the other.
Often they do not even notice the contradictions between
these rival approaches, though sometimes the two rivals are
engaged in fierce and open controversy, as is evident in some
contemporary philosophy. One strategy for reconciling the
rivals has been to claim for pure reason a limited territory
which has always been common to all human beings, while
conceding the remaining territory to a variety of historically
conditioned perspectival communities, each with its own
internal criteria for truth. Thus some truth is "true-for-
everyone" but most truth is "true-for-us." What is true-for-
everyone is allegedly true in abstraction from all historical
contexts, true for any human being at any time and any
place. What is true-for-us varies from community to community, each with its own perspective, which has been
shaped by the countless factors of its historical context.

This way of settling the conflict between impersonalism
and perspectivalism can be attractive to both camps, for it
draws a boundary between them and allows each to reign
supreme within its own territory. My own proposal differs
from this in various ways. First, although I do grant to pure
reason a "territory," it does not reign supreme there, but

must be in dialogue with other perspectives. For example, in Chapter VIII I draw up a list of universal human needs and interests concerning which it is plausible to claim that everyone else might agree—provided that they, like me, are using pure reason. On this basis I propose a minimal moral code. This code, however, should be both complemented and corrected by insights concerning human needs and interests which arise from other perspectives, including the spiritual.

Second, I must concede that although pure reason aspires to gaining universal acceptance for its conclusions, it does not as yet provide truths which everyone recognizes. Indeed, pure reason appeared only recently in its *present* form as a dominant perspective within much of Western culture. Pure reason is the perspective of one community and it exists alongside rival perspectives held by other communities. Truth concerning our changing human nature emerges gradually as these perspectives are pooled together, complementing and correcting and including each other. As more communities participate in dialogue, people change, and a truth which is "true-for-us" may grow in the range of its "us," though this is at the price of its isolationist purity. For example, more human beings may both apply and exemplify pure reason as this is enriched and modified by passionate reason and spirited reason. And the emerging truth is not merely a pooling of perspectives that moves toward an overall coherence among diverse perspectives, for it is also based on the direct experience of individuals within the various communities. Their *intra*personal dialogue involves a shaping and shaking of conceptual structures in response to experience.

Such an intrapersonal dialogue occurs concerning *spiritual* reality, as I have already indicated. All our knowledge of experienced spiritual energies and spiritual presences is knowledge *through* perspectives that we bring *to* these realities. Earlier, however, I said that although we almost always perceive reality perspectivally, through a conceptual or symbolic "grid" which we bring *to* reality, the one exception is when we let go of this grid completely in mystical surrender. But is this possible? Can anyone let go of the grid complete-

ly? Mystics of different religious traditions agree in answering "Yes."[6] Their testimony should be taken seriously. It is
not that they refuse to take the insights of perspectivalism
seriously. On the contrary, no human beings have been more
aware of the power of human perspectives over the human
mind. They have known firsthand the difficulty in letting go
of our attachment to the familiar mental frameworks which
we impose on our experience of the Ultimate and of things
and people. Nevertheless they testify that eventually one
can "empty the mind." Then there is a state of being conscious, but not conscious *of* anything, for one's consciousness has become indistinguishable from the Ultimate consciousness. Alternatively, they report that what one is
conscious *of* can be described only negatively, as an absence
of light or of sound or of any particular content. Perhaps
these are two different ways of referring to the same mystical state, or perhaps the second refers to a penultimate state.

Some mystics also report a way of experiencing things and
persons that does not discard perspectives but, as it were,
holds to them very loosely.[7] In this case the mystic experiences things and persons through perspectives, but the perspectives do not block access to reality, for the mystic does
not cling to them. Whatever conceptual or symbolic framework is in the mind is subordinated to a contemplative
openness of the mind. For example, in a typical "I-Thou"
encounter with another human being it is not the case that
all "I-It" conceptual frameworks have disappeared. Rather,
one lets go of all attachment to "I-It" preconceptions and
intuits the real presence of the person, while nevertheless
thinking in I-It ways.[8] Similarly, if the encounter is with a
discarnate spirit, there can be a subordination of description
and interpretation to the direct awareness of the spirit.
Without such subordination, and the letting go that makes it
possible, what one "encounters" is mostly what one imposes, not the reality itself. And the same principle applies if
what one encounters is a leaf or a rabbit.

Contemplation, with its subordination of our mental preconceptions to an openness toward whatever we are experiencing, is a crucial element in any intrapersonal dialogue

between interpretative perspective and direct experience. And such intrapersonal dialogue, where perspective and experience correct and complement each other, is itself an essential resource in both intracommunal and intercommunal dialogues, which otherwise tend to become mere mind games, out of touch with experienced reality. Thus the ongoing discovery-creation of human nature is a dynamic process which must be grounded in a contemplative openness to direct experience if perspectives are to be modified not only by each other but also by reality itself. Pure reason is in this respect an inadequate resource. Although pure reason provides an important perspective in the dialogues which lead us into truth, it lacks contemplative openness. Its impersonalism involves a leechlike attachment to the intellectual dimension of the self. This restricts reality to that which fits the frameworks which the intellect imposes on experience.

One species of pure reason is *science*, which has its own special strengths and special limitations. In the next chapter I will show how scientific method can have at most a limited application in studies of the paranormal hinterland of genuine spirituality. In Chapter VI, when we consider genuine spirituality in contrast with the paranormal, we will see that scientific method is out of its depth. In both chapters I will be challenging positivism, which is the dogma that scientific method is the only way to knowledge of reality. The explorations of scientific method and the paranormal may seem to take us a long way from the "edifying discourses" of Section 1, but a reflective spirituality needs to know how to respond to science, and a genuine spirituality can arise out of the paranormal.

V * * * Positivism and the Paranormal

In the nineteenth century Saint-Simon and Comte claimed that scientific method is the only way to knowledge or reality. This claim, which they labeled positivism[1] and which others call scientism, has become an unquestioned assumption not only for many scientists but also among people generally.

Positivism is a species of impersonalism. We recall that impersonalism is the dogmatic rejection of any truth that requires personal transformation to be adequately understood and appraised. All truth claims can and must be tested by reference to impersonal criteria, that is, criteria in principle comprehensible and acceptable to all intelligent human beings, regardless of personal differences in attitudes, emotions, values, character and so forth. All such personal variables can and must be set aside if pure reason is to be our way to truth.

Impersonalism is an operative ideal for many philosophers, legal theorists, literary critics, linguists, and historians. In each field scholars propose impersonal methods which allegedly could, in principle, give rise to universal intersubjective agreement. None of these impersonal methods, however, is as plausible as scientific method in achieving this goal. So there is a pressure to modify methods in the direction of science. This has already happened in various studies of human beings such as psychology, sociology, and economics, which claim to be "social sciences," though in each discipline some investigators resist this trend.

Is scientific method the only way to knowledge of reality? Obviously scientific method is one way. Science has achieved universal or nearly universal agreement concerning many matters, thereby transcending profound personal and ideological differences among human beings. And science has had amazing success in enabling us to transform our world. But this does not justify the positivist claim that scientific method is the only way to knowledge of reality. We have already implicitly questioned this claim in Chapter IV. There we saw that all species of impersonalism are being merely dogmatic when they reject the possibility that some truths cannot be adequately understood or verified unless individuals undergo an appropriate process of personal transformation. Since positivism is a species of impersonalism, its unreflective dogmatism concerning this issue has thus been challenged. There are additional reasons, however, for challenging positivism, insofar as it imperialistically claims an unlimited and exclusive scope for scientific method. In this chapter I will be charting some of the limits of scientific method in relation to the paranormal.

Some readers may have little interest in scientific method, and others may feel that it is alien and even threatening. I invite such readers to persevere, nevertheless, for science secretly influences all of us in our ways of thinking, so we need to become more clearly aware of it. And if you see science as an enemy you should realize that the slogan, "Know your enemy" applies. A further reason for persevering through my somewhat technical presentation of scientific method is that the chapter also lays the basis for a distinction between the paranormal and the genuinely spiritual, a distinction crucial for anyone embarking on a mystical path.

Four Principles of Scientific Method

There are various versions of scientific method, each one differing slightly from the others. A thorough study would note not only these variations but also the complexities that arise for scientific investigators in various fields. For our purposes, however, a brief and simplified presentation is appropriate.[2] Four main principles are prominent:

1. Isolation: Isolate genuine causal factors by using control groups.
2. Repeatability: Devise an experiment that anyone can repeat, and accumulate data on the basis of which one can establish either (i) Invariant Laws: whenever anyone produces A, there is B; or (ii) Statistical Corre-

lations: whenever anyone produces A, there is such and such, a probability of B.

3. Quantifiability: If possible, describe A and B in terms of measurable units rather than in purely qualitative terms.

4. Theoretical Plausibility: Relate your investigation to, or create, a theoretical framework that (i) brings together many laws or correlations concerning observables; and perhaps (ii) refers to nonobservable theoretical entities that help to explain the laws or correlations.

Let us consider each principle in turn. Isolation can be easily illustrated in medical research. If a new drug is being tested for its efficacy in treating cancer there might be three groups, X, Y, and Z, all of whom consist of people who have the same kind of cancer at the same stage. Group X would be injected with the drug, group Y would be injected with a saline solution, and group Z would receive no treatment. Groups Y and Z are "control" groups. If they improve as much as group X, this indicates that the new drug is not shown to be the source of any improvement in group X. Improvement may come equally in groups X and Y because the injection of anything which the patient thinks might help is a "placebo" for the patient, inducing a confidence which itself beings improvement. Improvement may come equally in groups X and Z because the particular kind of cancer common to both groups is open to spontaneous remissions, independent of any treatment. If, however, group X's rate of improvement is significantly better than group Y's or group Z's (or if Y and Z both get worse), the new drug is genuinely a causal factor in group X. And, more important, if the researchers had no control groups, but simply injected group X with the new drug, any improvement in group X could not be attributed scientifically to the drug, for maybe the change occurred because the injection acted as a placebo, or maybe the change would have occurred without any treatment.

In my presentation of the principle of isolation I have depicted scientific method as an attempt to identify *causes*. This is an oversimplification. Sometimes scientists are satisfied even though they cannot establish a causal connection, provided that they can establish a significant correlation which enables them to make reliable predictions. What more is being claimed when someone claims not only a significant correlation but also a causal connection? This question has evoked much controversy in philosophy of science and in metaphysics. It is not appropriate to explore this controversy here.[3] For our purposes I should note only that there seem to be two main paradigms of causality: *mechanical causality* (one billiard ball hitting another one) and *agent causality* (my purposively moving my arm, which holds the billiard cue).[4] The second paradigm, agent causality, lies outside scientific method. Where a scientist claims to establish a (mechanical) causal connection, two kinds of consideration seem to be relevant. The first consideration is whether the investigation fulfils the principles of isolation and repeatability. The second consideration is whether the evidence itself, or the entities in the relevant theoretical framework (for example, molecules), are connected mechanically; that is, by local impact or at least by some analogous kind of local contact. (Later we will see that some of the new physics does not involve mechanical causality.) Issues concerning mechanical causality and agent causality will periodically arise in this chapter, but here I want to note mainly that the scientific principle of isolation aspires ideally to identify causes, though it will accept significant correlations.

Repeatability has been depicted by me in its ideal form, where a scientist does not merely observe A and then B, but *produces* A and then observes B, in an experiment which he or she and anyone else (with appropriate training) can repeat. In a less ideal version of the principle, the scientist makes *observations* that are repeatable both by him or her and by others; for example, observing that such-and-such cloud formations and changes in barometric pressure are frequently followed by rain. Such scientific compilations at best enable us to *predict* rain but not to *produce* it. Both kinds of repeatability provide bases for universal intersubjective agreement concerning truth claims, but experimental repeatability provides bases for techniques of control, for knowledge as power over. Where the experimental repeatability yields only statistical correlations rather than invariant laws, the degree of control is correspondingly less, but it is nevertheless very important.

Quantifiability is in one sense a part of the principle of Repeatability. What one produces or observes must be an item (A) that is repeated as the same kind of item for such and such a *number* of times, with such and such a *number* of instances of (B) following. The principle of Quantifiability that I am noting here, however, goes beyond this element of measurability. In its most rigorous form this principle insists that both (A) and (B) must themselves be described in terms of measurable units rather than in purely qualitative terms. For example, if water is described not merely as "very cold" but as "at zero degree Centigrade," then the generalization "at zero degree Centigrade water freezes" involves *one* quantified variable. The concept of freezing, however, remains purely qualitative. Since there is minimal possibility of disagreement among observers concerning what counts as freezing (in contrast with the possibility concerning what counts as "very cold"), the generalization is acceptable to most scientists. Some scientists, however, aspire toward a science that includes only generalizations where both A and B are describable numerically. For example, in some research on sexual orgasm, personal testimony concerning experienced satisfaction tends to be replaced by data concerning measurable physiological changes or, less radically, people are asked to rate their satisfaction on a scale of one to ten. Or, in researching the effects of a new expressway within a city, any effects on the quality of life for citizens that cannot be quantified (for example, beauty and ugliness, or the sense of community within a neighborhood that would be divided) either tend to be omitted or to be given some artificial numerical significance so that the investigation can seem to provide "scientific" bases for a town-planning decision.

Quantifiability is not universally required by scientists,[5] though it remains as an ideal for many. The move toward it seems to arise from two distinguishable considerations. First, as I have already noted, quantifiability tends to reduce the possibility of disagreement concerning what *counts* as *A* and *B*. Second, there is increased scope for the application of *mathematics* to science if all the items are measurable units. In its extreme form, quantifiability seems to imply that all of science can be reduced to physics, the science that can most fully implement the principle. But less rigorous applications of the principle pervade a great deal of contemporary science.

Theoretical Plausibility is the scientific principle which gives rise to most disagreement among scientists; and the more remote the theories are from particular empirical observations, the more disagreement there tends to be. In this aspect of science the creativity of individual scientists is most evident, both in sometimes devising new theories which are simpler, more consistent, more comprehensive or more elegant than existing theories and in sometimes devising crucial experiments whose outcome decisively shows the superiority of one rival theory over another. (Scientific method provides no recipe for scientific creativity. It provides principles for *testing* scientific claims that often originate in the minds of creative scientists.)

My listing of theoretical plausibility with the first three principles of scientific method is potentially misleading, for science sometimes proceeds in the *absence* of any relevant explanatory theory. Sometimes scientists can bring about changes or predict changes on the basis of observed correlations without citing any theory. But although scientists can get by without being able to invoke theories as they carry on some of their investigations, the absence of an adequate theoretical framework can nevertheless often be a serious drawback, and an intrinsic part of scientific method seems to be the commitment to provide, eventually, such an explanatory framework. Thus although the results of a scientific study should not be dismissed purely on the ground that no adequate theoretical framework exists to help explain the results, the need for such a framework is an important consideration.

Consider an example from parapsychology. Experiments have been done to see whether a self-described spiritual healer has some effect on the rate of healing of mice or the rate of growth of plants.[6] If there is a significant difference between groups where his hands were a few inches from the mice or plants and groups where other hands were, and groups where no hands were, this suggests that somehow he was affecting them. In his own experience he is transmitting healing energies, but for the scientific investigator such energies are at most a postulated, nonobservable theoretical entity. Perhaps the energies postulated to explain what happened fit with those already postulated within existing scientific theories; but perhaps not. If not, then perhaps eventually parapsychological research will require the construction of some new theories, postulating some new energies. If, however, these energies are very remote from any energies postulated in the rest of science, parapsychology will remain somewhat suspect, on the periphery of science. (My own hunch, based on my own direct experience of various kinds of energies, is that some of these may fit what science now postulates, some may come to be included in a future revised super theory of energies, and some, for example, the healing energies of specific discarnate spirits, may be beyond the range of scientific investigation.)

I should note that, when some scientific theorists postulate nonobservable items, they do not assert these to be metaphysically real, in the sense that the observable items which theories explain are metaphysically real. Rather, these theorists see the nonobservables as formal fictions, useful in providing an intelligible unifying picture, and perhaps fruitful in suggesting further possible generalizations for scientists to investigate. In Chapter VI, however, we will see that other theorists (David Bohm, for example) think that their nonobservable items are quite real. We will also see that the new physics, insofar as it replaces miniature material objects by energies as the fundamental nonobservables, can be construed as being more congenial toward mysticism. We will also see that some radical innovators such as Bohm propose theories that seem similar to what mystics claim. (I will indicate why I am much less excited by all this than are some other advocates of mysticism.)

Although scientific theories are important for science as a whole, in most scientific investigations they are not prominent. Only rarely do scientific investigations involve any testing of scientific theories. Instead, the theories are presupposed, and even this implicit reference to theory varies greatly in its importance. Some concepts such as "electron" are heavily loaded with scientific theory in their meaning. But although one experiment may involve talk about electrons, another may be designed simply to find out how quickly oak burns, as compared with elm. The meanings of the terms *oak burns* and *elm* minimally invoke any reference to scientific theory.[7]

Commonsense Verification

This concludes my brief exploration of four principles of scientific method. Before we go on to consider more thoroughly the application of scientific method to various paranormal and spiritual truth claims, we should consider several other approaches to truth, beginning with *common sense.* What counts as common sense in our culture is deeply influenced by science, but there is still much that is nonscientific. This is evident in a court of law, especially if we set aside the ways in which the legal system imposes its own distinctive framework in determining what is legally relevant or irrelevant when a judge or jury come to a verdict. What we find is a commonsense focus on a particular event, for example, a murder. Here truth is not typically established by repeatable-at-will experiments involving control groups, quantifiable data, and scientific theories. Rather we assume in court, as in everyday life, that human agents can cause events[8] and that particular instances of this agent causality can usually be verified—as they were before the rise of modern science—without any appeal to modern science. In court a typical issue is whether a particular person did indeed cause a particular event, for example, another person's death. Sometimes scientific testimony may be sought concerning whether or not such and such a kind of action could cause such and such a kind of effect, but much of the relevant testimony is nonscientific. If we want to establish whether an observable event really occurred or who or what caused it, we find ourselves appraising the testimony of nonscientific witnesses. Such appraisal, whether in a law court or in everyday life, involves the application of three criteria: (a) reliability of witnesses (in contrast with possible fraud or self-deception or stupidity), (b) convergence of independent testimony (in contrast with nonconvergence of testimony or convergence where witnesses conspire to agree in their testimony), and (c) conformity with the current convictions of common sense concerning what does happen or what can happen (in contrast with testimony that seems "farfetched" to common sense, for example, "I clairvoyantly saw Jones murder Brown").

It is obvious that in our culture criterion (c) counts against testimony concerning the reality of paranormal and spiritual phenomena. Later on, however, I will argue that criteria (a) and (b) can sometimes work in favor of such testimony. That is, although the *dogmas* of our common sense (which arguably have a legitimate emphasis in a court of law) preclude the reality of the paranormal and the spiritual, the application of two commonsense *methods* of appraising testimony from psychics and mystics can indicate that perhaps the testimony is credible. Indeed, we will later see that these methods, with their focus on the honesty and sanity of psychics and mystics and the convergence or mutual corroboration of their reports, are more relevant in testing paranormal and mystical truth claims than scientific method is.

Eventually, in Chapter VI, I will be examining various ways of testing the truth claims of mystics, but in this chapter we will consider the truth claims of psychics. I distinguish psychics not only from mystics who report a unity with the Source at the soul, but also from people who are

involved in a "genuinely spiritual" process of personal transformation, open to whatever spiritual realities help them to
become more loving and less narcissistic. Thus far in this
book, however, I have included both psychic-paranormal and
genuinely spiritual elements in what I have called the *spiritual unconscious* and the *spiritual dimension*, without differentiating the two elements. In these chapters I will be dis-
tinguishing them. There are two quite different reasons for
doing this. First, the two elements are not related to scientific method in the same way. In this chapter I will show that
scientific method is to some extent relevant in testing some
kinds of psychic claims. In Chapter VI, however, I will show
that it is virtually irrelevant in testing genuinely spiritual
claims. Second, in the daily lives of some people the paranormal and the genuinely spiritual are at cross purposes, so
in Chapter VI a resolution of this conflict will be proposed.

Some people are psychic or, in my own case, have become
psychic. That is, they can either directly experience *normal
phenomena in paranormal ways*, or they can directly experience *paranormal phenomena* that are not accessible to ordinary sense experience. For example, they can either feel telepathically what someone else is feeling miles away and see
clairvoyantly what is happening miles away, or they can discern such paranormal phenomena as the transmitting of
healing energies (whether by themselves or others) and the
presence of a discarnate spirit near another person. Where
paranormal phenomena are involved, different issues arise,
as we will see later. Here I will merely note that a nonpsychic such as a scientist who investigates psychic healing of
mice and plants cannot directly check reports concerning
paranormal phenomena such as healing energies; at most
the publicly observable evidence might lead the scientist to
postulate such energies. Reports concerning the paranormal
access to normal phenomena, however, can be directly
checked by nonpsychics: "Yes, I was feeling terrified at 6:00

p.m. yesterday" or "Yes, your grandfather did die at 6:00 p.m. on March 11." We will consider such cases first.

Paranormal Access to Normal Phenomena

There is nothing paranormal about feeling terrified. It is possible, however, that one's feeling of terror might not be observable to others, who then have to rely on one's testimony. So let us consider an example of a clairvoyant[9] vision of a publicly observable event.[10] Let us suppose that the granddaughter's vision of grandfather's death was very detailed. That is, not only was the time correct, but granddaughter "saw" who was with him at the time (his housekeeper, pastor, and grandson), what they were wearing, where they stood and sat, what flowers there were, and so on. The more detailed the report, if confirmed by those present at the death, the more convinced the granddaughter is likely to be that her vision was not merely a matter of chance, but was somehow caused by the event. Especially significant are any details that she had no reason to anticipate, for example, the presence of a grandson who had been away for many years, or the fact that all the roses except one in the vase on the bed-table were dead.

Is the granddaughter's conviction rational? Clearly, it has no scientific basis. She has not considered any statistics concerning the frequency with which she (or people generally) have had *false* visions, and this is her first true vision. If the only item she had gotten right was the time of death, such considerations might seem relevant and she might conclude, "Well, maybe it was just a coincidence." But the more detailed her veridical vision, and the more items that she had no reason to anticipate, the less relevant any such considerations seem to be. If we ask, "What is the statistical probability of this particular convergence of miscellaneous qualitative details in vision and event?" it is not clear how the question could be answered. How much less probable does the inclusion of the roses or the grandson make the vision; that is, what numerical weight does one give to an item which, unlike the presence of the housekeeper, the granddaughter had little reason to expect?

Someone who rejects the possibility of paranormal causation may nevertheless insist that, in principle, a probability could be calculated and that even if this were one in a billion, we all must concede that highly improbable events sometimes do occur. Such a tenacious adherence to a worldview will seem rational only to other adherents (other true unbelievers!), for it involves a commitment to reject *any* appeal to a single case of the paranormal, however impressive the details may be and however improbable the occurrence may be. On the other hand, if the granddaughter on subsequent occasions has spontaneous clairvoyant or telepathic intuitions that are confirmed in considerable detail, surely it would be irrational for her *not* to believe that paranormal causation sometimes occurs.[11]

When I speak of paranormal "causation" here, what I have immediately in mind is something remotely analogous to whatever causation is involved in our normal perceptions of material objects. In understanding such perceptions more must be invoked than the causal influence of an apple tree on my brain. As my colleague Peter Hess has pointed out to me, seeing a tree which has 15 apples and 3127 leaves is not the same as seeing *that* a tree has 15 apples and (a rare occurrence) seeing *that* a tree has 3127 leaves. A *cognitive* element is involved in perception as well as a causal element. But insofar as there is a causal element, what could be the analogous causal element in the case of the granddaughter's clairvoyant perception? Two different kinds of theoretical explanation might be suggested, one analogous with mechanical causality and the other with agent causality. On the one hand, we might postulate a medium through which, in spite of the distance, the events in grandfather's room are in local connection with the granddaughter's consciousness, either via her brain or somehow directly. On the other hand, we might postulate some kind of synchronicity or preestablished harmony secretly arranged by a cosmic agent or mindlike arranging context, so that some changes in one part of the universe are instantaneously accompanied by corresponding changes in another part, without the changes being transmitted through any connecting medium.

The analogy drawn from agent causality has two important components. The first component is the intelligibility of a change, or a pattern of changes, in terms of intention or purpose. The second component is the direct initiation of physical change by a change in a mind: a new decision, a new attitude, and so forth. Concerning this mind-over-matter component,[12] we should note that even if we accept a scientist's claim that, say, my arm moves because of a change in my brain, we need to acknowledge that the change in my brain has itself a mental origin except where my movement is a mere reflex. My arm moves because I *decide* to move it. In a similar way, when my confidence in a placebo treatment helps me to overcome an illness, some mind-over-matter causation is at work even if a scientist shows that the originating physical change is the release of such and such a substance into the bloodstream, for the originating physical change has itself an origin in my confidence.

We should specially note that if my confidence gives rise to *two* distinct changes in different parts of the brain, both of which facilitate the same healing, we do not have to assume that one of these physical changes *causes* the other; both these changes can be initiated by my mind, connected in a purposive pattern by my mind.

In Chapter VI we will see that some radical innovators in science such as David Bohm seem to rely on some such an analogy in their explanation of instantaneous correlative changes in diverse parts of the world in the absence of a connecting physical medium. For many scientists, however, such theorizing seems quite fantastic. Indeed, if we return to consider attempts to give some causal explanation of the granddaughter's vision, we should realize that many scientists find both kinds of theorizing quite implausible. Whether one postulates a hidden medium which connects the event with the vision, or postulates a mindlike arranger, the explanation seems to them quite fantastic. This is one reason why many scientists are very skeptical concerning not only clairvoyance but also the paranormal in general.

And, as we saw earlier, some scientists are not merely cautious but irrationally dogmatic in their rejection of the paranormal. Fortunately a few proponents of scientific method are not dogmatic skeptics and are not constrained by the difficulties of theorizing about the paranormal. Instead they are willing to devote time and energy to doing parapsychological experiments in which statistical evidence is built up which shows that, for example, some people are much better than others at cardguessing. (Sometimes their research can even follow the principle of quantifiability.) Such a scientific approach is relevant where a person's psychic powers of awareness can be exercised *repeatedly* and *at will*,[13] for example in some alleged cases of what is called *remote viewing*, or in some alleged cases of what is called *psychokinesis*, where some people claim to have the ability to bend metal objects at will without physically touching them.[14] But where psychic powers are not available repeatedly at will, a scientific approach is not possible. And where psychic powers generate a very impressive single case, a scientific approach is not needed if someone is to have a rational, commonsense basis for believing that some paranormal explanation is required.[15]

I have already proposed a hypothetical case, the granddaughter's clairvoyance. I can also cite some examples which I have witnessed personally, when students in a group investigated psychometry (telepathy and clairvoyance facilitated by holding in one's hand someone's personally significant possession such as a watch, necklace, ring, or wallet). Often, though not always, one student would intuit correctly a very detailed event in another student's life even though the two students had no previous contact other than sitting in a large class together. One student "saw" a fellow student receiving her necklace near a lifeboat from a dark-haired man with a beard on a pleasure cruise; another student "saw" a fellow student getting married across the ocean in a small English church on a sunny summer day. When the student has no reason to suspect that the fellow student who confirms the vision is being dishonest, it is rational to believe, at least tentatively, that the convergence of vision and event was not merely a coincidence but was in *some* sense caused.

Is it possible that the professor leading the group (in this case, it was me) might have persuaded several students to agree to whatever "vision" the other student reported? Yes, of course it is possible, though in this case not true. Should the two students have investigated this possibility of fraud? More generally, how thorough should we be in checking out all possibilities of fraud where an apparently paranormal event has occurred? Some skeptics are so certain that no paranormal event *could* happen that they will postulate fraud even when the *only* specifiable basis for suspecting fraud is their belief that paranormal events are impossible.[16] Such a stance is not prudence, it is paranoia fed by fanaticism. A more rational and open stance is one in which fraud is not presupposed as likely unless one has specific reasons to suspect it in a particular case. Then the extent to which one checks out possibilities of fraud depends on the strength of the reasons. For example, where a professional psychic's income and prestige are at stake, and where his alleged feats are similar to those which professional magicians can replicate, great caution is appropriate, and one might well demand that the feat be subjected to scrutiny by a magician. But when a parapsychologist reports his or her findings, the possibility of fraud, although not totally irrelevant, should not be given more weight than when scientists report their findings in other controversial areas, unless there are specific reasons for distrusting the particular parapsychologist. Should the visionary students have checked out the possibility that I had set them up? Only if they had a specific reason to distrust me. An undiscriminating distrust is irrational.

We have also seen that it is irrational to insist that the *only* way to rule out mere coincidence is by repeated experiments or observations that provide statistical data, for this means rejecting in advance any evidence from a particular case, regardless of how impressive it may be in its detail. Similarly it is also irrational to insist in advance that every paranormal phenomenon that is not a matter of fraud or chance must be explicable by some as-yet-unknown "normal" cause. Like a fundamentalist Christian who offers $10,000 to anyone who can convince him that a statement in the bible is false, some fundamentalist materialists make similar offers to anyone who can convince them that a paranormal event has occurred. The offers involve no risk of loss, for no evidence could convince them. Their fundamentalist convictions are unfalsifiable.

It seems clear to me that the case against dogmatic skepticism is conclusive. No other firm conclusions, however, can be drawn from the various considerations I have noted. We are not left with a clear way to settle disputes concerning the reality of paranormal intuitions. Even if in a particular case both the possibility of fraud and the possibility of finding a normal explanation seem negligible, how impressive must the discernment be (for example, how detailed and unanticipated the clairvoyant vision's contents) if a nonpsychic is to be rationally convinced? I cannot formulate any abstract set of criteria for deciding this, criteria which all intelligent people can accept as "rational." Reasonable people can reasonably differ concerning particular cases. It does seem clear nevertheless that there is a point at which skepticism would be merely an irrational dogmatism, though people do not agree concerning where that point is.

To summarize the discussion thus far; I first distinguished between paranormal ways of discerning or producing *normal phenomena* and paranormal ways of discerning or producing *paranormal phenomena* that are not publicly observable. We have been examining truth claims concerning the former, and we found that science or common sense can sometimes test such truth claims, where something that is publicly observable is allegedly discerned or produced in a paranormal way, whether this be a deathbed scene, the bending of a metal, or the rapid growth of a plant. We saw that *scientific* testing is possible only where the psychic intuition or intervention can be repeated at will. In other cases, where an intuition or intervention is an isolated or spontaneous event, we saw that there are no universally accepted criteria for deciding whether or not an event is indeed paranormal. Even where an appeal to fraud or to an as-yet-unknown "normal" cause seem implausible, people can reasonably differ in their commonsense judgment concerning whether the particular details of the event are *sufficiently* impressive to warrant a tentative belief, or even a firm belief, that the event has a paranormal cause. The situation is analogous to a "hung jury" in a court of law, where, on the basis of the evidence, some jurors are convinced beyond a reasonable doubt that Jones murdered Brown, some believe only that Jones is the most plausible suspect, some cannot make up their minds, and one (like the dogmatic skeptic rejecting in advance any paranormal cause) never thought it was even possible that Jones could have done it.

Paranormal Access to Paranormal Phenomena

The possibilities for agreement among nonpsychics are even more remote where a psychic allegedly intuits or produces phenomena that are not publicly observable. Even if the psychic could do this repeatedly at will, a nonpsychic scientist cannot test the truth claim. Nor is there, as there was in the case of the granddaughter's vision, a place for commonsensical judgments concerning whether it was paranormal in origin. Consider two typical examples of intuitions of nonpublic phenomena. I recall somehow discerning, though my eyes were closed, that David was receiving a gentle feminine energy through the crown of his head and that as it descended it was blocked in the area of his throat. And I recall that a mischievous but not malevolent spirit with a yellowish aura entered the room when Ian arrived for a seminar lecture. In neither case did I expect that a nonpsychic could confirm my intuitions, but in both cases two other psychics did, volunteering reports before I said anything.

In general I do not bother to check out such intuitions with another psychic unless I have a particular reason to do so. For example, I may feel less confident than usual concerning a particular intuition, or I may think it would help the other person to have his or her intuitions confirmed, or something especially important may be at stake (for example, a friend has had a violent death and I want to be sure that my own intuition is correct; namely, that he is not earth bound and that he needs no psychic counseling). My usual confidence in my own intuitions of paranormal phenomena depends somewhat, but not mainly, on having had them corroborated occasionally by other psychics in the past. Sometimes another basis for confidence is my having had many years of deep psychotherapy. This enables me to distinguish between symbolic creations of my emotional unconscious and experiences which are paranormal in origin. For example, sometimes I distinguish between two kinds of imaginative dreams or visions: those which originated in my infancy and those which originated in a past life. The main basis for confidence, however, is a subjective certainty and a sense of obviousness that accompanies many of the intuitions, as they also accompany almost all of my ordinary sense experience in everyday life. Mistakes occasionally occur, as they do in my everyday seeing and hearing, and psychic experiences are more frequently fuzzy and sparse; but in general life energies and spirits seem just as real to me as desks and sounds.

Is it rational for a nonpsychic to believe in the reality of life energies or spirits? It seems to me that a wide range of stances are rational, from tentative disbelief through agnosticism to tentative belief. What does seem irrational is a nonpsychic's having an unshakeable confidence in either the unreality or the reality of life energies or spirits. Such a confidence in their *reality* is warranted only if one has direct experience of them. Such a confidence in their *unreality* would only be warranted if—as is the case where people have hallucinations of material objects—there were a way of *disproving* their reality by appealing to ordinary sense experience of other observers.

Often a nonpsychic understandably is far less skeptical concerning one kind of paranormal claim than another kind. I remember listening to a woman (let us call her Mary) after she had received a message from a spiritualistic medium at a gathering that we had both attended. The medium, whom Mary had never seen before, described Mary's deceased mother in a vaguely fitting way and relayed some rather banal messages. This was not at all impressive. But the medium mentioned that mother was holding a red rose in her hand, and this was very significant to Mary, for just before Mary had closed her mother's casket she had placed a red rose lovingly on her mother's chest. What Mary wondered about aloud as she talked with me was not whether some fraud had been perpetrated or whether reference to the rose was merely a coincidence. She wondered whether the medium was telepathic, somehow tuning in on her last memory of her mother, or whether the medium had really been aware of her mother as a discarnate spirit. For Mary, the former interpretation was more plausible, more economical, simpler. In general, Mary's choice understandably seems rational to many people, for whom the main plausible alternative to "other-worldly" interpretations of many paranormal phenomena is a "this-worldly" interpretation; that is, one which involves no belief in the reality of discarnate spirits who continue to live after death or who are reincarnated in successive human lives. For example, some "past-life" testimony that cannot easily be dismissed as fraud or as mere coincidence is interpreted in terms of this-worldly paranormal powers such as telepathy, clairvoyance, retrocognition, or access to a collective human memory. Suppose, for example, that a woman's testimony is that she was killed during a pogrom in a crypt under the chapel of a specific church in 1189. Even if there is no evidence that the woman could have read or heard about the pogrom, she could have unconsciously tuned in telepathically on any medieval historian who did know about it. If at the time of the testimony no crypt was known to exist under the chapel, but one is discovered two years later during renovative excavations, a this-worldly interpreter cannot appeal to telepathy, but can postulate clairvoyance.[17] If the reporter described not how the crypt looks now, but how it would have (according to expert historians) looked then, the interpreter can postulate powers of retrocognition or access to some collective human memory. Is it more rational to postulate such unconscious *this-worldly* paranormal powers or to accept the reporter's own *other-worldly* account, in which she reexperienced the events leading to her death in 1189? Some people are so certain that reincarnation is impossible that no testimony could convince them. Others are undecided. Once someone has had a past-life experience, however, the subjective similarity to other kinds of vivid remembering is usually convincing. Similarly if Mary were to have an experience similar to the medium's experience, she would probably be convinced that her mother continues to exist as a discarnate spirit.

One way in which there can be a *psychic* transition from this-worldly to other-worldly consciousness is through the experience of life energies: first the life energies of ordinary human beings and then the life energies of discarnate spirits. In my own case, many this-worldly experiences of life energy occurred during the 1970s through Reichian psychotherapy and meditative yoga. I learned how to become aware of other people's life energies as well as my own, how to tune in on their auras of light and vibration. Later, in the early 1980s, when I started to become aware of many *discarnate* human beings, what I "saw" and "felt" was quite similar. There was no big leap in consciousness. Some psychics, however, do not make this transition. Indeed, some Reichian therapists who are very aware of people's energy fields would deny that they themselves should be called "psychic." They reserve that label for people who claim to perceive discarnate spirits.

In general, if a person has had no direct experience of either life energies or discarnate spirits, there are only three kinds of possible bases for believing in their reality. First, one may appeal to parapsychological evidence where observable correlations at best suggest the plausibility of postulating life energies as nonobservable entities within a theoretical explanatory framework. Second, one may appeal to impressive particular events where at best a paranormal explanation seems to some observers to be the most plausible. Third, one may appeal to the testimony of people such as myself who claim to have experienced life energies and spirits, a testimony sometimes corroborated in detail by other psychics. Concerning this third kind of evidence people can reasonably differ, for example, in their appraisal of my honesty and of my freedom from self-deceptive tendencies. They may also differ concerning the weight to be given to specific corroborations in relation to the credibility of the other psychics, the extent of detail, and so forth. Even where an appraisal is very positive, appropriate conclusions might range from "I still neither believe nor disbelieve" through "maybe there's something in it after all" to "I'm sufficiently convinced to take steps toward experiencing whatever this is for myself."

Meaning and Method of Verification

The third response rightly implies that direct experience is required if one is to understand and to test such psychic truth claims adequately. The meaning of psychic talk about life energies and spirits is closely connected with its appropriate method of verification, which is essentially psychic rather than scientific or commonsensical. Readers who are acquainted with philosophical controversies during the middle of this century will realize that that when I connect meaning with method of verification I am ironically alluding to a slogan proposed by a modern species of positivism called *logical positivism*. The slogan was, "The meaning of a statement is identical with its method of verification." I differ from the logical positivists, however, in two ways. First, I speak only of a *connection* rather than in identity. I should note, however, that eventually some of them did likewise. They realized that if they *identified* meaning with method of verification this could lead to a subjective phenomenalism. That is, the reality of things such as chairs or stones could be reduced to the phenomena which occur in the consciousness of the person who acts in accordance with the method of verification. My second difference from logical positivism is much more radical, for I claim that some methods of verification are psychic and some are genuinely spiritual. No self-respecting positivist could ever concede that such methods of verification exist! I concede that my use of the expression "method of verification" is partly polemical, for whereas I am using the term *method* very broadly, alternating it with *way*, a positivist means something very specific: a *technique* which is *repeatable at will*. I am challenging the positivist assumption that the only way to verify any truth claims is by applying *such* a method. There are many different ways or methods, each one corresponding to the kind of truth claim being made. When we consider truth claims concerning the genuinely spiritual in Chapter VI we will see that the appropriate way or method is not a technique but a process that requires receptivity. My first task in Chapter VI will be to distinguish between psychic and genuinely spiritual methods of verification.

VI * * * Positivism and the Genuinely Spiritual

Genuinely spiritual experiences, in contrast with experiences that are merely psychic or paranormal, occur only where a person is consciously committed to a process of personal transformation which involves a deepening receptivity to whatever spiritual realities help one let go of a self-centered preoccupation with power and status and become more expansively loving. As one is enabled to let go of narcissism there is a deepening surrender into spiritual energies and presences that are unconditionally loving, and this gradually facilitates a surrender into the Source of all that exists, whether material, communal, psychic, or spiritual. One lets go of one's own self-separating will, with its need to dominate and control, so as to become an unimpeded channel of unconditional love, lived at the soul by the Source.

Psychics can be aware of energies and presences that are inaccessible to sense experience. Some energies and presences are usually not accessible to them, however, unless they commit themselves to a process of spiritual transformation in which self-preoccupied states that prevent such access are exposed and removed, for example, as an obsession with boosting one's ego and controlling one's world or a fearful fascination with the paranormal. Exceptionally, however, a psychic who is not involved in a process of spiritual transformation may have a vision of someone, such as Gautama Buddha or Jesus Christ, who is unconditionally loving. Such a vision is very different, however, from an encounter in which one is open to being transformed by the indwelling presence of Buddha or Christ. Instead of enabling one to become more loving, the vision will merely reinforce one's narcissism if, consciously or unconsciously, such reinforcement has been what one has been seeking in one's psychic ventures. This rule applies not only to visions but also to ordinary meetings with extraordinarily humble and loving persons. A man once *proudly* told me that he had conversed with the Dalai Lama! Sometimes, however, as in the experience of St. Paul on the road to Damascus, a powerfully loving presence can crash through our defenses to draw forth our unconscious willingness to be transformed. Indeed, for many people the *initial* genuinely spiritual experience is what begins for them the genuinely spiritual process of transformation.

Thus what I said at the beginning of this chapter is not quite true. Sometimes a genuinely spiritual experience occurs *before* a person is consciously committed to a process of spiritual transformation, for the experience initiates the commitment and the process. My main point, however, is that although merely psychic visions of spiritual masters do occasionally occur, a genuinely spiritual *content* of consciousness usually presupposes or facilitates a genuinely spiritual *mode* of consciousness which in turn is linked with a genuinely spiritual *mode of being*: a letting go into love.

Since a genuinely spiritual experience arises from or contributes to a specific process of transformation, any truth claims concerning genuinely spiritual realities require an involvement in this process as part of the method of verification. If, for example, someone reports an experience of unconditional love energy in his or her heart, what is claimed is utterly remote from scientific testing. Like the basis for a psychic's intuition of life energy, the unconditional love energy is not accessible to normal experience. And, more important, the unconditional love energy is not usually accessible to psychic experience as such, for it presupposes a genuinely spiritual mode of consciousness as this arises within a transformative process. Moreover, the spiritual experience cannot be produced at will; one can only let go of the will and receptively await the transformation experience, which may or may not then take place. If it does take place, one then actively assimilates it into one's everyday life. But one has no "method," in the sense of a technique that is repeatable at will, for producing spiritual experiences.

In contrast with this we saw in Chapter V that some *psychic* truth claims (though perhaps only a minority) are amenable to scientific methods of testing, for the psychic can allegedly produce a publicly observable effect at will, for example, bending metal bars or healing mice without touching them. Or the psychic can allegedly *observe* public events paranormally at will, for example, by "traveling" out of the body and witnessing events in designated distant places. Often, however, psychic truth claims cannot be tested scientifically, as we have seen in the case of the granddaughter's vision. And where what is reported is an energy or a presence that is not accessible to sense experience and has no publicly observable effects, scientific method is quite irrelevant. Thus, for example, if James had a near-death experience involving an awareness of a "being of light" in whose presence he reviewed his life, the truth of this report cannot be checked scientifically, though it might be checked by a psychic who was tuned in to James at the time. If, however, James reported events that took place in the operating room while he was unconscious and nearly dead, allegedly observing them from the ceiling, it is appropriate to ask the doctors and nurses who were there whether the report is accurate. (Such a check, however, is not a matter of science but of common sense.)

Such paranormal phenomena as out-of-body experiences evoke a great deal of interest in some circles, but people who are involved in a genuinely spiritual process often have little interest in paranormal phenomena or in proving the reality of such phenomena to the general public. What matters to them is the process of personal transformation and the spiritual realities involved in this process. Such people often gain increased paranormal powers as a byproduct of the process, but the temptation to focus on these powers is viewed as a distraction from the process. Like one's other talents, such powers must be subordinated to the process. This can happen in two main ways: as an expression of loving service to others, where one's psychic intuitions and spiritual healing may be of help, or as a tool in the process of personal transformation itself, where one's intuitions and healings can help one to clear away obstacles within oneself.

Often paranormal powers are not byproducts of a spiritual process, but either arise spontaneously or are deliberately uncovered and developed through a training process. Such powers resemble other human powers, including those acquired through scientific techniques, in that they can be used either for good or for ill, to help or to harm. Often psychic powers reinforce our narcissistic need to inflate ourselves and to impose our will on others. The training process through which one enhances one's paranormal abilities need not involve any commitment to a process in which one becomes more loving and less narcissistic. On the contrary, the training sometimes promotes ego trips and power trips that carry one in the opposite direction from a genuinely spiritual process. Hence many spiritual paths in many traditions warn against any deliberate cultivation of paranormal powers and against any fascination with such powers if they arise as byproducts of a spiritual process.

This warning is well warranted, but it should not lead to a total prohibition against starting with the paranormal. There are two reasons for this. First, many people in our culture (though not in other cultures untouched by the Enlightenment) have a constricting world-view that precludes not only paranormal but also genuinely spiritual experiences. Such a world-view is not usually changed by arguments—even if the arguments are as sound as, I believe, those presented in this book! Sometimes the only way that such a world-view can be undermined and shattered is by a powerfully impressive paranormal experience which the skeptic undergoes. I have seen this happen in workshops designed to evoke various paranormal powers of intuition. The whole reality issue shifts when one is no longer skeptically appraising other people's psychic testimony but trying to make sense of one's own psychic experience. Sometimes, of course, this happens spontaneously. Even a positivist philosopher may suddenly have an out-of-body experience if he nearly dies. This might, or might not, lead him to move beyond the paranormal into a genuinely spiritual quest, but such a quest was previously ruled out by his positivism.

A second reason for sometimes beginning with the paranormal follows from the first reason. Sometimes a person's pathway into the paranormal is to some extent open to the genuinely spiritual, for although the person is partly motivated by curiosity, there is also some desire to become more loving. For such people, (and there are many of them), rudimentary psychic beginnings can pave the way toward spiritually profound transformations. For example, a psychic meeting with one's personal spirit guide can eventually lead to an openness to transformation by the indwelling presence of Jesus Christ. Or an initial past-life experience with a trivial content such as a flirtation in an eighteenth century French court can eventually lead to an openness to a crucial past-life experience which reveals the main inner obstacles and the main spiritual resources in one's *this*-life process toward surrender into the Source. Psychic encounters with spirits and psychic past-life regressions do not necessarily lead to an openness to genuinely spiritual versions of such experiences, as a person may not be committed to becoming more loving and less narcissistic. But psychic experiences can provide a first stage which is helpful to many and perhaps necessary for some. Indeed, the distinction between psychic experiences and genuinely spiritual experiences is not always clear. Obviously there is a difference between Uri Geller bending spoons and St. Francis uniting with Christ, but there may be no difference between a self-described psychic who is *somewhat* open to being transformed by her loving spirit guide and an ostensibly spiritual person who is *somewhat* open to becoming more like his loving spirit guide. And both people might have a vision of Christ and respond to it in a way that is a mixture of narcissism and openness. My main point, however, is that a pathway that initially is predominantly psychic can lead into one that is predominantly genuinely spiritual.

In presenting reasons for cultivating paranormal awareness, in spite of the dangers and defects of the paranormal when viewed from a genuinely spiritual perspective, I have been assuming that both paranormal and spiritual experiences are, in general, real. This assumption can be challenged, however, by a skeptic. Let us consider the challenge.

The Skeptic's Challenge

For a skeptic all paranormal and spiritual experiences are *subjective* and *hallucinatory*. They are all allegedly subjective in the sense that a pain sensation in my left elbow is subjective. If I report such a pain my claim can not be falsified by any objective investigation, for my report may well be honest and true even though no physical cause of the pain can be observed. And a skeptic alleges that paranormal and spiritual experiences are hallucinatory in the sense that a psychotic's seeing a pink elephant in the drawing room is hallucinatory. That is, he mistakenly takes his experience to be an experience of a reality which exists independent of whether or not he experiences it, like the gray elephant in the local zoo. If I say that I see a pink elephant or that I am aware of a ghost or that I am aware of the risen Christ the skeptic would not deny that I am actually having a subjective experience, just as he would not deny that I am feeling a pain in my left elbow if I report it and he has no reason to think that I am lying. What the skeptic denies is that the pink elephant, the ghost, and the risen Christ actually exist to be experienced. On the contrary, they are creations of my own mind, private fantasies that have no real reference beyond my own stream of consciousness.

The skeptic's account may seem plausible at first, but let us examine it carefully. First of all, what is meant by *ghost*? Sometimes when people claim to have seen a ghost what they mean is a publicly observable object that is like an elephant in that anyone else whose eyes are functioning normally would be able to see it and a photographer could take a picture of it. In most instances, however, when a psychic says, "There's a ghost in the drawing room" she does not mean by *ghost* a publicly observable object. On the contrary, what she means is an entity whose reality is discernible only psychically. The meaning of her statement is linked to its appropriate method of verification, and the method is not scientific or commonsensical but psychic. So it is no longer clear what the skeptic can mean by calling the psychic's experience of any discarnate spirit a *hallucination*. In the case of the pink elephant, the skeptic and anyone else can prove that it is a hallucination by bringing in any Tom, Dick and Harry (or Joan, Jane, and Mary) to scan the drawing room. But such testing is irrelevant to what the psychic is claiming. The skeptic can not prove that the psychic is mistaken.

Can the psychic prove her claim to the skeptic? If, as sometimes happens, the presence of the ghost were accompanied by some publicly observable and puzzling phenomena such as dishes flying about on their own, the skeptic might be moved to consider various hypotheses, including the presence of a ghost. The only convincing proof, however, would be if he became a psychic himself, either spontaneously or by undergoing an appropriate training. Then he might well be able to detect a variety of discarnate spirits and realize that they, like chairs, exist independently of our experience of them. He might also check his findings with other psychics. Meanwhile, however, he is not in a position to claim that all psychic experiences of discarnate spirits are hallucinations, in the sense that a vision of a pink elephant is an hallucination.

A skeptic is similarly not in a position to call all genuinely spiritual experiences *hallucinations*. If Jones says, "The indwelling Christ is enabling me to share in his unconditional love for humankind," his claim can not be verified or falsified by bringing in Joan, Jane, and Mary to observe Jones. What Jones *means* is linked with the spiritual process of personal transformation which he is undergoing, and only someone who undergoes an analogous process can adequately understand what he means. Jones might be mistaken—completely or, as is more likely, partly—but this would only be directly discernible to a perceptive spiritual counselor. He is not mistaken in the same way as a drunk who sees pink elephants, for his claim cannot be confirmed or falsified by ordinary sense experience. (His subsequent observable conduct may tend to confirm or undermine his claim, but not conclusively, for good behavior can occur without any such spiritual encounter having actually preceded it, and bad behavior could occur because Jones subsequently turned away from Christ.)

If we move on to consider a mystic's ecstatic utterance, "I am God," which expresses a merging of human and divine consciousness, the skeptic's charge that this is a hallucination becomes even less appropriate, for the mystic is not saying that he is conscious of a reality that is distinguishable from consciousness. The reality *is* this consciousness.

Even if skeptics are involved in category mistakes when they dismiss alleged spiritual realities or the unity of soul and Source as "hallucinations," this does not mean that a skeptic must stop being a skeptic and accept all such mystical truth claims. Nor does it mean that only a mystic is in a position to make any appraisal, however tentative, of such mystical reports. Nonmystics have four bases for making some initial appraisals.

Appraising Mystical Claims

The first basis is the testimony of the mystics. We have seen that for various reasons mystical truth claims are not confirmable or falsifiable by scientific method or by such commonsense procedures as bringing in Tom, Dick, and Harry to have a look. But insofar as appraising such claims is a matter of appraising testimony, the formal criteria are similar to those employed by common sense in everyday life or in a court of law. The situation is somewhat analogous to deciding whether to believe reports from people who have visited a distant planet and who have brought back nothing from the planet for us to examine—only their obscure descriptions of strange inhabitants. Basically it is a matter of assessing the credibility of the witnesses and the convergence of their independent testimony. The credibility of a mystic, like that of the traveler or anyone else, depends on soundness of character and clarity of intelligence. A person who in all nonmystical dimensions of life is very honest and not prone to self-deception might nevertheless be lying or be self-deluded when providing mystical testimony, but some weight must be given to the testimony. Similarly a person who is very shrewdly intelligent in dealing with a wide range of nonmystical matters might nevertheless be stupid concerning mysticism, but such testimony also deserves serious consideration. Since many mystics have actually been very impressive in both character and intelligence, their testimony ought not to be cavalierly dismissed, though one's conclusion might well be no stronger than, "Maybe there's something in it after all." And because there is also an impressive convergence of testimony from mystics in various cultures that in some cases have had no known interaction, there is further evidence in support of such an openness.

Convergence or corroboration or testimony, however, is a more complex consideration than one might first realize. For one thing, mystics in different traditions differ considerably in their testimony. And even if we then explain the differences in testimony by referring to the influence of the traditions on the symbolic frameworks that the mystics brought to their experiences, the remaining similarities in testimony do not point unambiguously to a common experience of the same spiritual realities. Maybe what is common can be explained by referring to some common psychological or sociological tendency in human beings. And this "maybe" is not merely a skeptic's last-resort appeal to some as-yet-unknown factor. Some specific explanations have been offered. Freud, for example, explains a mystical "oceanic feeling" as a recollection of experience in the womb, and this has considerable plausibility. Indeed, having myself experienced regression back into infancy and earlier, I would confirm that what Freud claims is to a great extent true of some rudimentary mystical experiences, though Freud does not realize that the fetus and infant typically experience life energies, so the issues are much more complex than what Freud envisaged. Another depth-psychological account of commonly reported mystical experiences is provided by Jung, whose archetypes from the collective unconscious are operative cross culturally. For most mystics, spiritual energies and spiritual entities are "real" in the sense that they do not depend on the existence of human psyches, individual or collective, for their existence. Jung's archetypes are not set forth as "real" in this sense, so Jung—for all his marvelous sensitivity to spiritual experience—is providing an alternative account. Since Jung is not denying such a reality, but is remaining methodologically agnostic concerning it, a dialogue between Jungians and mystics is very feasible. Such a dialogue can be illuminating not only to Jungians but also to mystics, for it is clear that archetypes often do shape our experience of spiritual realities (and vice versa, a mystic would add). But on the issue of whether converging testimony from mystics indicates the reality of what they report, Jung provides an ambiguous contribution, for although he explores a spiritual dimension within the human psyche, it is not clear whether, for example, Goddess energy or Jesus Christ or angels exist for Jung independent of the human psyche.

Speaking of angels, we can now consider the convergence of testimony from many (not all) mystical traditions that there is a realm of angels which are ranked in a rigid hierarchy of increasing status and power up to the throne of God. Does this convergence of testimony strongly indicate that there really are angels and that they exist in such a hierarchy? Not necessarily, if a plausible sociological explanation for the belief in a hierarchy of angels can be provided. And it does seem plausible to explain the hierarchy of angels as a projection of earthly communal structures in ancient and medieval times on to a heavenly screen, thereby legitimizing the earthly authority of kings and courtiers. I find this account plausible as an explanation of the belief that angels have a hierarchical structure, but not as an explanation of the belief that angels exist. My own conviction that angels exist, however, depends on my having frequently experienced them, and I can see why my testimony does not convince a skeptic. And since in my experience of angels their communal arrangements seem to be nonauthoritarian, I have an additional reason to agree with the skeptic's explanation of the belief in hierarchy, though I must also explore the possibility that my own experience may be shaped sociologically by my own cultural context and its dominant ideologies. And I can see why a nonmystic, lacking any experience of angels, may find a skeptic's sociological explaining away of angels quite convincing. A dialogue between mystics and sociologists could be illuminating to both sides.

In general, since we human beings bring *to* mystical experiences a variety of different kinds of perspective that shape the experiences, nonmystics reasonably question any convergence of mystical testimony by looking for some convergence in the perspectives (psychological, sociological, or religious) that mystics share. For mystics it is different and more complex, as I noted in Chapter IV, for a mystic can have his or her own *intra*personal "dialogue" between interpretative perspective and direct sense experience of material objects. In both mystical and everyday awareness we perceive *reality both directly and perspectivally.* What we perceive we experience directly, that is, in such a way as to be assured that the spirit or the table are really there; but we perceive reality through a perspectival "grid." Direct experience limits what grid we can impose, and the grid influences the direct experience.

There is one exception to this. As we saw in Chapter IV, one kind of mystical experience allegedly does not involve perceiving reality perspectivally, through a gird, namely the "empty-mind" state, where one has so completely shed all attachment to any of our human perspectives that one is conscious, but not conscious *of* anything, and one is sharing in a divine or transcendental mode of consciousness. If one does then become conscious *of* anything, while continuing this mode of consciousness, one's awareness is presumably completely pure and direct. Mystics of many diverse traditions converge in testifying to the possibility of attaining such a mode of consciousness. Skeptics may find descriptions of the state unintelligible and for that reason inexplicable in nonmystical ways. But since no nonmystical explanation is offered, and since the unintelligibility to many nonmystics is not surprising if the "empty-mind" state allegedly occurs only at or near the end of an arduous personal process of transformation, the convergence of mystical testimony concerning this state remains to puzzle, though not to convince, any honest inquirer.

If the testimony of mystics provides a basis for only a tentative appraisal of mystical truth claims, the second kind of basis is even less conclusive, for it is an appeal to one's own experience. After all that I have said in this chapter concerning the need to be involved in a rarely undertaken mystical transformation if one is to adequately understand and convincingly verify mystical truth claims, such an appeal will seem very surprising. But, as I pointed out in Chapter IV, an initial understanding and a tentative appraisal of truth claims is usually possible even where some process of personal transformation is required for an adequate understanding and a conclusive testing of reports concerning a human dimension. And in the case of mystical truth claims most people do have some conscious experience, however limited and rudimentary, that is relevant to some of these truth claims. Even a psychic experience of life energy, for example, is somewhat analogous to a genuinely spiritual experience of unconditional love energy, and many people have had some version of the former, though perhaps mixed in with other experiences (for example, when listening to music or making love).

I also pointed out in Chapter IV that I believe that everyone has had at least an unconscious contact with the spiritual dimension, for the dimension is part of who we are. Even if we have repressed our awareness of spirit and of soul, this unconscious contact does provide an obscure preunderstanding which can facilitate recognition when one is in the presence of a mystic, and even when one is merely reading his or her reports.

Mystics differ, however, in their reports. Although they tend to agree concerning the kind of personal transformation that is needed, in that it involves a shedding of narcissism, self-centeredness, self-separation, self-preoccupation, and so on, they disagree concerning the final goal and how to get there. For example, some mystics depict the "empty-mind" state as the goal, whereas for others it is only a stage on the way. Some mystics stress transformation by the indwelling presence of a fully surrendered Master, whereas others do not. On what basis can one choose between them? The time of choice may arise for a nonmystic making an uncommitted initial appraisal of rival truth claims, or for a potential mystic choosing an initial spiritual path. In either situation one can consider the credibility of the rival mystics in terms of their character and intelligence. One can also give some weight to one's own experience, which includes some obscure intuitions of what one has not yet experienced clearly. If we are potential mystics seeking an initial teacher we probably have had some paranormal or spiritual experience which has stirred us deeply enough to make some commitment. We are then in a similar situation to a musical beginner who is looking for a coach in piano or singing. If we fully appreciated the musicianship of two alternative coaches whom we are considering we would be as advanced as they are and we would not need them! But we do have some rudimentary musical appreciation, and this helps us to make a choice. Similarly a mystical tyro can appeal to a rudimentary sensitivity in picking a teacher.

There is, however, a third basis for appraising mystics; namely, their *comprehensiveness*. This is specially relevant where a mystic sets forth the goal, the ultimate state. Has the mystic had a profound and genuine experience of most of the other states that rival mystics proclaim as ultimate? Or is the claim made from a *narrow range* of experience or a *shallow exploration* of various allegedly ultimate states? A mystic's range is important, for a mystic who is in a position to compare only state *A*, which he or she says is ultimate, with state *B* is in general less credible than a mystic who can compare *A* with all the main contenders for ultimacy from *B* to *Z*. Comprehensiveness of range is also relevant where mystics differ concerning what states are useless or helpful on the way toward the ultimate state. A mystic who dismisses a state (for example, all past-life experiences) which he or she has never known is less plausible than one who dismisses it after exploring it. Thus merely by reading or hearing a mystic one can as a nonmystic get some sense of the range of the mystic's experience.

Initially, however, one's impressions concerning the depth and genuineness of the mystic's experience can only be very tentative. Only later, as one proceeds along a mystical path and comes to know firsthand what previously one had only heard about, can decisions between mystics be increasingly based on one's own experience. One may, for example, come to question whether so-and-so ever knew a genuine "empty-mind" state; perhaps it was only an awareness of a still center within himself.[1] Or one's own fleeting experiences of receiving and radiating unconditional love may make more credible one mystic's claim that a profound and continuous experience of this is the ultimate goal.

We have seen, however, that, for the nonmystic who has not yet embarked on a mystical voyage, there are only three bases for making tentative appraisals of mystical reports: first, the personal credibility of a mystic and the convergence of independent testimony; second, one's own rudimentary experience, which provides some intuitions that one can to some extent trust; and third, the comprehensiveness of a mystic's range of experience.

Mystics and Modern Science

There is, however, a fourth basis on which nonmystics can make tentative appraisals of mystical truth claims: the congruence of mystical reports with the cosmological world-view of modern science, especially physics. It may seem surprising that mysticism could be supported by science, for we have seen that three elements in scientific method (isolation, repeatability, and quantifiability) have only a limited applicability in testing paranormal claims and none in testing spiritual and mystical claims. The fourth element, however, does seem to be relevant; namely, theoretical plausibility. I have already hinted at this when I suggested how a parapsychologist might explain why a healer can influence the growth of plants. Maybe he can postulate the very same energies that the healer says he experiences. Such a possible account is more feasible in this century, for physicists have partly or entirely replaced a mechanistic world-view, in which material objects arise from ultimate entities pictured as tiny billiard balls. Instead of miniature material objects, or as an alternative model alongside such a picture, one refers to energies of various kinds. Maybe even the spiritual energies experienced during a mystical process of transformation are versions of the energies that physicists postulate as ultimate realities in the universe.

Maybe, but maybe not. It is quite possible, I think, that some psychics can directly discern or manipulate some of the energies which modern science postulates, for example electromagnetic energy, but I know of nothing in scientific thinking that postulates spiritual energies which are unconditionally loving or postulates the existence and transforming influence of discarnate spiritual Masters or postulates the origination of everything, including all energies and entities, from an ultimate consciousness.

There are, nevertheless, some radical innovators among contemporary scientific theorists whose postulates do resemble some of the reports that mystics make.[2] For example, when Rupert Sheldrake postulates an invisible "morphogenetic" field to explain why the crystallization of a new organic compound in one location expedites such crystallizations around the world, this fits with mystical experiences of an interdependence which is not restricted to local-connective causality. Perhaps something analogous to such a field provides the context for the influencing at a distance which occurs not only in psychic telepathy but also in mystic awareness of nonseparation from anyone or anything in the cosmos. And when David Bohm says that each thing is a hologram of everything, "explicating" the "implicate order" of the universe in varying degrees, this fits with the mystical experience of oneself as a microcosm of the macrocosm, embodying the nature and the origin of the universe in a self-conscious "hologram." Thus it can make sense that the more deeply we go inside ourselves the more widely inclusive is the felt resonance with the vast ranges of reality outside ourselves, from primal cosmic energy through mineral, vegetable, and animal entities to primitive humanity and on through our evolutionary history to this day. And when Ilya Prigogine depicts the universe as an irreversible creative process in which order and chaos interact dynamically, this fits not only with universal mystical experience of a void which is creative but also with specifically Western mystical experiences of history as a process which has a direction, so that significant new developments are possible. Such a scientific world-view seems to confirm much of the mystical orientation of this book, which implicitly rejects not only a scientific resignation to a dismal future when everything eventually will succumb to entropy, but also an Eastern mystical flight from natural and human history, which allegedly can bring nothing significantly new.

Why then do I not attach much weight to Sheldrake, Bohm, and Prigogine as allies when I advocate mysticism? There are three main reasons. First, mystical experience provides a *sufficient* basis for believing mystical reports. No other basis is necessary. If, as could happen, the theories of physics were to change in the next century, reverting to mechanical models, this would make no difference to my mystical convictions. So it would be dishonest on my part to appeal to contemporary physicists to legitimize my own mystical claims. It would be like citing someone else's testimony in support of one's own testimony concerning some event while secretly knowing that if the other person were to disavow the testimony it would make no difference to me. Second, the *only* sufficient basis for believing mystical reports is mystical experience, for the meaning of such reports is closely linked with their appropriate method of verification, which is a mystical process of personal transformation. It is obvious, as I have noted, that some mystical reports refer to energies or entities or states (for example, loving energies, the risen Jesus Christ, or divine consciousness) for which there are no postulated scientific counterparts that even seem to be analogous. And even where there are postulated realities that seem analogous to the realities some mystics report, we cannot assume that what the physicist and the mystic *mean* is the same, for the appropriate methods of verification are very different. Can a physicist understand what a mystic means even though the physicist has not undergone a radical process of spiritual transformation? And, conversely, why should a mystic be able to experience that which enables physicists to predict and control what occurs in the everyday world? I am not insisting that what the physicist and mystic mean must be utterly different. Spiritually sensitive scientists such as Sheldrake, Bohm, and Prigogine may draw on their own mystical experience as they create their theories, but these theories eventually will have to be tested *scientifically* rather than mystically. And although what some mystics mean may be intelligible in a rudimentary way to nonmystical scientists, the apparent analogies between mystical and scientific cosmologies are more remote than what one might initially suppose, for the methods of verification appropriate to them are vastly different.

My third reason for not appealing to the new physics to support mystical claims depends on my philosophy of physics. Like many contemporary physicists and philosophers of physics, and unlike David Bohm, I regard the theoretical entities and energies of physics as formal fictions rather than as realities. In such a philosophy of physics, physics tries to explain what goes on in the real observable world, and does this by postulating energies or entities within theoretical constructions. These constructions are accepted solely because they are useful in providing an intelligible unifying picture and in suggesting further areas for research.[3] If, however, I were to assume that what physicists set forth as their theoretical items should be regarded as metaphysical realities, then of course it would matter a great deal whether these realities jibe with what mystics claim. If there were a conflict, I would have to choose between two competing metaphysical cosmologies. This would be a difficult situation, but since, as I noted earlier, science provides neither a necessary nor an adequate way of testing mystical claims, I would still find it rational to continue to be a mystic.

The situation for a nonmystic, however, is different. The new physics and such radical innovators as Sheldrake, Bohm, and Prigogine do provide some reason for nonmystics to give serious consideration to mystical truth claims. Even if physics proposes only formal fictions rather than metaphysical realities, the fact that these scientifically useful fictions are in some ways analogous to the alleged realities which mystics report can rightly move some inquirers to say, "Maybe there's something in mysticism after all." On the other hand, if scientific fashions were to change so that the dominant theories were as uncongenial to mystical reports as Newtonian science was, this quite-possible change would not be an unmitigated disaster spiritually. Insofar as mysticism becomes intellectually respectable, many people tend to *substitute* scientific-mystical speculation for the arduous personal journey which real mysticism entails.

Overall, the methods of science do not enable it either to negate or to affirm the reality of spirit and soul. At most, science can provide some indirect support for the plausibility of some mystical claims. Conversely, mysticism can provide some indirect support for the plausibility of some scientific claims. For example, where physicists set forth theories that are remotely analogous to mysticism rather than utterly alien, a mystic is not in a position to judge whether the theories are superior in their usefulness to science; that is a matter other scientists will have to decide. But a mystic is in a position to say that the theories are superior metaphysically; that is, that they are closer approximations to ultimate reality than are the theories which are utterly alien to mysticism. Such an approach assumes that mysticism is the best way to knowledge of ultimate reality. Insofar as physicists postulate ultimates (whether as fictions or as realities) their claims can be appropriately tested metaphysically (though not scientifically) by mystics.

If I regarded the theoretical items of physics as realities, I would be more inclined to regard metaphysical discussions between mystics and physicists as a dialogue between equals. I do not regard them as realities, however, both because I was convinced by the arguments of nonrealist philosophers of science long before I became a mystic and because now as a mystic I see scientific method as the least appropriate of all the perspectives we have considered in dealing with metaphysical issues. We come to know the real as we ourselves become more real, more completely human. For example, we come to know the reality of human freedom or unconditional love or spirit as we ourselves become more existentially responsible or more loving or more spiritual. In sharp contrast with this, the scientific method constricts our access to reality, whether in the cosmos or in ourselves. Hence, for example, behavioristic psychology is remote from human reality in ways that Jungian nonscientific psychology is not, for Jungians are learning about reality as they become more real. Jungians, unlike behaviorists, are themselves involved in an enriching, reality-opening process of human transformation. Thus, as I have noted, Jungians and mystics can learn from each other and correct each other.

Mystics have little or nothing to learn from physicists concerning ultimate reality. There can, nevertheless, be some mutual illumination in a dialogue between mystics who reflect metaphysically concerning their experiences and physicists who reflect metaphysically concerning their theories. Analogous conceptual issues may arise for each thinker. For example, a reflective physicist may ask whether Sheldrake's "morphogenetic field" and Bohm's "implicate order" are to be construed as *connecting media* through which one event can influence a distant event, or as *mindlike contexts* which somehow arrange for simultaneous correspondences between events. That is, which hidden underlying paradigm of explanation is at work: mechanical causality or agent causality? For Bohm it seems to be the latter. The distinction between the two paradigms becomes blurred, however, where mechanical causality, though locally connected, involves energies rather than miniature material objects, and where agent causality, though purposive, involves a context rather than a person.

Analogous issues may arise for a metaphysically reflective mystic who asks how his mystical experience of being connected with everyone and everything is to be understood. Here, too, a choice between two explanatory paradigms may seem necessary. Indeed I would suggest that both kinds of account are appropriate, though in relation to different mystical experiences. On the one hand, I know that I am not separated from anyone or anything because of mystical experiences in which my own spirit is connected with everyone and everything through a *cosmic spirit* that is a pervasive *medium*. On the other hand, I know that I am not separated from anyone or anything because of mystical experiences in which my own conscious soul is united with the *conscious Source* of everyone and everything, which *simultaneously* lives in us and as us. We should note, however, that although *cosmic spirit* is experienced as *energy*, it is also experienced as being analogous to one's own *agency*, though this agency is experienced spiritually in ways that involve blurred boundaries between agents. And although the *conscious Source* is less unlike an agent than it is unlike a mechanism, it is more like a *context* than it is like an individual person.

As a metaphysically reflective mystic I can try to understand my experience in such ways. My main conclusion in this chapter, however, is that scientific method is quite inappropriate in testing claims concerning the reality of spirit and Source, though it can be applied to some claims concerning the paranormal, where psychics can allegedly discern or produce publicly observable phenomena in paranormal ways *at will*. And my main contention is that the meaning of claims concerning spiritual reality is linked with their appropriate "method" of verification: a process of personal transformation.

In Section 2 as a whole I have provided reasons for questioning the dogmatic assumptions of impersonalism, perspectivalism, and positivism, but I have not demonstrated the reality of spirit. I hope, nevertheless, that I have persuaded some skeptical readers to admit, "Maybe there's something in it," since it is no longer unintelligible that intelligent and reflective persons can come to believe in the reality of spirit.

The spiritual dimension is only one of many dimensions in human nature. We saw in Section 1 that it is intimately interconnected with psychotherapy, and in this section we have explored some of its complex relations with reason. In the next section we will see what difference the inclusion of a spiritual dimension makes to morality and reflections concerning the origin and nature of good and evil in human beings.

Section 3

Spirituality and Ethics

VII * * * Mystical Humanism and Morality

The conception of human nature emerging in this book can be appropriately called *mystical humanism*. It is *mystical* in that it includes a spiritual dimension in each person and it envisages the whole person being lived by the Source. It is *humanistic* in that it includes much that is advocated by secular humanists. In particular, this chapter will reveal my agreement with secular humanists who claim that a minimal morality can be based on a sense of our common humanity even if there is no spiritual dimension and no Source. I shall also claim, however, that a mystical humanism is more comprehensive and thereby more adequate as a rational basis for morality.

Any dialogue with a secular humanist is for me partly a dialogue with a secular-humanist "voice" within myself. It is more challenging, however, to be in dialogue with a real, flesh-and-blood human being, in this case Kai Nielsen.[1] Among contemporary atheistic philosophers I have found him to be the most persistent and passionate in his probing of issues concerning religion and morality, and I have a deep respect for the personal integrity and the philosophical clarity with which he writes. Unfortunately he has been so prolific that perhaps only a dedicated doctoral student could undertake the task of reading all his published books and essays. My own outline of his thought in this chapter is based on a careful study of a fair sample of articles published within a five-year period.[2]

The chapter is in two parts. In Part I, I will set forth my own perspective in such a way that in Part II my agreements and disagreements with Nielsen can be clearly outlined.

I

First I should outline my own conception of morality. A moral judgment is, first of all, a claim concerning how *any-*

one ought or ought not to *be* or *behave*, for example, "anyone ought to be a loving person" or "anyone ought not to torture another human being." Second, a moral judgment must also be justifiable by reference to some factual statements concerning conditions or constituents of human fulfilment, individual or communal.[3] Anyone ought to fulfil his or her true nature as a human being and anyone ought to behave in ways that promote rather than hinder such fulfilment or well-being in others. There are universal human needs and interests, though many of these are not yet recognized by everyone. Fortunately a few seem evident to virtually everyone, so that almost universal agreement can be achieved concerning a requirement for *some* restriction and regulation of human conduct pertaining to the taking of human life, infliction of injury, truthfulness in testimony, keeping of promises, protection of property, and sexual relations. Although moral codes differ considerably in detail concerning these matters, there is a rational basis here for a minimal moral code. The basis is in common human needs for elementary bodily security and for the rudimentary social cooperation that survival requires. Even if a human being is no more than "an intelligent physico-chemical mechanism in self-directed motion"[4] there would be a rational basis for a very minimal moral code. This would be true even if there were no spiritual dimension in human nature and no relation of humankind to a divine Source. Such a morality thus does not require a basis in religion.

Indeed, I see some possibility that beyond such a minimal code we human beings may eventually develop a broader consensus concerning human needs, and with it a wider and more concrete moral consensus, on the basis of secular social science and humanistic studies of humanity. My own optimism concerning this is tempered by the conviction that the more scientific the method, the narrower is the range of the human that is deemed suitable for investigation and thereby implicitly deemed to be real. Yet the less scientific the method, the less likely is the apparent prospect for universal intersubjective agreement, for divergent moral perspectives are associated with divergent psychological and social theories.

If, however, the protagonists of nonscientific secular studies of human nature acknowledge their perspective as partial and in need of supplementation and correction by other perspectives, the probability of an emerging comprehensive secular view of human nature greatly increases. And whether or not such an emergent view is likely, it is necessary as an important step toward a fully rational morality. At this point I should explain what I mean by *rational* in this context. A moral judgment is rational if (a) the alleged factual statements concerning human nature provide an adequate basis for the moral judgment and (b) the alleged factual statements are true. In such an approach two *conflicting* moral judgments could each be "rational" in both these respects but each could be based on different true statements concerning human nature. On the other hand, the *same* moral judgment could be based on different true statements concerning human nature; for example, a prohibition of torture could be based on our human need to avoid excessive pain, or on our human need to be treated with respect, or on the psychological trauma usually produced by torture, or on our human need to be lovers rather than torturers; or a prohibition of torture could be based on all these human facts together.

A moral judgment is the *most rational* among *conflicting* judgments or it is the *most rational* among *identical* judgments, when the conception of human nature on which it is based is not only true but also the most comprehensive and coherent. For example, one secular conception of human nature might be relatively narrow, confined to one sociopolitical perspective such as socialism. But another secular conception might include a wide variety of mutually complementary and mutually correcting perspectives, for example, other social-political perspectives, a variety of psychological perspectives, ecological perspectives, creative-artistic perspectives, existentialist perspectives, rationalistic and scientific perspectives, and so forth. Such a comprehensive conception of human nature would provide moral reasons

for some moral judgments not justified in a narrow conception, and it could provide a richer, overdetermining set of
reasons for other moral judgments.[5] And when the reasons
are more than adequate rationally they may well be more
efficacious *motivationally* for many or most people. For
example, even if a conception of human beings as much
more than merely sentient beings is not required rationally
to justify prohibition of torture, such a conception may be
more effective motivationally in restraining people from torture. Whether or not this is so will depend on what additional perspectives on human nature are included. Many "isms,"
both secular and religious, have been invoked to both justify
and encourage torture. But it does seem likely that a cumulative piling up of accepted reasons for the same prohibition
is likely to reinforce motivation.

My main interest here, however, is not motivation but
rational justification. Unlike some religious people, I envisage both the possibility and the desirability of a secular
morality based on a variety of nonreligious perspectives concerning human nature. But I also believe that such perspectives are usually mistaken, not in what they affirm, but in
what they omit or deny concerning the religious dimensions
of human nature. I hold that the most rational morality
would be one which, while including the best of secular
morality, also goes beyond it by including a conception of
human beings as spiritual and as ultimately fulfilled in their
relation to the divine Source. Sometimes such a mystical
humanist morality will go beyond most or all secular morality in the additional or revisionary content of its moral judgments, especially concerning answers to the question,
"What ought I to *be*?" Sometimes, however, it will go
beyond by adding a *reason* for the *same* moral judgments.
The latter is more often the case concerning answers to the
question, "What ought I to do?" For example, a mystical
humanist conception of human nature provides an additional reason for refraining from torture.

Are religious statements required to justify moral judgments? Not always, indeed not usually, if the moral judgments pertain to external behavior in relation to a minimal

moral code, for there are secular statements concerning human nature that are rationally adequate to justify such a code.[6] Religious statements may, however, provide further justification. And in some instances, for example, the moral judgment that all human beings ought to be treated with respect and care regardless of their differing characteristics, no secular justification seems to be completely adequate. (I will discuss issues of egalitarianism later on, for Nielsen explores them extensively.) And some moral judgments concerning what one ought to *be* require religious justification because what one ought to be includes religious elements.

What do I mean by *religion* in this context?[7] I mean whatever pertains to God or whatever pertains to the spiritual dimension of human beings and the cosmos. God is distinguished sharply from the spiritual dimension in that God is the ultimate Source not only of whatever is spiritual but also of whatever else can be experienced as a content of consciousness. I will first discuss the spiritual dimension and then try to talk about the divine Source.

The spiritual dimension is discernable to some extent by almost all human beings, the main exceptions being those whose world-view precludes recognition of it in any form because they restrict reality to what can be experienced through common sense and science. Spiritual discernments can occur from time to time spontaneously but they usually occur frequently only when they are cultivated through one of the wide variety of meditative practices or through some psychotherapies such as bioenergetics. My own cumulative personal experience has convinced me beyond any reasonable doubt that we are all not only physical bodies and centers of consciousness who are passionate and reflective but also spiritual bodies, patterns of vibrating life energy. As physical, emotional, mental, and spiritual beings, any change in one dimension affects all the others. Some spiritually minded people foolishly try to ignore their bodies and emotions and intellects as well as their involvement in the power structures of society; but it is equally foolish to try to ignore our spirits, even if our dis-ease seems to be entirely physical or entirely emotional or entirely mental or entirely political. Moreover, the spiritual dimension links us *directly* to other human beings in telepathic influence for good or ill. It also links us to discarnate human beings now in spirit form, and through it we can learn directly from spiritual masters both living and "dead." And we can learn to resonate to the most sublime spiritual energies in the cosmos, thereby becoming recipients and channels of unconditional love, abundant life, and blissful peace. And through learning how to "go with the flow" of spiritual energies at various levels we learn the rudiments of receptivity that eventually can become surrender to the ultimate Source.

Thus the spiritual dimension has many facets and many levels, from the merely psychic or so-called paranormal to the loving energy that most intimately reveals God. Most human beings, except a minority in the post-Enlightenment West, have been aware of this realm in some way, though often superficially and usually with much projection of personal fantasies and cultural expectations. All religious experience is, I am convinced, an experience of spiritual energies of some kind. The energies themselves vary greatly, and the human projections on to them also vary, both in degree and in kind. Even the Jewish and Christian experiences of God as the mysterious presence "out there" have arisen from encounters in the spiritual realm. Some forms of energy, for example, unconditional love, *reveal* God better than others do, and that is the truth in traditional theism at its best, for example, in Martin Buber. But none of them *are* God, the divine Source.

The mystical God cannot be experienced, for an experience is always an experience *of* some content, whereas God is not a content, however sublime. God is the creative pure consciousness, the pregnant void, out of which all particular existents continually arise. God as such is known only in a state of pure consciousness, devoid of all particular contents. Such a state is possible for human beings and in it the realization is that there is only God. But paradoxically human beings can also be in such a state while also being aware of particular existents, including oneself as this particular person, arising from God and in God: being God and being lived

by God. This realization is the ultimate in human fulfilment. It is a transfiguring surrender of the self-separating
particular self. One becomes a luminous being, outshone by
the Source that one ultimately *is*. This culmination can
occur only when the whole self—body, passions, mind, spirit—has been united together in surrender to the Source. The
whole self includes our threefold interdependence: with
other persons in the power structures, both just and unjust,
of society; with everything else in the cosmos that like us is
mineral, vegetable, or animal; and with all that inhabits the
spiritual plane. The whole self includes whatever human
needs and interests can be uncovered by both secular and
spiritual perspectives on human nature. And the whole self
is united by the human *soul* as a metaphorical point where
the self arises out of the divine Source. We all have or are a
soul, but in most of us it is rudimentary and barely developed (or, in another view, barely uncovered).

Much more should perhaps be said about religion as
awareness of spiritual reality and as transfiguration in the
mystical God. But if any such religious claims are meaningful and true, it is obvious that they provide additional
"facts" about human nature on which moral judgments can
be based. Thus, even though a minimal or better-than-mini-
mal moral code for society can be justified without bringing
in religion, religion may be rationally relevant to morality.
But are any of the religious claims that I sketched earlier
true? Indeed, are any of them even *meaningful*?

Here a general issue of understanding and intelligibility
arises. How do any of us come to understand human nature
more deeply than we do at present? Whether the approach is
secular or religious it seems evident to me that *much* of any
deeper understanding is not scientific or purely rationalistic,
but on the contrary requires that each of us undergo a process of personal transformation—relatively superficial or
radical—in which a new dimension of human nature is
uncovered within *us*, in spite of our initial repression and
resistance to it. An obvious example of this is the uncovering of the emotional unconscious through psychotherapy,
but a similar need for "conversion" is at times evident when

a person acquires an ecological conscience or when he or she is politicized through participation in a struggle against oppression or—I would add—when the spiritual realm is derepressed and allowed into consciousness. In all these cases people understand in *varying* degrees. It is not a matter of either understanding fully or not understanding at all. And usually there is some initial intelligibility, however confused or superficial, even before the "conversion." So if a sincere inquirer finds a claim *unintelligible*, this is a serious challenge. In some areas, nevertheless, especially those involving intimate personal experiences such as psychotherapy and spirituality, a charge of unintelligibility by an outsider or nonparticipant has little weight. For example, in a debate with Benoit Garceau, Kai Nielsen protested that Garceau's religious language is not sufficiently intelligible for Nielsen either to deny or to take on trust. Garceau had said, "No one would think of denying God if those who believe in Him manifested Him as *an unlimited space of light and love.*" Nielsen commented, "We do not understand what that word-string means."[8]

My response to Nielsen's protest is that only a religious believer who has been very radically transformed will manifest God in such a way, and that only a person who is at least beginning such a transformation will discern something of what such a transformed person is manifesting and thereby find such language somewhat intelligible. The fact that Nielsen does not find the language intelligible is very much to be expected. The reason for this is not that all or most of our private experience is in principle incommunicable. When, in his debate with Garceau,[9] Nielsen rejected such an assumption, I agree with him. Even where a rare experience is not communicable to most people, it is in principle communicable to someone else who has had the experience. The point is that if one is to understand the language which expresses some rare experiences one must have had the experiences. And if one is to have the experiences it is necessary, in some cases, that one undergoes an appropriate personal process of transformation. For example, if I am to understand adequately the expression, "repression of infantile longings," I usually need to undergo psychoanalysis or some analogous process. And similarly if I am to understand adequately, or even initially, what a Christian or Buddhist contemplative means by "an unlimited space of light and love," I must usually undergo an arduous process of purificatory and meditative discipline. Then an experience for which Garceau's phrase seems appropriate will perhaps occur. Indeed, there are two different experiences, each arising along a different meditative route, to which the phrase might apply. In one route, I first become aware of vibrations or energies that have various colors and are associated with various human emotions, including love. Then an experience of loving light may be so intensified that there is a sense of expansion beyond any boundaries. Alternatively, a meditator may first enter an unlimited void, an emptiness without boundaries, and then become aware of energies of light and love arising out of this void.

A Buddhist contemplative, pondering Garceau's phrase, might say, "I can relate what you say to my own experience, though I differ in that I would not use the words 'manifestation of God' to describe it." A fruitful Buddhist-Christian dialogue might ensue, including clarification concerning which of the two experiences outlined earlier is being considered. The dialogue between Garceau and Nielsen, however, came to an impasse, for Nielsen did not concede that perhaps this difficulty in understanding arises from his not having had the relevant experience. Had he made such a concession, he might then have inquired how he might come to have the experience. And the answer to such an inquiry might include learning from an exemplar, a spiritual master, who can guide in the process of personal transformation that leads to having the relevant experience.

Thus issues concerning the intelligibility of religious language can lead to issues concerning how we can learn from others who have superior spiritual wisdom. If I accept someone as an exemplar in a particular dimension of human fulfilment, or more comprehensively as an exemplar of human fulfillment, do I thereby lose my freedom? The word *freedom* may refer to (a) freedom *from* external or internal com-

pulsions or impediments or (b) freedom *to* fulfil one's potential (freedom as ability) or (c) freedom *as* acceptance of personal responsibility. Some disciple-master relations involve
a loss of freedom in all three senses. But this is not the case
where no coercion is sought or received, where the master is
genuinely more fulfiled than the individual in the relevant
respect and where the individual accepts responsibility for
continuing or discontinuing association with the master. At
best, the individual is completely liberated in sense (b)
through a gradual process of personal transformation that
involves an ever deepening freedom-*from* (cf. [a]) and free-
dom-*as* (cf. [c]).[10]

To choose an exemplar one need not already fully understand the virtues which the exemplar possesses and which
one hopes to acquire by imitating her or him. All one
requires is what Basil Mitchell calls "an incipient awareness
of what is worth imitating."[11] This initial understanding
may be very confused and distorted and meager and yet be
adequate both as a rational base and as a psychological
motive. Thus when Kant says, "Even the Holy One of the
Gospels must first be compared with our ideal of moral perfection before we can recognize him as such,"[12] this is true
only if we acknowledge that our initial ideal may be very
inadequate and that we may need to be influenced by the
Holy One of the Gospels and gradually transformed into His
likeness, if we are to come to understand fully what *His*
ideal means. A similar point applies if Kant or anyone else
approaches the Buddha or a Hindu saint or a Sufi spiritual
master. And a similar point applies if the issue is how we
come to understand what the word *good* means when it is
applied to God. We can understand only to the extent that
we become *like* God though initially we apply *some* concept
of "good" to God.

And if we turn from saints and God to colleagues and
friends, and consider how we learn about human nature
from them, this too may involve not merely an impersonal
exchange of ideas and arguments, but an openness to be
changed as the other person enables me to uncover previously hidden dimensions of my human nature. At best, a dialog-

ical process presupposes and includes a process of transformation of the individuals who are involved in it and openness to be influenced not only by the arguments but also by
the personal example, the lived insights, of others in the dialogue. Such a dialogical process enables people to regard
their own conceptions of human nature, whether scientific-
secular or nonscientific-secular or religious, as *partial* and
incomplete perspectives which can and must be supplemented and corrected by other perspectives. Out of such dialogues can eventually come a much more substantial universal consensus concerning human nature. Meanwhile
such dialogues provide both concurring and overdetermining
reasons for a minimal moral code and cumulative, complementary *additions* toward a comprehensive conception of
human nature. This conception would not be expressed in a
punitive moral code but rather in a flexible universal ideal
toward which we each can aspire in our own individual
ways. And in the very process of such dialogues a *new*
human nature is to some extent evolving.

Although I am emphasizing the possibilities of consensus,
I acknowledge the obstacles. People are reluctant to regard
their own perspectives as partial, incomplete and open to
some correction. And even where the reluctance is overcome, there are important *conflicts* between perspectives
that are difficult to resolve. Moral philosophy tends to focus
most attention on the interesting and troubling cases where
there seems to be unresolvable conflict. These should not be
ignored, but in a context of genuine dialogue there is hope
for eventual resolution.

II

Having sketched my own perspective I now turn to consider my agreements and disagreements with Kai Nielsen's
perspective. First, *because* I am a mystical humanist, I share
much of Nielsen's atheism. God as understood and denied
by him is also denied by me. This is the God of much conventional, nonmystical theism, depicted as an infinite individual, a Transcendent Person "out there" who as an all-

powerful world Creator, utterly distinct from and separate from the world, issues divine commands that human beings must obey or else suffer punishment. For Nielsen this God simply does not exist. For me, the experience and conception of such a God arise from a distorted awareness of spiritual reality. The distortion arises in two ways. First there is a mistaken identification of this spiritual reality, this mysterious and powerful life energy, with God; but God as divine Source is beyond experience. Second, as Thomas Merton has shown,[13] there is a projection of human narcissistic and megalomaniac self-fantasies onto the cosmos, a projection "out there" of the god whom each of us would secretly like to be.

In contrast with this, I use the term *God* to refer to the creative pure consciousness out of which all particular existents continually arise. And what this means is understood only to the extent that one is radically transformed to realize that one is, paradoxically, both this creative pure consciousness and one of the particular existents which arises from it and in it. I agree with Nielsen[14] that God as such cannot be experienced. So would many mystics, for whom God is not an item or particular, however sublime, which human consciousness can detect. God is not like a person or an angel or a field of energy or a radiant light, though each of these may reveal God in some way. God is known as God in a state of pure consciousness, devoid of all particular content. Whatever can be experienced is at best expressive of God, revelatory of God; it is not God as such.

Thus I share Nielsen's atheism, denying the existence of the God whom he also denies; but this is because, unlike him, I have faith in (and to a limited extent know) a different, mystical God. Another area of agreement is in his critique[15] of the claim that divine commands provide a necessary and sufficient reason for making moral judgments in accordance with those commands. From "God commands *X*" it does not follow logically that I ought to do *X*. Whatever the powers of God as a postulated Infinite Individual, His commands could only be accepted as moral if either we judge them to be moral already or we have brought our own moral concepts to bear on God and judged God to be so morally wise and good as to be worthy of obedience even in instances where we do not initially concur with what is commanded. I have already argued, in contrast with Nielsen, that such a judgment that God is good need not make God's moral goodness redundant. Our own concept of moral goodness is not, and need not be, completely adequate already. But I agree that morality cannot be totally and solely derived from divine commands of an Infinite-Individual God even if there were such a "God." On the contrary, religion as worship of an Infinite-Individual presupposes a human judgment that this Individual is worthy of worship, a judgment that includes—as Nielsen rightly insists—the moral judgment that this Individual is morally good.

Thus I agree with Nielsen that such a God's commands are neither necessary nor sufficient premises for moral judgments. I also agree that if such a God existed, human integrity and dignity would require our exercising our own autonomous freedom, making our own moral decisions, rather than yielding to a coercive heteronomy, doing whatever the Big Boss in heaven says we must do. Issues of human autonomy in relation to God change significantly, however, if our understanding of self and God moves away from Nielsen's context toward, say, Buber's conception of I-Thou encounter, which I see as a step toward mystical humanism. Both Buber and mysticism reject a Kantian picture of the self as an isolated individual whose freedom is reduced by *any* influence received from another individual, especially an Infinite Individual. Both Buber and mysticism see this as a self-induced fantasy, a human creation. For Buber, God may still be experienced nonmystically as an external personal presence, but this time not as another individual, especially an Infinite Individual, but rather as the loving, noncoercive spiritual reality which pervades all persons and all things. Such a God is remote from the projected concoctions of human egoism that have perverted much traditional theism. But in my view even this view is incomplete and partly distorted. Eventually it can and must be subordinated to a mystical awareness in which one surrenders, not to an external Agent or even to a pervasive Presence, but into the divine Source. The human soul is the metaphorical "place" where the whole self arises out of the divine Source, and where the whole self can freely surrender into the divine Source to *be* and to *be lived by* the divine Source. One surrenders into what one ultimately *is*.[16]

Thus far I have considered two elements in Nielsen's atheism: his not believing that an Infinite Individual exists, and his insistence that from belief in such a God morality need not, cannot, and should not be derived. A third element where I am again in considerable agreement (though again partly for different reasons) is his critique of the motivation underlying such religious belief. He draws implicitly on Freud concerning how religion arises from an infantile sense of powerlessness along with a craving for a protective parental authority figure.[17] And he draws on Marx concerning how religion arises from the needs of the ruling classes to legitimize their privilege and authority through ideologies that encourage the lower classes to accept their subordinate place.[18] I agree that much religious belief can be partly explained in these ways, though I think that as more and more believers become aware of such motivation, it loses much of the power it had when it was entirely unconscious. But I would want to add to such psychological and sociological accounts of religious motivation a *mystical* account which I have already sketched, citing Thomas Merton. The very same narcissistic, self-isolating, self-inflating desire to be "god," which is the main human obstacle to knowing the true God, is also the main source of the false idea of God which has corrupted much of Western theism.

A fourth area of agreement with Nielsen is in sharing his abhorrence of some of the ways in which Christianity has influenced people: its reinforcing of our infantilism; its sanctioning of oppressive regimes, imperialism, and war; and its frequent violations of even minimal moral codes in an appeal to religious values that allegedly override those based "merely" on nonreligious human needs. I find some consolation in the fact that within Christendom there have nearly always been minorities who have followed St. Paul in putting away childish things,[19] or who have followed the prophets in denouncing oppression, or who have followed Jesus in his humanitarian challenge to religious fanaticism. Overall, however, I would find it difficult to substantiate a claim that Christianity, or religion in general, has done more good than harm in human history.[20] Nor do I feel any need to make such a claim, for by being a religious person I do not ally myself with all religion any more than Nielsen, by being a secular person, allies himself with all secularism, including its Stalinist and Nazi forms. But I did claim that a comprehensive mystical humanism would provide the strongest motivation not only for its own morality, but also, in general, for a minimal moral code. I would readily concede, nevertheless, that there are many secular persons who live much better lives, as appraised not only from their perspective but also from mine, than do many conventional religious believers.

Thus far I have noted some ways in which I share Nielsen's atheism, though partly for different reasons. Our focus has been on religion in relation to morality. Now we turn to focus on morality in relation to religion, first considering Nielsen's moral-social philosophy. I share with him[21] a commitment to work toward a society in which there is maximal freedom in the sense that people are treated as ends in themselves and not merely as means to be coerced or manipulated; and a society in which all persons are allowed to shape their own lives in accordance with their own ideals of human fulfillment (perfection, flourishing) insofar as this is compatible with the freedom of others. I differ from this liberalism in one important respect, however, and so to some extent does Nielsen. I believe that although people vary considerably in what fulfills them, there is a sizeable common core of human needs and interests, a human nature, to be discovered (though to some extent to be created as well), so that my stress on freedom to pursue one's own fulfilment arises not only because of a legitimate diversity in modes of human fulfilment and an abhorrence of coercion, but also because freedom is neces-

sary for the process of discovering for oneself the constituents of human fulfilment that are common to all.

Insofar as Nielsen himself has a universal ideal concerning what constitutes human fulfilment, it seems to include a
life conducted in accordance with practical reason.[22] This
involves, first of all, a calculative or technical reason.[23] Such
a reason involves choosing efficient means for a comprehensive cluster of compatible ends which reflect one's wants. It
also involves postponing decisions wherein one detects confusion concerning means or ends or concerning one's own
mental state. Here I should note that although I see such
technical reason as a constituent of human fulfilment, I
would emphasize it less. Indeed, I see the predominance of
technical reasoning as a major obstacle to recognizing and
developing much of our secular human nature and all of our
religious human nature.[24] But Nielsen himself sees some
limitations to technical reason, and his conception of practical reason includes much more. First of all, it involves a
capacity to recognize what he calls *moral truisms*[25] that pro-
hibit, for example, torture of human beings, cruelty to
human beings and animals, treating promises lightly,
exploiting and degrading human beings, breaking faith with
people, and so on. Anyone who does not recognize that these
prohibitions hold unless overridden by some very special
justification has no understanding of the concept of morality
and thereby—Nielsen seems to imply—lacks an essential
ingredient as a human being. I agree, though I do not regard
these moral prohibitions simply as truisms, for I think that
they can be justified by reference to facts about human
nature.

Nielsen's liberal social-moral perspective is also modified
by a realization that contemporary liberalism tends to ignore
the insights of Marx and others concerning how injustice
and oppression are masked by unacknowledged ideologies[26]
which claim that we already *are* free in the ideal ways that
liberalism eulogizes. I agree with this modification and I also
share another modification. He and I would both insist that
our individual fulfilment cannot be legitimately sought or
genuinely realized in abstraction from our relations with

others in the power structures of society. Indeed, our sense of alienation and helpless hopelessness arises partly from our entanglement in an alienating and oppressive society. Nielsen would, I think, say, "mainly and perhaps entirely" rather than "partly." As a socialist he presumes that our despair is not rooted in a common tragic condition, but in certain alterable social conditions.[27] My own view here differs in that I see alienating and evil tendencies as also arising in human beings independent of social conditions, in psychological and spiritual processes which are only partly influenceable by changes in social structures, and which tend to corrupt any initially superior social structures that are introduced. But I would also acknowledge much truth in Nielsen's emphasis. Even initially superior individuals who have dealt radically with the evil within themselves tend to be corrupted by self-deceptive ideologies and the hidden complicities of oppressive societies.

Nielsen's universal moral ideal for human beings thus involves living in accordance with a practical reason which includes respect for others' freedom, application of technical reason, sensitivity to moral truisms, and minimal self-deception by ideologies. He also advocates a kind of rationality which is needed for a particular kind of sociomoral *reflection*,[28] which I will now outline. Nielsen considers the possibility of a potentially universal sociomoral perspective, or at least an alternative to moral relativism and skepticism, emerging from a method of reflection that he adapts and revises from the distinguished contemporary philosopher John Rawls. This reflection brings together *considered moral judgments, moral theories* (especially moral principles), and *social theory* (including factual considerations). During the reflection elements in all three categories are open to modification so that eventually an overall coherence may be attained that brings "wide reflective equilibrium" (WRE). I should first clarify what he means by *considered moral judgments*; for example, "racial discrimination is wrong." For a moral judgment to be deemed to be "considered" it must not be made under emotional duress or without adequate information or in any arbitrary way.[29] In spite of these restrictions, the class of considered judgments is very much larger than that of moral truisms. Although moral truisms are almost universally accepted, considered moral judgments vary considerably between cultures and even within cultures.[30] Nielsen's hope is that more widespread rational agreement could ensue if people tested their considered judgments not only in relation to moral theories, but more important in relation to social theories, which include both "truth of an unproblematic sort"[31] (factual information that is apparently value free) and claims concerning human beings that *combine* factual and evaluative elements, including implicit moral judgments.[32] Nielsen envisages the method of WRE as going on among "emancipated and enlightened people" who have a "conception of human good (of a distinctive human *flourishing*)" because they understand "human needs and vital centers of interest" and their relative importance.[33] In other words, the method presupposes a value-laden factual conception of human nature.

Nielsen thus holds that a social theory can provide some bases or reasons for moral judgments even though it is not confined to neutral empirical facts accessible and acceptable to all rational social theories. His own hope is for a "rationally reconstructed theory emerging from the Marxist tradition."[34] But why not broaden the range of WRE to include not only some other social theories but also some theories concerning the human *psyche* and the human *spirit*? These also deal with human needs, human flourishing, and human interactions. The comprehensive humanism I suggested in Part 1 becomes in principle appropriate.[35] (Its mystical-surrender component raises different issues, which I will consider later.) Such a comprehensive humanism can include Nielsen's predominant concern, which is how to reduce social evils. But it can also go beyond this to enrich his universal moral ideal by adding to the life of practical reason dimensions of human flourishing drawn from psychological and spiritual conceptions of human nature.

I should note that sometimes Nielsen, contrary to the method of WRE with its appeals to social-theory claims about human nature and its implicit conceptions of human flourishing, reverts to his earlier noncognitivism in moral matters.[36] In such an approach, no facts can rationally justify any moral judgment, and allegedly morally significant "facts" concerning human nature merely mask hidden moral premises that themselves are unjustifiable. For a noncognitivist, morality is a matter of human resolve or commitment or creation. And not only morality but more generally all meaning and purpose in human life are created by human beings rather than being in any sense discovered.[37] In such an approach, however, even Nielsen's moral truisms are threatened, for they can be relativized as a merely coincidental consensus among human beings in their arbitrary moral resolutions and willful creations of meaning, a consensus that cannot be justified by any references to human nature. In contrast with this, Nielsen's method of WRE does appeal to value-laden facts about human nature.

So let us continue exploring Nielsen's use of WRE, focusing in particular on the issue that is for him a test case: egalitarianism. Nielsen agrees[38] with Kant's dictum that every human being has a right to be treated as an end (as something of intrinsic worth) and never merely as a means. This can be expanded into the explicitly egalitarian claim that every human being is equally worthy of concern and respect simply as a human being, irrespective of inequalities of birth or merit or moral sensitivity or other excellence or any other characteristic.[39] Nielsen is committed to egalitarianism,[40] but he interprets it in conflicting ways which all seem relevant and plausible. (I admire his willingness to risk inconsistency because of the pressures of intellectual and personal integrity.) Sometimes he interprets his egalitarianism noncognitively, as simply his personal *resolve* to treat human beings with equal concern and respect.[41] Sometimes he considers viewing it as a groundless *belief* which one need not relinquish, for justification does come to an end.[42] Sometimes he faces the force of elitist criticisms:

> What is the justification for treating them all as ends in themselves . . . when they are so very different? Why not reserve this for the creative elites who are genuine creators of

value? And is it not arbitrary to say that all human beings have the same intrinsic worth when they are plainly so different in intellectual capacity, merit,moral sensitivity, and goodness? It looks like a carry-over in a secular context of a non-rational religious attitude.[43]

Perhaps Nielsen here hints that egalitarianism might be justifiable from some religious perspective if any such perspective were rationally tenable. Since he rejects this possibility, he turns to the method of WRE to see whether it could show the superior rationality of egalitarianism over elitism. But unfortunately in his own application of the method[44] he at most refutes some superfluous defensive arguments that elitists may raise concerning the prevalence of human differences in past cultures and the probable continuance of these differences. He argues that elitists underestimate the sociohistorical factors which produced past differences and underestimate the possibilities of more equitable distribution in a technological culture. But the egalitarian position is not adequately defended by evidence which indicates that people in the future might differ much *less* in the characteristics elitists cite as bases for differential concern and respect. The egalitarian position is that any person, right now, in spite of relatively lacking such characteristics, is worthy of equal concern and respect: even if, for example, he or she has developed little individual creativity, or little of Nielsen's practical reason, or little awareness beyond a brutish sensitivity to pain and pleasure. And if an egalitarian alleges that all human beings have a *common*, invariable characteristic which justifies equal respect and care here and now, what is it?[45] Emerging characteristics of future persons in future societies are surely not relevant, except as indirect evidence for alleged *capacities* which all people now have, which give us all an equal intrinsic worth. But then we must ask whether there is any genuinely universal capacity among human beings which, by its very existence as a capacity rather than an actuality, provides intrinsic worth and rationally calls forth our respect and concern for the whole person who has this capacity. Secular egalitarians may cite capacities for individual creativity or for practical reason or for sensitive awareness. But in each case there seem to be inequalities in capacity as well as the more obvious inequalities in actuality; and in extreme cases the capacity may seem to be almost absent. Yet although such egalitarianism is thus limited, it is remote from extreme forms of elitism. We should realize that elitism and egalitarianism are not dichotomous opposites, but rather conflicting emphases along a continuum. The movement toward a more thoroughgoing egalitarianism continues if we combine together several such secular-egalitarian perspectives, each with its own reference to a quasi-universal human capacity.

For me, however, the most plausible secular basis for egalitarianism is an alleged universal capacity to treat others with respect and concern. The plausibility is based on the fact that this capacity is often partly actualized in *response* to being treated with concern and respect. If at first a person does not respond positively, some degree of persistence is usually quite rational, for often in the past a positive response has eventually resulted. And even when considerable persistence is in vain, a belief in the person's hidden moral capacity may be quite rational. In a few cases, however, there seems to be no secular evidence at all that the person has this capacity: he or she seems totally evil. For a secular egalitarian the existence of the capacity must then be a matter of secular faith. Although I find such a *faith* admirable I think a reliance on noncognitivist *resolve* to treat the person *as if* he or she had intrinsic worth would be more intellectually honest—unless, as is often the case with such saintly secular humanists, their faith is being secretly confirmed by blurred discernments of the evil person's *spirit*.

If, however, a person is genuinely spiritual in the sense that he or she has undergone the radical personal transformation that brings a deep discernment of human spirit, the existence of a moral capacity for respect and concern, even in a very evil person, is not a matter of faith but of spiritual insight. One can see within the person a loving and radiant light, though the person has deeply repressed and constricted and distorted this light. And not only is this light in the person a potential motivating source for having moral respect and concern toward others; it rationally calls forth one's own respect (indeed reverence) and a concern to help it to blaze forth unimpeded. Of course spiritual insight varies greatly. Much less is needed to discern the radiating light of a saint than the hidden light of a Darth Vader. Only a saint can see the latter, and he or she must have undergone an arduous spiritual journey in which he or she has faced up to his or her own "dark side" and discerned light even there.[46]

Even a profoundly spiritual perspective, however, is still limited in its egalitarianism. If respect and concern are based on the spiritual light discerned in all human beings, a varying respect and concern seem appropriate because people do vary in their spiritual light. Also, people's variations in nonspiritual characteristics do seem to warrant differentiating treatment. In humanistic mysticism, as distinct from a purely spiritualistic mysticism, we are to treat not simply the person's spirit with respect and concern but the whole person. If so, we cannot ignore the varying imperfections. Hence the focus of respect and concern must be the soul, which is the whole self united (to a greater or lesser extent) at the metaphorical point where it arises out of its divine Source. The soul is not a part of the self, like the mind or spirit. Any attempt to unify the self by a part of the self is a form of internal division and tyranny. The soul is the metaphorical place of freedom where the whole self surrenders to being lived by the Source and being the Source. This involves becoming an open channel of the unconditional love which arises immediately from that Source. Only such transfiguring surrender enables us to become completely thoroughgoing egalitarians, like Jesus of Nazarath, unrestricted by any human differentiating characteristics in our respect and concern, whether the characteristics be capacities or actualities, whether they be spiritual or nonspiritual. A few people who have been transformed by the purifying and awakening disciplines of a great religion exemplify this. And some secular humanists are closer to it in their lives than many conventionally religious people. Such religious people have religious beliefs, but not the spiritual awareness and the transfiguring surrender presupposed for an adequate understanding of these beliefs.

How is such conventional religion possible? This question shifts our attention to some epistemological issues with which I conclude this chapter. My answer to the question is that although both conventional believer and atheist can typically use the word *God* correctly in a religious "language game," not violating what Wittgensteineans call its *grammar*, such *linguistic* understanding requires only minimal *experiential* understanding.[47] The believer trusts his or her tradition in its claim that the language does have an experiential base, and he or she may gain some experiential understanding by being committed to the way of life associated with the language. In contrast with this, the atheist focuses on the apparent lack of experiential base and the apparent contradictions in some of the religious language. Both believer and atheist, however, are dealing with *exoteric* religion, not with the spiritual and mystical transformational core of *esoteric* religion. As Nielsen correctly points out,[48] if a person who was religious becomes an atheist, he or she may still understand the religious language, though I would note that with the decline of religious practice any acquired experiential understanding may disappear altogether. And what Nielsen says is true only when the shift to atheism is from conventional belief. When a person has had profound spiritual experience of divine love and has begun to surrender to the divine Source, the move to atheism as a denial of both spirit and God is a turning away from spiritual experience and from a surrendered mode of existence, so that gradually one virtually ceases to understand the esoteric core of religion, leaving only the exoteric shell to be rejected. Such a form of atheism is quite intelligible to anyone undergoing a serious esoteric religious process, for the process usually involves many mini-reversions toward atheism in which one "forgets" (that is, represses) today what one knew yesterday.

But during such an esoteric process, how can one tell whether a putative experience of spiritual reality, including an experience of "God" as understood nonmystically, is real or illusory? Nielsen claims that there is no way one can tell in any religious process, because all religious experience allegedly has only a psychological reality as a subjective private experience, for it lacks public, intersubjective confirmation.[49] I would agree that many experiences of spiritual reality lack "public" confirmation in the sense of confirmation by ordinary sense experience, though various low-grade spiritual discernments may receive partial confirmation through parapsychological research. If there were a spiritual realm such as has been described in esoteric religious traditions, such a realm would, by definition, not be detectable by ordinary sense experience except indirectly when it impinges on the nonspiritual world so that its operations might thereby be inferred from changes in that world. Perhaps all spiritual discernments involve some nonspiritual changes as well, but this is not obvious, and the former are often discerned by themselves through spiritual insight. Moreover, there is often considerable intersubjective confirmation of spiritual discernments among people of spiritual insight, for example, concerning the presence and the characteristics of a discarnate spirit in a particular place at a particular time.

Appraisal of spiritual discernments is not a simple matter. As we saw in Chapter VI, even if one's experience is confirmed by others, this is not itself a sufficient condition for truth. Many explanations that skeptics use as alternatives to spiritual explanations may be relevant, for example, the expectations of the group and the jointly held fantasies of individuals. Sometimes these nonspiritual explanations may be totally adequate; sometimes they need supplementing by the realization that the human mind can create real spiritual entities; but sometimes they deal at most with some characteristics projected on to an already-existing spiritual reality; and sometimes there is minimal projection. In making such distinctions there are two kinds of criteria: intersubjective and personal. On the one hand, confirmation by others, though not strictly a sufficient or necessary condition, is very important, especially when the other is a spiritual teacher whose wisdom one has come to have reason to trust. On the other hand, there is one's own growing self-knowledge, perhaps after many years uncovering both one's own self-deceptions and one's own spiritual truth. Included among the intersubjective and personal appraisals there are, or should be, *moral* criteria that are relevant to judgments concerning whether the discernments pertain to a spiritual reality that is both important and exemplary. This is crucial, for much spiritual exploration is amoral or even so immoral as to be psychopathic. Indeed, the most decisive moral struggles occur, largely unconsciously, on this plane, both for individuals and nations. There are, however, spiritual energies which, as they emerge immediately and undistorted from the divine Source, are unconditionally loving. And a radical moral-spiritual transformation is possible in which one becomes an unobstructed channel of that love and eventually realizes one's ultimate identity with the Source. This transformation, however, requires a letting go of all attachment to the human self as separated from its loving Source. Without such letting go, even the best of human morality, whether secular or spiritual, tends to become perverted and corrupted by the narcissistic desire to be one's own god. So in an *ultimate* way morality does depend on "religion" for its correction and fulfilment: it depends on religion as transfiguring surrender. Here is the truth that is perverted in divine-command theories of morality and in self-righteous religious attacks on atheism. Here is the ultimate nature and origin of evil in human beings, as we will see in the next chapter.

VIII *** On the Nature and Origin of Good and Evil in Human Beings

The most important issues in philosophy are, perhaps, ethical, and the most basic ethical question is, "What is the nature and origin of good and evil in human beings?" In this chapter I will outline my own answer. You will notice that the answer presupposes the critique of impersonalism that I set forth in Chapter IV, though here the limits of impersonal philosophical and scientific approaches are emphasized, not primarily in relation to our knowledge of spiritual reality, but rather in relation to our experiential understanding of the nature and origin of good and evil in ourselves. Also, having in previous chapters uncovered narcissism as self-preoccupied motivation, as resistance to loving energies and as recoil from the divine Source which lives us, I will in this chapter introduce the possibility that some degree of narcissism is an ineradicable tendency in human nature.

I do not hope to generate universal agreement concerning my account, which is in any case tentative, but it does seem to me that it is worth considering. Mystical humanism can provide a distinctive and inclusive perspective on the origin and nature of good and evil in human beings.[1]

First, let us consider the claim that the question of origin is appropriately answered by objective and scientific study of the *causes* of good and evil in human behavior. Such an approach typically assumes that there is a clear distinction between the issue of *nature* and the issue of *origin*. The issue of the nature of good and evil is typically viewed as an evaluative issue in contrast with the issue of origin, which is a factual issue. Allegedly the two issues are entirely separable. Some broad human agreement is assumed concerning the nature of good and evil. Then the investigation focuses on the origin of good and evil, where origin is construed in terms of causes. By *causes* I mean either necessary and sufficient conditions or, less rigorously, influences or factors that tend to bring about good or evil behavior. If a one-cause theory such as "the ownership of the means of production" or "parental influence in early childhood" seems inadequate, a combination of causal theories may be offered.

Such an approach is often challenged on the ground that even though various psychological and sociological and biological and historical factors influence us toward good and evil, there is an element of *freedom* in our choice. This freedom or free will may be severely restricted by such influences, but it is not eliminated. Indeed, freedom can be expanded in its scope by our growing knowledge of these influences and our deliberate decision to consent to them or to resist them. Where such freedom is stressed, an uncovering of the origins of good and evil in human beings involves not only looking at external and internal influences on our choices but also, and more crucially, at the exercise of freedom in our choices. And this involves a shift in our perspective on not only the origins but also the nature of good and evil in human beings. Good and evil are no longer simply human behavior as evaluated by a conventional moral code. Rather, they are also, and crucially, a matter of free choices where we receive or resist this or that influence. Radical good and evil thus both originate in free choice and consist in what we freely choose. And if we look at the nonradical good and evil that is publicly observable in human behavior and ask for an explanation of its origin, free choice is a factor alongside the various influences investigated by the social and biological sciences.

On what grounds is freedom plausibly introduced as a revision of a totally scientific-causal account? Consider, for example, the present impasse in criminology where, it is alleged,[2] no method of changing human behavior has been established as working better, statistically, than any other. One interpretation of this impasse is that it is merely a temporary difficulty in the inexorable progressive march of science, which eventually will discover the complex of factors that produce good and evil behavior. This interpretation assumes determinism, though the determination to go on looking for causes need not do so. In another interpretation, although improvements in scientific explanation of human behavior are possible, freedom is a postulate that scientists can legitimately bring in to explain both contemporary and ultimate limitations on their own explanations. That is, even if most people tend to respond in such and such a way to such and such treatment, some people choose to resist the influence, and this choice need not itself have a cause. But outside of science free will is not tentatively postulated on the basis of gaps in science, but firmly asserted on the basis of evidence from introspection. When I look within myself I find myself making choices and at times defying known influences. And not only does introspective evidence contradict determinism, I cannot really believe in determinism at the moment when I am making a choice, though I may *"entertain"* the theory of determinism concerning myself and *believe* in it concerning everyone else.

Thus far we have looked at objective knowledge of causes and introspective awareness of free will. Many thinkers see some version of these as exhausting the relevant possibilities. Both of these, however, are challenged by a discovery that comes from a further, more rigorous introspection: the discovery of *self-deception*. That is, I discover that I have been actively obscuring my awareness of my own fundamental motivations, and this willful ignoring has been distorting my supposedly objective scientific discernment of external and internal influences. It has also been radically restricting my own freedom. Choices that seemed completely free were not completely free, but arose mainly from fundamental motivations which were unacknowledged and hence not deliberately, fully consciously chosen. It is here in the uncovering of radical self-deception, which is neither a mere ignorance or unawareness nor a fully conscious deliberate willing, that some thinkers locate radical evil, which combines both the origin and nature of evil in human beings. What is the hidden fundamental motivation or way of being in the world? As we saw in Chapter III, existentialists, depth psychologists, and mystics sometimes concur in depicting radical evil as a hidden narcissism. Narcissism is characterized as self-centeredness, self-preoccupation, self-separation, self-enclosure, or egocentricity. It involves a competitive concern about one's own possessions, power, and status as compared with others. Later in this chapter I will be showing that the convergence on narcissism as radical evil involves important differences of interpretation. Here I am stressing similarities, and using the term *narcissism* to refer to these similarities.

If radical evil consists of a hidden narcissism which we self-deceptively conceal from ourselves, it has to be uncovered and dealt with. Otherwise our discernment of both good and evil will remain distorted. One cannot assume that the question, "What is the nature and origin of good and evil in human beings?" can be appropriately dealt with impersonally, by objective scientific research—or, for that matter, by impersonal philosophical argument and analysis. One cannot assume that the question is like a question in engineering ("Why did the bridge collapse?") or in metaphysics ("Must there have been a First Cause?"). Whether impersonal investigation can help, and if so, how, will become clear only if first I become to some extent aware of unacknowledged evil within me, distorting my discernment of both the nature and origin of good and evil by interpreting these in ways that help me not to look at my own narcissism. Nor will a relatively superficial introspection concerning my own apparently free choices suffice. There must be an exposure and acknowledgment of radical self-deception, shattering my resistance against acknowledging my fundamental narcissism. Such an uncovering involves a change in the uncoverer, a personal transformation. It is an uncovering of a way in which I have been deceiving myself, actively obscuring an awareness of my own narcissistic motivation. Uncovering this motivation is a necessary condition for reducing it or eliminating it. It is not a sufficient condition, however. (I will explain this later on.)

On what basis do I claim that radical evil—that is, both the ultimate origin and ultimate motive of evil—is a basic motivation appropriately labeled *narcissism*? My basis is a combination of my own experience and the testimony and reflection of others whom I regard as wise, including some philosophers who are genuine lovers of wisdom rather than mere technicians of argument. Of course my initial selection of thinkers as "wise" depends on trusting my own wisdom when I discern their wisdom. For this reason, and also because their testimony unfortunately diverges on important matters, as we shall see, I ultimately have to appeal to my own experience in ongoing dialogue with their testimony and reflection. Such dialogue involves being open to whatever personal transformation is required to understand their claims adequately. Then one can appraise and adjudicate these claims. This seems to me to be the most appropriate method for a philosopher who is investigating radical good and evil, though a more impersonal and less dialogical and less esoteric method may be the most appropriate concerning other issues, say logic or in philosophy of science.

When I investigated the difficult notion of self-deception as it arises in psychotherapy (see the beginning of Chapter III), I did not focus on trivial examples which help us to contrast self-deception with sheer ignorance. But almost everyone has in everyday life come to realize, for example, not only that I *am* feeling angry but also that a few minutes ago I *was* feeling angry and was *actively resisting* my awareness of this, refusing to acknowledge it not only to others but also to myself. This is experientially different from realizing that I am feeling angry whereas a few minutes ago I had no awareness whatsoever of feeling angry. Similarly if my most basic motivation, like everyone's, is narcissism, and I have been deceiving myself concerning this, then when I uncover or depress it, I realize that it not only now is, but also has been, my most basic motivation, and that I have been actively resisting awareness of this up to now—a few minutes ago, months ago, years ago.

How can anyone test the claim that we all are fundamentally motivated by narcissism? All those who make such a claim insist that the appropriate test is a mode of reflection that gradually enables the inquirer to uncover a radical self-deception. This mode of reflection deeply and personally involves and changes the inquirer. Some philosophers can

guide the reader toward such testing by mapping and commending a path of personal probing in which we gradually
expose and remove the layers of resistance to self-knowledge. I am thinking of such philosophers as Kierkegaard,[3]
outlining the stages in the uncovering of despair; or Marcel,[4]
inviting us to join with him in what he calls *secondary
reflection*; or Lavelle,[5] offering aphoristic and edifying meditations on Narcissus. Such philosophers, however, are in the
minority today. Most philosophers presuppose that we
humans can adequately understand the nature and origin of
good and evil without being involved in a process of personal
transformation which uncovers whatever distorts human
discernment of good and evil. We can allegedly rely on an
analytic method or a phenomenological method or a meta-
hermeneutical perspective, in each case counting on our
detachment and our rigorous reasoning to prevent distortion.
But if only a few existentialist or contemplative philosophers can help us to uncover radical evil within ourselves,
we must also investigate other paths, whether mystical or
depth psychological. And this, I maintain, requires not merely reading about the paths but actually participating in
them. For example, one can read the works of a great contemporary spiritual master, exploring Narcissus with Da
Free John[6] or the egocentricity of "spiritual materialism"
with Chogyam Trungpa,[7] but their writings are merely intro-
ductions to a process of radical personal change without
which what they say can only be superficially understood
and superficially tested. And although we can read in Freudian texts that the megalomanic self-centeredness of infancy
is still operative in adult life, what this means can be understood only superficially and tested only superficially unless
one undergoes a deep therapy in which infancy is reexperienced through regression and then as it intermingles with
the feelings and motivations of adult life in the present.

   If a philosopher who is investigating the nature and origin
of good and evil in human beings does not personally participate in a path of self-transformation which reduces repressed
self-awareness or does not in his or her writing appeal to
alleged insights gained through such a process, this is under-

standable, for such an appeal has little cogency and perhaps little meaning for those who have not undergone such a process. Rational discussion becomes difficult. Fortunately participation in relevant processes is a matter of degree rather than an either-or, so some mutual understanding is often possible. Nevertheless a philosophical method that does not presuppose such a personally varying basis for mutual intelligibility and intersubjective appraisal obviously has merits—even if, as I would maintain, it also has limits in that it does not reveal the heart of the matter. If I may borrow two terms usually applied to religion rather than philosophy, there is a difference between *esoteric* and *exoteric* philosophy, and each has its merits and demerits. Even if an esoteric philosophy is more profound in dealing with radical good and evil, its special conditions for adequate understanding and testing make it less open to widespread rational appraisal.

An esoteric philosophy, however, can include much that is set forth in various exoteric philosophies and also much that is set forth in scientific or causal accounts of the origin of good and evil, provided that these are not regarded as ultimate explanations. For example, an exoteric philosophy may claim, on the basis of observation or elementary introspection, that what it calls *egoism* is universal in human beings. And from social science there may come psychological and sociological explanations of why such egoism varies in intensity among individuals and groups. In both cases *egoism* is understood as "being motivated by what one sees as one's own self-interest." This is, I maintain, merely a superficial glimpse of the radical narcissism which is uncovered and understood adequately only when the investigator is personally involved in a self-transforming path of depression. But such claims of exoteric philosophy and of social science are not totally false. They are to some extent true.

The esoteric claim that all human beings are radically evil in their narcissistic motivations raises two immediate questions that have not previously been considered in this book. First, if we are to explain the differences in character and action between most people and, say Hitler on the one hand

and Mother Teresa on the other hand, must we reject the claim that narcissism is universal? Is narcissism present or predominant in only a few human beings? Second, is there any nonnarcissistic motivation, any radically *good* motivation, in some or all human beings? This second question is obviously also relevant to the problems raised by variations in viciousness among human beings, but we will not try to answer it until we have explored the first question. That is, we are asking whether radical evil is equally at work in all, or almost all, human beings, or whether it is only at work in a minority, though it is a possibility or even a temptation for all.

Martin Buber,[8] following Jewish tradition, distinguishes between people at two different stages of evil: "sinners" and "the wicked." Only the wicked are involved in radical evil. They differ from mere sinners in that instead of indecisively drifting away from the good from time to time or even most of the time they decisively reject the good and affirm themselves narcissistically as gods, utterly self-enclosed and self-preoccupied, sovereign centers of the universe, claiming as good whatever they will. For Kierkegaard in *The Sickness unto Death*,[9] however, narcissism is not a *change* for the worse which occurs in a few people but rather an already-operative demoniacal motivation at work in everyone, but which is uncovered by only a few. In Kierkegaard's *The Concept of Dread*,[10] on the other hand, the demoniacal or "dread of the good" seems to be a change undergone by some people rather than a universal radical evil which everyone should uncover. My own view concerning the issue is similar to Buber's in that I hold that there are *two* motivations, good and evil, at work in all human beings, and that only in a minority is the good almost totally eclipsed by the evil. I differ from Buber, however, in holding that the evil motivation has the same narcissistic character in all human beings, though it varies in intensity along with the degree of closedness to the good, for narcissism includes being closed to the good, as I shall maintain later on. And I agree with both Buber and Kierkegaard in seeing another variable: our free *response* to our awareness of our own narcissistic motivation. Insofar as I become aware of my own narcissistic motivation I can freely choose either to consent to it, thus reinforcing it, or to resist it, thus weakening it. If I consent to it, I become *more* evil than I was both in basic motivation and in my behavior arising from that motivation. An extreme case of this is what Buber calls *wicked* and Kierkegaard calls *demoniacal.*

Thus variations in degree of evil among human beings depend on at least two variables: the extent of their clear awareness of their own evil motivation, and the direction of the choices made in response as that awareness becomes clear. Freedom obviously enters into the choices but it also enters, though less obviously, into the process of becoming aware, for each of us is actively obscuring and resisting the awareness, and at any particular moment we could stop doing this to some extent. At any particular moment some aspects of our narcissism are in the background or threshold of consciousness, and these could be granted our active attention; it is up to us. Although further, deeper aspects of our narcissism are not hovering in the background or threshold of consciousness, but are at the moment inaccessible, these will eventually become accessible as more and more layers of narcissism are successively uncovered. Thus freedom is involved at each stage of uncovering in the long process that eventually leads to a full, stark clarity concerning our radically evil motivation. Freedom is involved at each stage in two ways: in uncovering or not uncovering the motivation and also in then reinforcing or resisting the uncovered motivation.

But freedom is not the only factor giving rise to differences in evil among human beings. External influences can reinforce both one's narcissism and one's unclarity concerning it. The more empty and unloved one feels, whether consciously or unconsciously, the more difficult it is not to be narcissistic and also oblivious to one's narcissism. Since an uncaring familial or social context, especially during childhood, tends to reinforce such feelings, such a context tends thereby to reinforce narcissism. Such evil contextual influences are not themselves radical evil though they do contribute to radical evil, that is, individual narcissism. Only the individual, ultimately, can reduce or eliminate his or her own narcissism, but the individual not only has a responsibility to try to do this but also, I believe, a responsibility to reduce the evil influences which reinforce narcissism in others, both because they thereby reinforce radical evil and because they are evil in themselves. If external social influences can be so important, perhaps the focus on radical evil as exclusively a matter of *individual* motivation must be revised. Later on we will consider this possible revision, and the importance of *social* evil.

Here, however, we will continue to focus on the individual rather than society. We have partially accounted for differences in evil among human beings by noting both social influences and individual freedom as these affect individual narcissism. Another factor might be differences in *good* motivation. So now we ask whether there is any nonnarcissistic motivation, any radically good motivation, which is potential or actual in some or all human beings.

An initial indication that perhaps there is a good motivation is that as evil motivation is uncovered it is *contrasted* with good, for without some such contrast we could not recognize evil as evil. Hence if evil is narcissism, the uncovering of narcissism can not occur unless there is at least an obscure awareness of what a nonnarcissistic motivation would be. Without this, narcissism would either not be detected at all or, if detected, would appear as a brute fact about human beings, a natural and unavoidable tendency rather than radical evil. Indeed, some thinkers view our glimpses of nonnarcissistic motivation as mere illusions. We like to imagine ourselves as being nonnarcissistic, but we are not. Those who hold such a "cynical" view claim that we cannot eliminate or even reduce our narcissism, though we can modify its behavioral expressions in ways useful to ourselves or others.[11]

In another view, we humans really do have a capacity and inclination to be motivated nonnarcissistically. This motivation, like narcissism, is repressed and can only be uncovered if a person is involved in a process of self-transformation.

Then we can freely grant it our consent, and it begins to operate much more powerfully. This motivation, let us call it *love*, is in perpetual *conflict* with our narcissism, which cannot be eliminated. In this conflictual view, we ought to try for a preponderance of love over narcissism, or—a very different goal—a reconciling synthesis of love and narcissism. We may well fail in our attempt, for love and narcissism are opposites. Where love inclines and enables us to engage in the mutual giving and receiving of "I-Thou" encounters with other human beings, narcissism's self-enclosure precludes such intimate encounters.

In contrast with both the cynical and conflictual views is a third view, where love is the most fundamental motivation and narcissism is a derivative distortion of love. On such a "monistic" view, narcissism can be reduced and eventually, in principle, eliminated, as love is uncovered and expanded to replace it. Even if in some people only narcissism is now operative and even if in almost everyone there is a struggle between narcissism and love, this internal division within human beings is not inherent, for narcissism is a derivative perversion of love. Our most basic motivation is a desire for affectionate intimacy,[12] but when this desire is frustrated we become self-preoccupied. Hence narcissism is not an inherent human tendency with a power of its own. We are not aptly pictured as having two independent motors, each propeling us in a different direction. There is one motor, which naturally carries us in one direction, but we humans have introduced a steering apparatus, the egoistic self, which points us in the other direction.

Thus far I have sketched three *secular* views of love as the radically good motivation: the *cynical*, in which love is an illusion; the *conflictual* or dualistic, in which love is real and has to compete on equal terms with narcissism; and the *monistic*, in which love is the only real motivation, since narcissism is merely a distorted and derivative perversion of love. My next suggestion for consideration is that we add to both the conflictual and the monistic secular views a component which I will call *spiritual*, according to which love is viewed not only as a human inclination and capacity but

also, and primarily, as a cosmic spiritual energy which pervades both the person and his or her surroundings, an energy
in which human beings can participate insofar as they are
open to it. Such openness can be more appropriately pictured
as a sail which catches the wind rather than as a motor
inside us, though where there is a motor it could cooperate
with the wind and sail. To be motivated by love is then not
so much to turn on an inner motor, though it could include
this; rather it is to open oneself to being moved by loving
energies. And to be motivated by narcissism, whatever else
it may include, is to *resist* being moved by loving energies,
thereby experiencing them in distorting, self-preoccupied
ways, for example as anxiety, hatred, or obsessive ambition.[13]
According to a monistic view, narcissism is a defective steering apparatus which we have concocted so that we can shut
out the winds of the spirit; it has no power of its own, and it
can gradually be dismantled and eventually eliminated.
According to a conflictual view, however, we can never
eliminate narcissism, for being human includes having a
narcissistic inner motor; hence attempts to dismantle it are
either impossible or inhuman. But although this is different
from a monistic view, a conflictual view that is spiritual can
rationally hope for a predominance of love over narcissism,
since love as a human inner "motor" has cosmic energies on
its side, whereas narcissism is merely an inner motor.

I find myself leaning toward a spiritual monistic view, but
I see a spiritual conflictual view as a strong alternative, for
perhaps there is an inherent human tendency toward narcissism. At the end of this chapter I will consider this possibility, but here I wish to examine spiritual monism further. Evil
is viewed by spiritual monism not only and not mainly to be
contrasted with good, as if there were two independent
alternative paths, like turning left or turning right at an
intersection. Evil arises from the *failure* to recognize and to
be motivated by the good, and from the substitution of an
alternative motivation in place of such participation.
Gabriel Marcel,[14] for example, sees what I call *radical evil* as
an "egocentricity" which arises from a lack of participation
in being, an inner emptiness. This hidden void evokes too

much terror and anguish to be acknowledged as such, and therefore it is pseudo-remedied by egocentricity, with its attachment to perverse and empty substitutes for full being: possessions, power, and status. Insofar as a person is open to participation in being, the inner emptiness decreases and the attachment to these substitutes can also decrease.

What does "participation in being" mean? Whatever Marcel meant, my own experience and dialogue with a variety of thinkers lead me to distinguish two meanings. These are not contradictory, for a person who is a mystic can participate in being in both senses. In the first sense, which I have already anticipated in talk about love as a cosmic energy, "being" is understood in a similar way. Being is experienced as life energy or spirit, that is, a universal cosmic power and presence that pervades the human being and his or her environment, blurring the boundaries between them. Being includes the person's social and natural environment, so that participation in being both requires and brings about an intimacy, a nonseparation, in both community and cosmos. In the second sense, "being" is understood as "being-itself," that out of which all beings are continually arising—all things, events, and forces, including being qua life energy or spirit. Different mystical traditions give different labels for being-itself: the creative void, the hidden Godhead, the ultimate Source or Ground. Do all these traditions mean the same? I assume that the most deeply transformed mystics in each tradition do, but this could be verified only by becoming such a mystic. A less controversial claim is that participation in being, whether this be spiritual love energy or mystical Ultimate, requires a letting go of one's narcissism; but it also enables us to let go of it, for participation in being replaces narcissism.

Talk about participation in being raises a crucial epistemological issue that I must mention here. The dominant perspectivalism in contemporary philosophy precludes any *direct experiential* basis for such talk. Even Paul Ricoeur's brilliant and sensitive investigations in *Fallible Man*[15] and *The Symbolism of Evil*[16] are restricted by his linguistic perspectivalism. He talks about a feeling relation to the world in which there is what he calls *in-being*, but this can be discerned only indirectly because, he says, we live in a subject-object duality that has structured our language, and we understand only *through* language.[17] Similarly our understanding of evil as "defilement" (and presumably also of good as "blessing") comes through an imaginative reflective analysis of *symbolic language* used by religious people. Allegedly both we and the people we study can have no immediate prelinguistic or postlinguistic experience of defilement, and all talk about an invisible fluidlike force that enters us is irremediably symbolic.[18]

In response to this I claim that both talk about "in-being" and talk about "defilement" and "blessing" arise from direct experience of fluidlike vibrations of life energy or spirit. Even a rudimentary practice of some forms of meditation can enable some Western rationalists, who powerfully repress such experiences, to become aware of these vibrations. It soon becomes obvious that the language of "defilement" and "blessing" arises initially from experiences of intrusion of energies which are alien and disruptive, on the one hand, or benign and enhancing, on the other hand. As seen with the eyes closed, the former are typically dark and the latter typically light. The language of "defilement" and "blessing" arises initially from such experiences, as our words for color arise from our experiences of color. Of course language then goes on to create much of the framework within which the experiences occur and are understood, and here Ricoeur's analysis is extremely illuminating. But the crucial epistemological issue here is whether there can be prelinguistic or postlinguistic experiences of being and of spiritual energy. My contention is that such experiences have been commonplace in most human cultures. As I noted in Chapter IV, the main exception is the post-Enlightenment West, which deeply represses such experiences and treats any literal talk arising from them as sheer superstition.

This has been an important and controversial epistemological digression, but we must return to substantive issues. I was describing how participation in being is related to narcissism. At this point we should reconsider my account of narcissism as radical evil. I said earlier that although many thinkers do converge to a considerable degree concerning radical evil, my use of the term *narcissism* to represent all their views concealed important differences in conception. Consider the following alternative views.

First, there is a view in which narcissism is conceived primarily or even exclusively as *self-inflation*, so that it is appropriately elucidated as "pride" or "hubris" or "the desire to be god." The opposite of narcissism is then humility, where this is construed as *self-deflation* or self-humiliation or submission to the rightful authority of an external god or *polis*. Within this view, there are only two possibilities, self-inflation and self-deflation; these are allegedly evil and good, respectively. Stalwart Prometheans in every era understandably proclaim that if these are the only two possibilities in the traditional evaluation one of them must be rejected: "Down with self-deflation. Let us defy the gods and steal their sacred fire, even if eventually we must be punished for violating their law against impious self-inflation."

A second, less dramatic, view sees that narcissistic self-inflation is an evil to be avoided, a vain self-glorification, but so too is self-deflation or petty self-constriction. The good is to be found in an Aristotelian mean between the two extremes. This is a commonsense secular view that is attractive in its attempt to be realistic about both our human capacities and our human limitation. From my own perspective, however, it radically underestimates our capacities, for we can participate in cosmic love-energy and in the ultimate Source from which we arise. And on the other hand, it radically underestimates our limitations, for we are unconsciously moved by both self-inflating and self-deflating fantasies that undermine all our attempts at a golden mean, a simple realism.

In a third, more existentialist view, we all are inherently divided between self-inflating and self-deflating tendencies, tending to deny either our finitude or our freedom; evil or narcissism consists of either one of those denials. Good is the fragile synthesis we may occasionally manage when we somehow affirm in our lives both our radical freedom and our radical finitude. Our inner division never heals, but occasionally a suture holds together both sides of the wound that is human nature.

The view I present in this book resembles both the Aristotelian view and the existentialist view in that I see evil not only as a self-inflation that denies our finitude but also a self-deflation that denies our freedom. What I stress, however, is the way in which narcissism involves being caught up in an alternation between the two mutually reinforcing extremes, each of which is fuel and foil for the other. This dynamic swinging between two poles occurs because we have ambivalent feelings toward each of them: we both desire and fear to be like a god, and we both desire and fear to be like an infant. Where I differ most decisively from Aristotelian and existentialist views, however, is in proposing as the opposite of narcissism a participative way of being in the world that *transcends* the preoccupation with comparative status, power, and possessions and the high or low self-ratings this involves. Such a transcendence of narcissism is possible because narcissism is fundamentally a defense mechanism against the good, a self-enclosure to keep out the cosmic love energy which pervades human society and nature, a shut-upness that provides an illusion of independent existence rather than the reality of being lived by the ultimate Source. As we learn how to chip away at this defense mechanism, gradually letting go of it, it is replaced by a new love motivation. For as I noted earlier, participation in being not only requires a letting go of narcissism; it helps to bring about the letting go.

According to a mystical monist view, which I hold, the fundamental split that needs to be remedied is not *within* the individual human being who is allegedly both finite and infinite, but *between* that individual and that from which the individual is separating himself or herself. On such a view the "self" as usually experienced is mostly or almost entirely the narcissistic defense mechanism, an inhuman human concoction which constricts and perverts love. Only a few human beings, the saints, are selves who are unimpeded particular expressions of love in all their human dimensions. Only the saints are truly or fully human. And their testimony concerning radical good and evil must therefore be given far greater weight than the distorted perspectives of human beings in general, who are caught up mostly in narcissism with its inner dualism and its repression of genuine good.

From a mystical monist perspective, which fortunately is fairly intelligible even if one is not a saint, narcissistic self-inflation and self-deflation are seen in a new way. The desire to be god is not simply a defiant delusion, as the gods of Prometheus held. Rather, it is a distortion of a truth. All human beings are already divine in their depths, where they are not separate from the Source. And all human beings already participate in cosmic life energy which issues immediately from that Source; we need not steal the sacred fire, for it has already been given to us. And in an mystical monist view the awareness of radical finitude and dependence is not simply a submissive delusion, as Prometheus claimed. Rather it is a distortion of a truth, that each human being as distinct from the Source is merely a transient expression of that Source. And this dependency applies not only to the mortal body and everything else in us that readily reminds us of our finitude but also to the mind and will and spirit which have led us to delusions of godlike infinitude. The whole self, including its non-material dimensions, is radically dependent on the divine Source for sheer existence from moment to moment. On the other hand, the whole self participates in the divine Source and in the loving life energy which issues immediately from that Source. So each of us is both God and man or woman, paradoxically combining the divine Source and a particular expression of that Source. *The basic human paradox is the paradox of incarnation, not the paradox of combining opposed human tendencies in perpetual conflict,* whether these be finitude and alleged infinitude or narcissism and love.

The very notion of "God" is perverted by a narcissistic perspective. It seems as if one must *compete* for divinity: either I am the center of the universe and everything else is peripheral, or some deity is the center of the universe and I am peripheral. To aspire to be divine is to contrast oneself with others, excluding them from my own preeminent position, like the jealous God of much Western theism. Mystical inwardness, however, reveals a divine reality which includes and shares, a God who is both the center of every thing and everything's individual center. So although my attempt to be "Number One" in the universe is mistaken, I do have a dignity, as does everyone else, far beyond such status. What I see is not a complete illusion, like a mirage in the desert. I have a perverse perspective on something which is really there. I long to possess for myself a gleaming gold crown which I seem to see on a distant hill, but actually I am standing unawares with everyone else on streets paved with gold. Or, to change the metaphor, I am rooted in the same hidden divine bulb that lives not only me but all things. To become aware of that hidden Source is to be no longer separate from anyone or anything.

In a mystical monist view the *ultimate* origin of good and the *ultimate* nature of good are to be discovered by surrender into the divine Source and by openness to the cosmic energies from that Source. The Source is Love and the energies are loving, and both would exist even if there were no human beings, though human beings would not exist if there were no Source. The paradox of incarnation means, however, that human beings can both participate in the *ultimate* good through surrender and openness and develop a distinctively *human* love which is valuable in itself. This human love is an embodied love. For example, it can be expressed sexually in the physical body and socially in the body politic. Moreover, human love itself can be an expression of divine Love and of loving cosmic energies. Thus human life can combine ultimate good and human good.

Human good occurs not only in individuals but also in communities, for justice and liberty can be expressions of human love in social institutions. Such communal involvement arises from an awareness of our human interdependence within these institutions, but it can also arise from our participation in the divine Source within which we are all mystically united, and from our participation in cosmic energies which connect us intimately on a spiritual plane. Mystical unity and spiritual connection transform our communal interdependence within the body politic, but do not replace it. Here too the mystery of incarnation is at work.

Let us now turn from exploring good to consider *evil* again. Thus far we have viewed evil as a motivation within *individuals*. This view must be revised in response to what I have been saying about the social scope of good and in response to previous remarks concerning the importance of *social evil*. I noted earlier than an unloving social context can reinforce individual narcissism and is thus an "origin" of evil in that limited respect. But it is clear that institutionalized social injustice is an origin of evil in other ways as well. It causes much human suffering, both mental and physical, and by means of ideology which sanctions oppression it gives rise to many other evils such as callousness and ruthlessness. Moreover, it is not evident from human history that variations in the intensity of social injustice depend solely on hidden variations in the personal narcissism of individuals. Institutionalized impersonal social evil seems to have its own relatively independent momentum; indeed even relatively saintly individuals have been fundamentally self-deceived by communal ideologies which sanction oppression. So it is not obvious that even if everyone individually eliminated their individual narcissism this would eliminate institutionalized evil—unless such elimination of narcissism included a "participation in being" which transforms not only the individuals but also their society. But that would require a mysticism in which the *whole self*, including its inextricable interdependence within the body politic and not merely the private mind and will and spirit, is open to being lived by the divine Source. Such a mysticism has been rare. And evidence suggests that impersonal structures of possession and power and status in societies are a significant source of evil which is not simply derived from the narcissism of individuals. And social injustice is not only an origin of evil; it is itself evil, whether or not it originates from evil motivation in individuals. It is plausibly regarded as part of the *nature* of evil, for it reflects the inherently communal character of human existence when it pictures evil as *between* us rather than *inside* us.

But surely both pictures are needed. Social injustice is not radical evil if that means it is the sole origin of evil and the sole instance of evil. The elimination of social injustice would not bring the elimination of evil motivation in individuals. Whatever the social system, the temptation to narcissism remains. Indeed, historical evidence indicates that this temptation continues whether one's social context is oppressive or relatively benign. Where the temptation exists, we are free to respond to it with either consent or resistance. We are free, more generally, to be open or closed to the spiritual love energy and the divine Source that are present in *every* situation, though much more difficult to discern in some situations than in others. Since this stance of being open rather than closed, however much it is influenced by external factors, depends decisively on the free choice of the individual, a focus on the individual is indispensable in any adequate understanding of radical evil and radical good. But this does not mean that any attempt to transform the institutionalized structures of domination in society is a futile distraction from the purely private task of individual self-transformation. If evil is a state of affairs that is contrary to radical good, then social evil is no less evil than individual evil, for radical good is communal as well as personal. Moreover, even if we start with the individual, the self which is to be transformed consists partly of its real and inextricable entanglement in the impersonal structures of society, so that the full uncovering of individual narcissism includes an uncovering of various forms of group or collective narcissism in which the individual is involved. Another relevant consideration in support of not focusing exclusively on individual evil is that in the near future it seems unrealistic to hope for any widespread reduction of individual evil, and meanwhile the bulk of humankind exists within social systems of institutionalized injustice and oppression that can and ought to be challenged so that at least these systems do not become worse. On the other hand, there is ample historical evidence that any new and initially better social system is quickly corrupted by evil in the motivations of individuals. Hence some focus on motivation would be warranted even if evil were mainly construed as social evil.

From this discussion of social evil it seems evident that individual narcissistic motivation cannot be regarded as the only significant evil or the only source of evil. Rather, a focus on radical evil and radical good in individual motivation is best seen as a way of emphasizing the decisiveness of each individual's choice between being open or closed to a good which is not only individual but also communal and cosmic.

If it is true that we *choose* closedness or narcissism rather than openness or participation, is this because we are *tempted* in this direction because of some inherent tendency within us toward closedness or narcissism? Does narcissism remain as a temptation, though not as an operative motivation, even in the saint? In the "Postcript" I will note four reasons for believing that being human involves being prone to narcissism, but these reasons can help us to see why narcissism should be, and can be, *transformed* rather than eliminated. Becoming human has involved becoming gradually more aware of our individuality, and although it is true that our sense of individuality disappears as we surrender into the Source, a new awareness of individuality can reemerge as we begin to be lived by the Source. The basic human paradox is the paradox of incarnation, which means that each of us is both divine and human: both the Source and this particular, individual person, both identical with the Source and distinct from the Source. If our developing human individuality includes a tendency toward self-separating narcissism, it also makes possible eventual incarnation. Our "fall" into narcissism is not simply an unmitigated disaster. Rather, it is a necessary stage in a process toward a transformed state that will be better than what would be possible if we were still like innocent animals or if our individuality were ultimately unreal. Perhaps, then, both the "monistic" and "conflictual" views I presented in this chapter are too static, and the truth concerning good and evil lies beyond them, yet drawing on them. This possibility will not be explored in this book, but in a sequel.

In this book, however, I now turn to the final section. Thus far I have looked at the implications of my controversial conception of spirituality for depth psychology, for skepticism, and for ethics. Now I will investigate the implications for religion. Since my own religious background and my own central convictions are Christian, I will present three issues for Christians. Analogous issues arise, however, for people of other faiths. Indeed, when in the next chapter I pick up the concern about institutionalized evil that arose toward the end of this chapter, I present it in the context of a Christian-Buddhist dialogue concerning the connections and tensions between spirituality and social action.

Section 4

Spirituality and Religion

IX * * * Spirituality and Social Action[1]

The conception of spirituality which has predominated thus far in this book could be called *contemplative*, in contrast with one that is *social-activist*. Within Christianity there is a tension between these two emphases, neither of which should be abandoned or radically subordinated to the other.

What I call *contemplative* spirituality is more prominent in Orthodox and Roman Catholic Christianity than in Protestantism, and it is remote from a good deal of conventional Christianity, which tends to emphasize correct religious beliefs and individual moral behavior and thus is equally remote from "social-activist" spirituality as well. Contemplative spirituality has three elements common not only to Christian contemplatives but also to contemplatives in most of the great religious traditions. None of the three elements has any obvious link with social action, that is, with the recognition and reduction of injustice in the institutional power structures of human society. The three elements in contemplative spirituality can be labeled *appreciative awareness, spiritual awareness,* and *individual transformation toward egolessness*:

1. *Appreciative awareness.* Contemplative spirituality includes an appreciative awareness that everything is okay as it is—indeed, not merely okay but wondrous and radiant and harmonious and good—in an ultimate sense of "good" which transcends our usual dichotomy between good and evil. For Christians this awareness is sometimes linked with God's vision of creation as depicted in Genesis 1:31: "And God saw every thing that he had made, and, behold, it was very good." And for Christians this awareness is sometimes also linked with God's perfect and generous impartiality as depicted in Matthew 5:45: "He

maketh his sun to rise on the evil and on the good, and sendeth rain on the just and on the unjust."

2. *Spiritual awareness.* Contemplative spirituality also includes an awareness of a spiritual dimension in the self, in others, and in the cosmos. For example, one may become aware of one's own spiritual body as vibration or as light, and one may develop a similar awareness of others, whether these be ordinary human beings who have physical bodies or saints who have died and who are now spiritually active on earth. Such awareness, which varies from elementary psychic discernment and spiritual healing to subtle contact with heavenly realms and enlightened spiritual teachers, all seems indiscriminately "paranormal" to most Westerners. In most human societies, however, this whole dimension, or parts of it, have seemed quite "normal." Contemporary Christianity is relatively impoverished and ignorant in this dimension, not only because of the influence of Enlightenment philosophy and science, but for many other reasons, including the Christian repression of a feminine spirituality which is especially sensitive in such matters, a repression which included the massacre of millions of witches in the late Medieval and Reformation eras.

3. *Individual transformation toward egolessness.* Contemplative spirituality at its best includes and emphasizes a radical change in an individual's way of being in the world. In this process spiritual awareness and appreciative awareness may be intensified, but the intensification may in turn become an occasion for a regressive "ego trip," so that the person is worse off than before. The core of the transformative process is not new contents or states of consciousness but a letting go of the self-separating ego, with its gross and subtle forms of attachment. And the culmination of the process is the realization of our ultimate identity with that out of which everything is continuously arising, which is not an object I can

experience, but the mystery out of which I, too, arise, and the mystery which I ultimately am.

Christian spirituality at its best includes contemplative spirituality with its appreciative awareness, spiritual awareness, and transformative process of release from the self-separating ego, culminating in oneness with the Ultimate. For Christians, appreciative awareness is experienced and understood in relation to divine providence working for an ultimate good that transcends our usual dichotomies between good and evil, and in relation to divine impartiality dealing generously with both the just and the unjust. Christian spiritual awareness may include, but goes beyond, merely psychic and low-level spiritual discernment. The Christian begins to "see" and "feel" Christ's spiritual body as really present and to unite with Christ as our living spiritual master through whom we can become open to the Ultimate—because Christ is already completely open. And a Christian transformative process is experienced and understood as a letting go of the old, false self; the process culminates in our being lived by God. The whole self, united at the soul as it arises from God, is an egoless, unimpeded expression of God.

But note that it is the whole self, not merely the spiritual dimension of the self, that is thus surrendered to be lived by God. And this self includes not only the spirit and the body and the emotions and the mind of each of us as isolated individuals but also—and here is the crucial claim—*the individual in relation to human community and human history.* In a biblical understanding of human nature, I *am* these relations; they are not incidental or extrinsic. I am a part of all that I have met, and all that I have met is part of me. Western liberal secular thought depicts the human being as an isolated individual who may prudently set up social contracts with others for mutual benefit and who may choose altruistically to involve himself or herself with others, but who is essentially singular. In a biblical view, and in some communal secular views whether conservative or Marxist, this atomistic account is false. My language and culture and technology and religion and values and basic attitudes and personal virtues and personal vices all arose initially, and continue to arise, within a *communal history*. And in both a biblical and a secular-communal view I am inextricably involved in a network of institutional power structures that are mostly *unjust*. Moreover, I tend to deceive myself concerning the ways in which I benefit from institutionalized injustice. I ignore or rationalize my privilege and power. Thus social evil as a destructive historical-communal way of being in the world is also associated with a distorted way of being *conscious* in the world that corrupts even individuals who are decent and well-meaning in their individual dealings with others. Part of the answer to the question, "Who am I?" as asked by Don Evans, is "I am a white, male, middle-class, academic, non-'ethnic', Christian Torontonian; I am a citizen in a country which still promotes the dominance of whites and males and middle-class and academic 'experts' and Christians, a country which exploits the Third World, which practiced cultural genocide against its native peoples, and which is part of an alliance which threatens mass murder with nuclear weapons." Thus I must acknowledge that my perspective is distorted by my privileged position. But this is not enough. I need to see the world from the perspective of the underprivileged, the victims. And even more, I must be actively trying to reduce or remove at least some of the injustices in which I am entangled. Thus social activism arises from an acknowledgment that I am an historical-communal being rather than from an altruistic decision to assume some responsibility for others who are less fortunate.

Such a social-activist spirituality is in contrast and tension with contemplative spirituality as appreciative awareness, spiritual awareness, and individual transformation. Let us consider each in turn:

1. Appreciative awareness sees everything as okay, but this is challenged by the social-activist realization that *injustice* pervades human history and human community and that I am part of this injustice.

2. Spiritual awareness by itself can be an attempt to *escape* from surrender of the whole self to be lived by God. Instead, we identify the self with the spirit, ignoring not only the body and the emotions but also and especially human community and human history and our entanglement in oppression and strife.

3. Individual transformation by itself is not enough. A person does not stop participating in communal and historical injustice merely by a private change, however radical, in his or her own individual way of being in the world. This limitation applies even in the case of a supreme spiritual master, a Jesus Christ or a Gautama Buddha. Though their lives of poverty reduce such participation in injustice, they do not and cannot "opt out" of society even as hermits, for they share in a responsibility for whatever injustices continue in the society that reared and nurtured them. Even the purest of human beings cannot be complete or perfect until all injustice is eliminated. This cannot be denied unless we deny the inherently communal and historical character of human existence. Some Christians and some Buddhists do deny it, dismissing our involvement in society as merely a this-worldly and temporal aspect of human beings that can be discarded when each of us is individually "saved" or "enlightened," leaving this veil of tears to enter the Eternal Now. But for a Christian spirituality which is not only contemplative but also true to its biblical origins, the self as historical and communal is real, and I cannot be abstracted from a fellow human being who is suffering from injustice. There are two reasons for this. First, I am an historical-communal being linked with that human being through the power structures of society, though in some cases admittedly very indirectly. Second, I am being lived by an Ultimate which also lives that human being. Wherever God is, I am, and God is suffering that injustice *in* that human being.

Let me elaborate further on these two reasons why contemplative spirituality and social-activist spirituality come together for Christians. The first reason has to do with the *self*. The human self combines elements from each perspective. On the one hand, each of us is an individual who is basically okay and in harmony with other humans and with the cosmos; each of us is also a spirit living within a spiritual realm; and each of us, behind our false, egoistic self, is a true, open-textured self which is not ultimately separate from anyone or anything. On the other hand, each of us is partly constituted by our historical-communal relations in the power structures of human society; we are members of the "body politic."

The second reason why contemplative spirituality and social-activist spirituality come together for Christians has to do with *God*. The human self is being lived by a God, who is both transcendent and radically immanent. That is, God transcends the whole self as its ultimate source, beyond our dichotomy of good and evil. Yet God is also immersed or incarnate in that self, immanently suffering its injustice and its anguish. Thus, for a Christian, being lived by God involves on the one hand a blissful union with that out of which everything is continually arising. On the other hand, one identifies oneself with God's self-immersion in human communal history, actively sharing in the divine partiality for the poor and the underprivileged and the oppressed. On the one hand, being lived by God involves identification with that which transcends human existence, whether individual or historical-communal, as its mysterious source, beyond all distinctions between good and evil, justice and injustice, subject and object, I and Thou, past and future. Yet on the other hand being lived by God also involves identification with the immanent divine involvement in the messiness of human history.

I have pointed out various ways in which contemplative spirituality needs to be balanced and corrected by social-activist spirituality. The reverse is also true. Christian social activism needs the three elements of contemplative spirituality to balance and correct it. Otherwise it does more harm than good. Let us consider appreciative awareness, spiritual awareness, and individual transformation in turn.

1. Without appreciative awareness Christian social action degenerates into a crusader's zeal, polarizing the world and also the self into irreconcilable opposites of good and evil, viewing the process of communal and personal progress as inherently conflictual rather than as a transformation by inclusion. The Christian and his or her Western-secular mimic thus often causes at least as much harm as good in their ruthless attempts to eliminate evil. Christian and Marxist social activists sometimes proclaim that the point is not to understand the world, but to change it. Others may subsequently wish that these meddlers had left well enough alone. And when social activists reject appreciative awareness as a mere legitimizing of unjust power structures, they are mistaken, even if the appreciative awareness has been used in that way, for it is an absolutely necessary corrective to self-righteousness and destructive fanaticism.

2. Without spiritual awareness, Christian social action becomes dogmatically secular and materialistic, ignoring the powerful spiritual dimensions of good and evil in human life, and opposing all concern with them as a mere distraction from concern about oppression and hunger. Without spiritual awareness, Christian social action becomes virtually indistinguishable from secular social action except for a belief, not linked with any experience, that somehow a hidden power called *God* is at work in the historical process. And at worst, the poor are denied all spiritual consolation unless this somehow enables them to overthrow their oppressors.

3. Without individual transformation, Christian social action becomes an exercise in futility, for old oppressive power structures are merely replaced by new ones that are quickly corrupted by individual egoism,

generating new forms of oppression. This does not mean that no social action should be undertaken unless and until each of us is completely transformed. Nor does it mean that if each of us were completely transformed individually there would be no need for social action to eliminate injustice. What it does mean is that both kinds of change must be going on together.

More generally, what is required is a creative tension and a mutual critique between contemplative and social-activist perspectives. As I have indicated, there are grave dangers if either perspective is neglected. My presentation of these critiques, however, has been too abstract and too polemical. What is needed is sensitive and intuitive discernments by individuals and groups concerning which perspective should be emphasized in a particular life situation. I have presented a map, not a route. Each person will unite the contemplative and social-activist elements of the self in his or her own way, and each will discover, in his or her own way, the unity of the God who transcends us and is incarnate within us. Moreover there is also a need to recognize that people legitimately differ in their individual vocation or calling, so that Mary Jones may emphasize a social perspective and John Brown a contemplative perspective and together they can balance each other.

The word *vocation* leads me to consider another element in Christian spirituality as it issues in social action. The Bible contains many stories of how people were called to a particular task in relation to a particular historical community. This biblical conception of calling was expanded by Christian tradition, especially during the Reformation, so that *all* Christians have a vocation in their specific historical-communal context. If a Christian meditates on the question, "Who am I?" part of its meaning is, "What am I here for?" And whatever the specific answer to, "What am I here for?" there is a sense of being part of the Christian community and the human community which are involved in a historical process that has a direction and an overall purpose.

One's vocation is not always mainly a calling to social action in the sense of challenging unjust power-structures, but it does link my sense of who I am to some task of bringing about *change* in a specific sociohistorical context, though the change may be artistic or intellectual or spiritual rather than political. And a sense of vocation links this task with a larger historical pattern and direction toward a culmination in which not only individual sin and sorrow but also communal strife and exploitation will be no more.

In closing, I want to compare this Christian sense of vocation with a different kind of answer to the question, "What am I here for?" that may be associated with belief in *reincarnation*. During the past few years I have come not only to believe in reincarnation but also to experience past lives and relate them to this present life. I deeply regret that Christian tradition has been so closed-minded to this mode of human self-understanding, though I do not propose that it become a required belief. For me, a part of the answer to the question, "What am I here for?" is "I am here in *this* life to learn such-and-such which, I now realize, I failed to learn in various past lives." Often the learning is linked with a task in this specific sociohistorical context, so that often, though not always, this-life *learning* and this-life *calling* obviously coincide; perhaps at a deeper level they always coincide.

Both a biblical sense of vocation and a reincarnational sense of learning involve a real self which has a real past out of which I emerge (my historical community or my past lives) and a real future toward which I am moving. And both attribute to this real self a sense of being free and responsible: I can choose to fulfil what I am here for, or I can choose not to do so. If I choose the latter, a historical change which should have occurred does not occur, and I will face an analogous challenge in a future life. Each of us is a real, ongoing self, linked with the past and oriented to the future. All of us have the freedom and responsibility for our own direction in the concrete context where we are living. One kind of contemplative awareness, however, tends to deny the reality of this self: there is only God, only the Eternal Now, with no past or future, no distinguishable me or you or this or that, no choice, no task, no learning, no direction, no better or worse; there is only the One. On some spiritual paths this state of awareness is ultimate. Contemplation allegedly culminates when one's sense of self disappears, along with all temporality and multiplicity and one is totally transparent to the One. For Meister Eckhart, however, this is only an important phase, to be followed by another one, in which one is thrust back into the world, into history, into community, as this particular person, while somehow retaining the awareness of timeless unity with the One.[2]

The spirituality that I propose for Christians is not simply an awareness of the unity of soul and Source, but a surrender of the whole self, united at the soul, into the Source to be lived by the Source. And this whole self is not an eternal, unchanging reality, for it is in process through many lives, and is intimately interconnected with other human selves in the ongoing communal history of humankind. What needs to be transformed by surrender into the Source is the whole of our humanity. All our dimensions, including our historical dimension, are interdependent. Abstracted from the Source, we are unreal. Insofar as we are lived by the Source, however, we *are* real. Our human nature does not consist of an eternal essence which transcends and renders trivial or illusory what happens in human history, with its various eras and cultures and varied approximations of justice and peace. On the contrary, each of us is significantly linked with the whole of humankind, and the whole history of humankind, both past and future. Only at the eschatological End of history will there be a completion of our humanity and a complete revelation of the divine Source through that humanity.

Thus "contemplative" spirituality and "social activist" spirituality are inextricably interconnected in an historical process of individual and communal transformation.

X ✳ ✳ ✳ Spirituality and Christian Openness to Other Faiths[1]

In this book a complex and controversial conception of spirituality has gradually developed. In this chapter I apply it to issues of interreligious dialogue. Since I am a Christian, my focus will be on Christian openness to other faiths. Before I begin, it seems appropriate to note six features of my conception of spirituality that will either be noted or expanded in the chapter:

1. Human beings and everything that exists continually arise from a mysterious *Source.* If we surrender our selves into the Source, we are at first conscious only of the Source. Then, however, we can experience ourselves arising out of the Source as particular, embodied beings who are being lived by the Source. Usually, however, human beings live in narcissistic self-separation from the Source.

2. One dimension of human nature is *spirit.* An awareness of oneself as spirit and of spiritual presences and spiritual energies is a crucial element in the process that leads to surrender into the Source to be lived by the Source.

3. Nevertheless human beings are not only spiritual, and it is the *whole self* which is to be surrendered into the Source to be lived by the Source. This whole self includes the physical body, emotions, mind, and spirit, and also interdependence with other human beings in historical community.

4. Human nature is still evolving, as we uncover and create who we are, especially in dialogue with each other. Only at the *End* will humankind be complete individually and communally. Only then will humankind be a complete incarnation and expression of the Source. The process of change toward the End

involves not only a transformation of individuals but also a transformation of communal institutions and relations with nature.

5. Some of our knowledge is accessible impersonally, regardless of personal differences, for example, our knowledge of scientific facts and a minimal moral code applicable to everyone. Such impersonal knowledge is crucial for our ability to live together with some degree of cooperation in spite of profound differences in perspective. Much that is important about human beings, however, is not accessible impersonally, but requires personal *transformation* as a prerequisite for experiential understanding. This is the case not only for the emotional unconscious but also for the spiritual unconscious.

6. We impose various *perspectives* on our experiences and thus we see human beings and the world through our imposed frameworks. It is important to become aware of our perspectives, and much of our advance in knowledge comes from dialogue between perspectives in which mutual revisions can occur. We do nevertheless have some direct experiential access to reality, including spiritual reality, so that perspectives are not only revised by reference to other perspectives, but by reference to such experience.

Now that I have outlined these six contentions, I can begin my inquiry into Christian openness to other faiths. My first question is, "What is openness?" It is important to realize that there are different kinds of openness, and that these form a cumulative series of stages. The initial stage of openness, which is as far as many people go, is *tolerance;* that is, accepting persons whose beliefs we do not share, not coercing them to change their beliefs. The next stage, which is fortunately becoming more common in modern pluralistic societies and even globally, is *cooperation* in practical projects where we share common values; for example, in humanitarian concerns such as health, human rights, or peace. A third step, going beyond tolerance and cooperation, is *dialogue,* in which one tries to understand what the other person's faith means to him or her. Next, out of tolerance, cooperation, and dialogue there may emerge a fourth stage: an empathetic and respectful *friendship,* where for example a Christian encourages a person of another faith to draw on his or her own spiritual resources, so as to become a better Buddhist or Jew or native Canadian. The fifth stage is *intimacy,* which means including within one's own life many of the rich resources of the other person's spiritual tradition. Such intimacy initiates what some have called an *intrareligious dialogue,* a dialogue within oneself between Christian practices and perspectives and those of another faith. And insofar as one now sees the world partly from the other perspective, intimacy involves a revisioning of one's own Christian perspective. The change may be quite slight, but it may be radical.

Now that I have briefly sketched the stages of openness, I am going to propose five reasons why Christians should be more open to other faiths. One reason is that we can receive from other faiths a wider and deeper experience of what it means to be human. This is crucial for Christians because we are called to devote our whole selves to God through Christ, but thus far we have only included segments of our humanity in our self-offering. Other traditions include dimensions of human nature that have been largely ignored by Christians in recent times; for example, few North American Christians are aware of themselves as spiritual energy, living in a cosmos that teems with incarnate and discarnate spirits who can help us or whom we can help. If Christians in South America or Africa or India have more of this spiritual awareness, this is mainly because of "pagan" traditions that Christianity did not successfully eradicate. Similarly few North American Christians experience the "shamanic" dimension of our humanity: our resonance with the earth, our sense of interdependence with nature, which comes through an inner awareness of ourselves as mineral, vegetable, and animal. And few North American Christians have realized, with the mystics, that being human involves an awareness of a mystery at the hidden center of our being, where there is no clear boundary between being human and being that ultimate from which everything arises.

It is true that Christians can draw on Christian resources from our past to recover, to some extent, an awareness of oneself as spirit, as fully embodied and as not separated from our Source. But today these dimensions of human nature are often more readily accessible through direct contact with living people in other traditions. And it seems clear to me that some of the range and depth of being human is not recoverable from Christian tradition as such, and that it has been experienced and lived authentically by people of other faiths. This is specially obvious in the case of traditions which, paradoxically, Christians have persecuted for being more genuinely incarnational than Christianity has ever been, especially those modes of spirituality which are distinctively feminine. In the case of the other traditions the closedness of Christianity has been not so much an oppressive intolerance as an arrogant ignorance, for example, in relation to the rich heritage of Tibetan Buddhism, with its knowledge of the spiritual realm and its wisdom concerning ways to freedom from self-preoccupation.

Insofar as our experience of ourselves as human beings is constricted (a mind and will in a machine-body), we bring only segments of self in love to others and in surrender to God. Expanding our awareness is for Christians more than merely a noble humanistic aspiration. Beyond this, it is essential to the life of faith: being lived by the loving God in every dimension of our existence. We should be intimately open to other faiths so as to learn and live more of what it means to be human. Whatever is excluded from surrender to God in Christ does not disappear. It remains within Christians in perverse forms, as seeds of destruction.

The destructiveness of Christianity provides a second reason for more Christian openness to other faiths: *repentance.* Our history of oppression of Jews and native peoples and "witches" is so appalling that communal repentance is called for. And such repentance must include a searing scrutiny not only of Christian conduct but also of whatever Christian teachings have legitimized that conduct, sanctioning intolerance. And genuine repentance should go beyond tolerance all the way to an openness that involves intimacy. That is, we must not only stop treating people of other faiths with gross inhumanity, persecuting them for their beliefs; we must become open to recognize and acknowledge ways in which many of them manifest the fruits of the Spirit. At worst we have committed what Jesus called the unforgivable sin, attributing their powers of love and peace and healing to Beelzebub. Genuine repentance involves a new readiness to rejoice in, and to learn from, workings of the spirit in religions that seem initially alien to us.

Much more could be said about repentance, but I move on to propose a third reason for Christian openness: *humility* in matters religious, where no knowledge claims can appropriately be made in an absolute, unqualified way. Christians should have a humble realization that our awareness of religious reality is limited and distorted by the perspective we bring to it. Our partial understanding can and should be enriched and corrected by reports from others who have different perspectives. This is the case not only for us as individual Christians but also for the Christian community as a whole.

Such an epistemological humility is not the same thing as a relativism in which my religion is merely true-for-me and yours is merely true-for-you and no religion is really true. Relativism reduces religion to a matter of taste, or to what "works" for me. Hyphenated truth, truth as true-for-*X*, is agnostic concerning reality. It is like saying, "This water feels cool to me," where there is no way of determining whether the water really is cool. Or it is like saying, "When I believe this pill is helping me, it does," where there is no way of determining whether it really helps.

There is, nevertheless, a half-truth in relativism, for religious truth is not known by us in abstraction from the perspectives we bring *to* it. Realism in making religious claims must be tempered and qualified and humbled by relativism. One of the intellectual reasons for epistemological humility has arisen prominently in the so-called Second Enlightenment which Kant initiated when he explored the conceptual framework that the human mind brings *to* all experience. Various thinkers after him explored more concretely the profound and mostly unconscious influences that shape our perspectives: psychologically (Freud), socioeconomically (Marx), historically (Dilthey), and linguistically (Wittgenstein). Especially in matters religious, we can now see that we are limited by the perspectives we impose on our experience, perspectives shaped by a multitude of factors that are mostly unconscious. As we try to uncover these factors, we realize that we have been, and still are, prone to self-deception. What we mean by "God," for example, is influenced by experiences in childhood, by ideas legitimizing current power structures in society, by the historical-cultural context in which we are immersed, and by the "grammar" of the language in which the word *God* occurs. Indeed, the insights of the Second Enlightenment have come to dominate academia so pervasively that, as we saw in Chapter IV, many theologians and investigators of religion have restricted themselves to studying how and why human minds think as they do within various faith communities, abandoning all hope of any direct awareness of religious reality.

But the realization that our religious understanding is limited by the perspectives we bring to that understanding need not make us totally agnostic concerning whether there is a reality to be discerned. Consider, by analogy, what happens when one sees a physical object from a perspective. What one perceives is really there, but each perception is necessarily incomplete. Moreover, a perception from one perspective may be much better than a perception from another perspective. And propositions expressing what is perceived from the better perspective can be accepted as true, though not as infallible, complete, or absolute. Moreover, such propositions can be contrasted with others that express what is perceived from a very inferior perspective—propositions that can be rejected as almost totally false because of their distortions and limitations.

Although spiritual realities differ greatly from material objects, and our "perspectives" on them are such metaphorically rather than literally, I think it is clear that, in principle, realism and an acknowledgment of perspectives can apply here, too, provided that religious experience involves a discernment analogous to seeing. And such an analogy is what great religious traditions, especially in their mystical moments, have claimed—even if the seeing is mostly "through a glass, darkly."

Indeed, these traditions, for many centuries before the intellectual ferments in nineteenth century secular thought, have themselves taught a kind of humble acknowledgment of limitation by our perspectives. They have insisted that human beings are involved in "sinful" or "ignorant" ways of being and ways of being conscious which distort our perceptions of religious reality. A profound human transformation is required if we are to have an adequate awareness. Our understanding of religious reality is limited by, and relative to, the extent to which we let go of our self-preoccupation and allow ourselves to be transformed into, or revealed to be, the likeness of the Ultimate. Hence the meaning of a religious statement such as "God is love" varies greatly from person to person. Mary may understand it in a way that is mostly true, whereas John understands it in a way that is mostly false. This contrast occurs if Mary's living of love is relatively mature and if John's perspective is radically self-centered, severely distorting his discernment. In contrast with such a statement as "The cat is on the mat," which is simply true or false as understood by anybody, religious claims are understood with varying depth and varying distortion by different people, and their truth varies accordingly. This religiously based stress on personal prerequisites for understanding provides a profoundly religious reason for humility in making religious claims. Indeed, the secular perspectivalist critiques of human reason as rationalization, ideology, and historical product can be viewed by Christians as a "fleshing out," in greater detail and with new insights, of some dimensions in the perennial religious critique of human self-deception. So one basis for being open to other faiths is the humble realization, arising from one's own Christian faith and from secular insights, that all religious truth claims are made from human perspectives which involve limitations and distortions. If we are open to learn from others who have different perspectives, we can thereby both correct and expand our own perspective. The intimacy of an intrareligious dialogue with another faith can be a significant element in the ongoing process of personal transformation as a Christian, enabling us to uncover hidden distortions and to discern religious reality in new and deeper ways.

We saw that relativism by itself is only a *half*-truth, for it denies any discernment of religious reality. But it is a *half*-truth, for our discernments are limited and distorted by our perspectives. The fourth reason for openness that I now propose is also linked with a half-truth: *secular humanism.*

According to secular humanism, all that matters is what we humans have in common apart from religion, plus the moral imperatives which arise from this common humanity. Religion is at best irrelevant and at worst evil, so we should set religion aside and treat each other in mutual tolerance.

We saw in Chapter VII that such a secular humanism is untenable if, as religious people rightly maintain, human beings include more than the secular humanist allows, if we are spirit as well as body, emotion, and mind, and if we all arise out of an Ultimate Reality. Nevertheless we also saw that there is a half-truth which Christians must acknowledge here in response to secular humanism. Christians must acknowledge that there is a basic minimal morality based on our sense of common humanity. This morality should not be violated in the name of religion. It is wrong to harm someone because his or her religious beliefs and practices are not one's own. And more generally, in the post nuclear era our very survival as a human race now depends on discovering our common humanity and learning at least the mutual tolerance which arises with that discovery. I do not suggest that all of morality can or should be restricted to what most human beings—of all faiths and of none—can agree upon. What I am proposing is that such a consensus deserves a special priority, and that whatever broadens and deepens a sense of common humanity among humankind should be encouraged. The sense of our common humanity is the experiential basis for an active moral consensus. (My own work for such a "global ritual" as the minute of silence and moment of sound for peace on the UN Day of Peace arises from that conviction. In silence we set aside for a minute the differences which divide us, and in sound we celebrate the common hope and concern for peace which we have experienced. Then we return to deal with the differences in a new spirit.)

The universalism of secular humanism at its best, the commitment to treat every human being with respect simply because he or she is a human being, is a sound reason for Christians to be open to people of other faiths: tolerant, cooperative, and in dialogue. Insofar as Christians are human beings they should be committed to this. But they should also be committed to this as Christians. Historically, the universalism of modern secular humanism arose out of the Christian tradition, though detached from that tradition, which included not only universalistic elements from Greek thought, especially the stoics, but also universalistic elements in the teaching of Jesus. To take only one example, the parable of the Good Samaritan depicts the exemplary helper as a man from a deviant religious group, and the person deserving help is simply any person in need. Jesus was continuing and deepening a Jewish respect for righteous persons in other faiths and a Jewish concern for the welfare of the aliens within their society. More generally, if for Christians all human beings are created in the image of God, and if Christians are called to a neighbor love that is universal and unrestricted in scope, the half-*truth* of secular humanism is reinforced rather than undermined. And it is clear that a minimal social morality for humankind requires a good measure of mutual tolerance, considerable cooperation in humanitarian works, and extensive dialogue to facilitate mutual understanding between people of differing perspectives.

Beyond this, however, there is a fifth reason for Christians to be more open to other faiths, a reason that justifies openness as friendship and intimacy. As we consider this fifth reason, which draws on all the previous four reasons but goes beyond them, we need to introduce a dimension of human beings which thus far I have ignored: the communal. More specifically, Christian tradition includes a vision of the End in which humankind as a whole will have been transformed, not as individuals in isolation, but as an intimate, interdependent community. Using the analogy of the physical body as an organism, Christians have envisaged a universal "body politic" which will completely incarnate and fully reveal the indwelling Spirit of God as Love. Because of the intimate involvement between all persons at the End, *each person will somehow participate in the transformed humanity of everyone else* (though in varying degrees). But each individual and each group will contribute a distinctive way of being human, a distinctive way of incarnating and revealing God. To change the metaphor, the transformation of humankind at the End will be like the sun shining through a stained glass window, uniting thousands of distinct color centers in a unifying pattern of embodied light. In such context the Christian cannot say to the Jew, like the hand saying to the foot or the blue glass saying to the orange glass, "I have no need of you." Rather, the Christian will have encouraged the Jew, in friendly openness, to be a better Jew, and will have participated, in intimate openness, in a Jewish way of being part of transformed humanity.

Such a Christian eschatology implies that we do not yet fully understand human nature, for this will emerge communally as individuals and groups contribute their distinctive ways of being human, and as these ways are surrendered into the indwelling God to be lived by God. This will not happen unless people of diverse perspectives become more open to each other not only in tolerance, cooperation, and dialogue, but also in friendship and intimacy. Out of the mutual enrichment and mutual critique and the interiorizing of each other's perspectives there can gradually emerge a new humanity. With that new humanity there will emerge a new understanding of what it means to be human.

What I am considering here is not the minimal social morality which secular humanism can rightly proclaim as basic. And it prohibits anyone, whether secular humanist or religious dogmatist, from claiming now to sum up human nature from some allegedly undistorted perspective. Rather, what is proposed is, in intellectual terms, a pooling of human perspectives for mutual enrichment and mutual critique, like the proverbial blind men pooling their diverse reports as they touch the elephant in various places. And in terms of dynamic process, what is proposed includes more: a friendly and intimate openness to other perspectives, a personal surrender of self-preoccupation into the Ultimate, and an active commitment to deal with whatever in oneself or in society is an obstacle to the unimpeded expression of the Ultimate in humankind as a planetary community. Hence a fifth reason for Christian openness to other faiths is that this is an indispensable part of the process toward the End for which Christians hope, the salvation of humankind.

But is not Jesus Christ in some sense essential to the salvation of humankind? And does not the friendship and intimacy I have advocated require Christians to deny this? How can someone remain loyal to Christ while encouraging a Buddhist to be a better Buddhist, or while revising one's own Christian faith in response to what one has interiorized from Buddhism?

Many Christians have held that, to be saved, that is, rightly related to God, human beings must all be related to God through Jesus Christ. This is allegedly a necessary, indispensable condition. Second, many Christians have held that this relation to God through Jesus Christ is sufficient, that is, complete, final and unsurpassable. No other path is necessary, and no other path can in any sense add anything to salvation beyond what is provided through Jesus Christ.

Since such an exclusive position has been used to justify intolerance and even persecution—or at the very least, an arrogant attitude toward non-Christians—some Christian theologians have urged Christians to stop focusing on Christ as the one essential way to God. Rather, we should focus on God. What matters is a person's relation to God, which for Christians may well be through Christ, but for others is not. A "Christocentric" Christianity is an obstacle to genuine openness, so we must discard it. It does not matter, in this view, *how* we get to the ultimate religious goal once we are there. In the End we will all be face to face with the same God, and differences between religious paths will have become irrelevant.

Such a "theocentric" approach to other religions may indeed be more appropriate initially in dialogue with Jews and Muslims, for whom a vigorously Christocentric approach is difficult and even offensive. On the other hand, the focus on *God* assumes that Buddhists and Advaita Hindus are simply mistaken in their view of the goal as being beyond what most Christians mean by *God*.

If, however, we understand the ultimate religious goal in mystical terms, the view that "It does not matter how we get there once we are there" is very plausible, provided that the mystical goal is what I call *transparency*. What I mean by this is best understood in terms of an analogy.[2] Imagine that you are inside a cathedral, looking at two windows. One is perfectly clear and transparent, so that the sunlight shines through it without our being aware of any glass in the window. The other window is translucent, for as the sunlight shines through it, the colored patterns in the glass contribute to what we see, though we are still seeing sunlight. A translucent medium not only transmits light, it is also illuminated in a specific and characteristic way by that light, depending on its own qualities. If there is a third window in the cathedral, and it is translucent, but with different patterns of color, we can intelligibly compare the two translucent windows and evaluate one as *better* than the other. But if two transparent windows are both completely clear, they are *equally* transparent.

Let us first consider the *transparent* windows as analogies for salvation, or the ultimate religious goal. Suppose that in the process of getting the windows to be perfectly clear, different methods were used, with different states, so that during the process the windows were quite different. If all that matters is the end result, such differences prior to the end result do not matter. Similarly if success for religious tradition consists in enabling individuals to become transparent to the Ultimate, differences among traditions in the process which leads up to this do not matter. In a "transparency" view of salvation, there is a paradigm way of being a human person, namely, becoming so selfless that one is aware *only* of the Ultimate and so selfless that others can see the Ultimate *through* the person because there is no self in the way. If transparency to the Ultimate can occur within and by means of several different traditions (say Advaita Hindu, Theravadin Buddhist, and Orthodox Christian) then none of these three is *necessary* for salvation, and any one of these three is *sufficient*. The three traditions could still be evaluated in terms of their success rate as facilitators of transparency, and one tradition might conceivably emerge as the "winner" in this respect; but such a "winner" would not thereby be shown to be the only path of salvation. And the traditions could also still be evaluated comparatively by reference to *non*ultimate criteria, whether these be spiritual or moral or aesthetic or sociopolitical or intellectual. These criteria might be common to all the traditions or they might vary from tradition to tradition. In either case interesting and pertinent comparisons and dialogues might occur between traditions, but always with the agreement that these criteria are not ultimate. One tradition may be more spiritually knowledgeable, and another more sensitive to social injustice, but what really matters is enabling individuals to become transparent.

Although a transparency model of salvation has not been prominent in Christianity, I shall argue later that it should have an important, though subordinate, place. Let us here consider the implications of a *Christocentric* claim if a transparency model is presupposed. I see no problems arising from a Christian claim that a relation to God through Jesus Christ is for some Christians *sufficient* in their becoming transparent to God. Even if it were true that a particular Christian could become transparent more quickly by including some Buddhist meditation in his or her daily practice—or even by becoming a Buddhist—the Christian claim could still be tenable. But let us consider the claim that a relation to God through Jesus Christ is *necessary* for any human being to become transparent to God. Such a claim entails one or the other of two claims concerning other religious paths. Either no human being has ever become selfless except through Jesus Christ or, even if some human beings have done so, this has not made them transparent to *God*, whatever else they may have been transparent to. Thus either Gautama Buddha was not selfless, or if he was selfless this did not make him transparent to God, but to Nirvana, which is allegedly different and not Ultimate.

The claim that Christians have a monopoly on selfless transparency seems to me preposterous. Indeed, Christian tradition is not even the most likely "winner" in a competition among traditions as facilitators of transparency. But the question, "What have selfless Buddhists or Hindus or Sikhs been transparent *to*?" is both important and difficult to answer. It is clear, for example, that what Buddhists mean by *Nirvana* differs considerably from what most conventional Christians mean by *God*. But if testimony from Christian contemplatives is to be given great weight, and if they can sometimes describe God as "a limitless space of light and love," it becomes plausible to wonder whether *Nirvana* and *God* refer to the same Ultimate, for converging testimonies from Buddhist and Christian contemplatives become relevant. But there are also divergent testimonies, and in any case we cannot adequately understand what any contemplative, whether Christian or non-Christian, is transparent-to unless we become similarly transparent ourselves. So Christians are simply not in a position to claim dogmatically that no non-Christian has ever been transparent to the Ultimate, even if the Christian God is the Ultimate. If salvation means transparency to the Ultimate, it is implausible for Christians to insist that Jesus Christ is necessary for salvation. Instead, we should be more open to learn from other faiths what they have discovered concerning paths to selfless transparency.

A transparency conception of salvation, however, is not dominant within Christian tradition. Even within contemplative versions of Christianity transparency is at most a stage, and translucency predominates. So let us now consider an approach in which translucency is the appropriate analogy for salvation.

If salvation is like the shining of sunlight in a translucent window, the medium is part of the message. Christians can then intelligibly regard various *human* qualities of Jesus of Nazareth as very important, which would not be the case if he were like a transparent window. Indeed, if in general one person's way of being can be a better expression or embodiment of the Ultimate than another it is intelligible that a particular person could be in some sense the paradigm expression of the Ultimate, providing the normative standard for all others. And it is intelligible that a relation through that person to the Ultimate could be both necessary and sufficient for others to become analogously expressions or embodiments of the Ultimate. Thus some elements of the translucency model of salvation, in contrast with the transparency model, render intelligible the exclusivistic claims of a traditional Christocentric theology.

Other features of that translucency view, however, undermine a dogmatic exclusivism. I have indicated some of these already in my sketch of Christian eschatology, where salvation lies in the historical future and involves humankind as a whole. Humankind must be transformed not only individually but also communally. Whatever impedes the embodied expression of the Ultimate in human life has to be removed and replaced by individual and communal ways of being which genuinely and completely reveal the Ultimate. The media must be modified if the divine message is to be fully communicated. And the crucial medium is the whole human community. This includes *all* dimensions of the community, whether these be spiritual, moral, aesthetic, sociopolitical, or intellectual. And if salvation is the embodied expression of God it cannot fully occur in any one individual in isolation. Each of us is connected in interdependence not only with other human beings living today but also with all that exists in the material universe and in spiritual realms. In a Christian vision of the End, all this together, including everyone who has ever lived, will be transformed and transfigured so that the radiant glory of God can be displayed in all that exists.

In such an eschatological vision of salvation as a communal and cosmic expression of the Ultimate, the claim that Jesus Christ is necessary for salvation is still intelligible. That is, it is intelligible to claim that, in the End, a communal-cosmic transformation fully expressive of the Ultimate will involve everyone being related to God through Jesus Christ, participating in the particular kind of incarnation which Christ initiated. It is intelligible to claim that this requirement applies to everyone, even Buddhist bodhisattvas and Sufi saints and Hindu gurus. But it is also intelligible to claim that everyone will also have to be related to God through Gautama Buddha and various other human beings who have exemplified in their lives a distinctive and genuine expression of the Ultimate as well as a distinctive transparency to the Ultimate. Who these authentic exemplars and facilitators have been may not become perfectly clear until the End, when they will obviously be enabling everyone to contribute to the total "translucent window" which will embody and display the Ultimate.

I have shown that in the context of a Christian-translucent conception of salvation, the following three claims are intelligible:

1. Jesus Christ is the paradigm embodied expression of God.
2. Jesus Christ is necessary for salvation in the sense that at the End everyone will necessarily have participated in his embodied expression of God.
3. But the embodied expression of God in the lives of some people of other faiths will also be similarly necessary for salvation.

All three claims are quite unintelligible if one conceives salvation in terms of *transparency*, as some Buddhists do. Even 3, which may seem to Christians to be a radical concession, will be very puzzling if a Buddhist regards the founder of his or her tradition as dispensable, not necessary—like everything else. I should note, however, that it would be misleading to imply that all Buddhism presupposes a transparency model. Some Buddhists say that Nirvana *is* Samsara, for when they become aware of what transcends the everyday world they do not do so by bypassing that world. Such a Buddhist perspective is similar to Christian translucency in an important way. Indeed, it is closer to incarnational Christianity than either perspective is to many *other-worldly* forms of mystical religion. But Christian translucency differs significantly even from such a Buddhist this-worldly emphasis in two respects: (i) the insistence that full translucency will occur only at the End and that meanwhile there is much injustice and other evil, which must be reduced or eliminated; (ii) the insistence on the social-historical-communal character of the evil which impedes and the good which expresses the Ultimate. Hence social action can have Ultimate significance, not merely as it arises because individual Buddhists and Christians are moved by an Ultimate compassion, but also as part of a change in the cosmos that must occur if the Ultimate is to be fully expressed. Hence not only social action but also history and time are viewed in a different way, for translucency is a goal in the historical future as well as a partly realized state in the present.

But I digress. We were considering the Christian claim that a relation to Jesus Christ is *necessary* for salvation, and we found that it is intelligible within the context of a Christian-*translucency* model of salvation. What about the claim that Jesus Christ is *sufficient*? Such a claim implies that no other way is necessary for the full realization of the eschatological hope. But I have already argued that other ways may be necessary. If many human beings have in fact been translucent to God through other traditions, and if in fact this seems likely to continue to be the case, the exclusion of any necessary contribution from other traditions seems to me questionable. Indeed, since the End somehow includes not only people living at the time of the End, but all of humanity that has ever lived, a claim that all other paths are dispensable and have always been completely dispensable seems to me very dubious.

Furthermore, even if Christians were correct in claiming that no *other* path has been or is or ever will be *necessary* to the eschatological emergence of the City of God, it seems to me implausible to claim that none of these can *add* anything at all to that City. For this would mean that nothing of significance as expressions of God in human life has been added or could be added by other traditions. Perhaps the crucial point here is that the distinction between being "necessary" and being "addable" dissolves when we are envisaging a *full* expression of the Ultimate in human life. How could any genuine expression be justifiably omitted? Moreover, as I argued early in this chapter concerning the need for Christians to fill out their understanding of what it means to be human by learning from people of other faiths, it is obvious empirically that contemporary Christian understanding and living of human nature is incomplete.

Taking a different tack, I would also point out that within Christian tradition itself are teachings which suggest that what Jesus Christ was and is can be "completed" and in that sense "surpassed" as the Christian community expresses the divine reality more and more adequately, each individual Christian and group of Christians adding something distinctive to the total expression. By analogy, even if the way through Christ is in some sense central for humankind, individuals and groups from other traditions may add something which would otherwise be lacking in the total expression of the Ultimate, both now and at the End.

To sum up my discussion of the issues within the context of a Christian-translucency model of salvation, it seems to me that although the necessity of Jesus Christ for salvation is intelligible in that model (much more so than in a transparency model), the necessity of other persons or paths is also intelligible and plausible, which conflicts with claims that Jesus Christ is sufficient for salvation.

In effect, a Christian can say this to a person of another faith: "I believe that Jesus Christ is in a unique way the paradigm human expression of God, and that eventually it will be necessary for all human beings to participate through Christ in their human expression of God. But I am also convinced that the full human expression of God in humankind will also involve everyone participating in what many people in your tradition and other traditions have learned and lived. And some of these contributions may turn out to be much more significant than most of what has developed within traditional Christianity. So I try to be open in friendship and intimacy with you, while humbly commending a Christian path to you to the extent that you feel open to consider it."

But what do I mean when I confess that Jesus Christ is "in a unique way the paradigm human expression of God"? This seems to imply that Jesus Christ is in some *special* way necessary for salvation in contrast with, say, Gautama Buddha. One way in which a Christian's loyalty commitment to Christ is expressed is by seeing Christ as normative. That is, although much can and should be added to the particular expression of God in Jesus Christ, nothing should be added that is *incompatible* with that expression. Thus, for example, the fact that Jesus was not, and is not, a *woman*, means that much can and should be added from embodied feminine spirituality, but whatever is added should be compatible—and similarly in the case of an addition from shamanism or yoga meditation or Buddhist selflessness or Marxism or psychoanalysis and so forth.

But what counts as "compatible?" In the past, much persecution of other paths by Christians and much constriction of the Christian path itself has been legitimized by an allegedly obvious incompatibility between Christ and various ways of being human. And even if Christians now concede in theory that some other spiritual paths may be a *necessary* contribution to the full expression of God in humankind, the concession could lead to little real improvement in openness if these contributions have to satisfy a very rigid compatibility criterion. On the other hand, whatever a Christian experiences as impeding human participation in Jesus Christ as embodied expression of God should be set aside. Indeed, some sort of compatibility criterion is implicit in any serious commitment to Jesus Christ as necessary for salvation. A Christian is *loyal* to Jesus Christ, not merely open. If my proposal is valid, a Christian can be open to other faiths while being loyal to Jesus Christ. Indeed, it would be disloyal not to be open.

What I propose for Christians is a dialectical and flexible relation between one's experience of the risen Jesus Christ and one's experience of humanity as one becomes more open in intimacy to other faiths. This is not mainly an intellectual exchange between idea systems, though that is included. It is mainly a dynamic experiential process in which *whatever* one experiences of the indwelling Christ and the inclusive dimensions of our humanity is an occasion for personal transformation that has two stages: one surrenders one's self-preoccupied self into God and then one is reborn as a particular, embodied expression of God in intimate interconnection with other human beings and with nature.

At the conclusion of this chapter I am suggesting that the Christian life is both a surrender of self into God and an expression of God through the self. The surrender includes a detachment from everyone and everything. The expression includes an intimate interconnection with everyone and everything. The surrender can be pictured as transparency. The expression can be pictured as translucency. Transparency is not a final goal; it is a stage, a prerequisite for translucency. We need to let go of all attachment to self and world and become aware *only* of God, thereby enabling others to see *through* us to God, as if we did not exist. But then such self-surrender can make it possible for God to live *as us;* our whole selves in intimate interdependence with the whole world can then be God's embodied expression.

Although Christian tradition has rarely endorsed transparency as the goal of the Christian life, various versions of it have been seen by Christian contemplatives as the necessary penultimate stage in Christian life, the "Dark Night" prior to living the life of God in the world. Conventional Christians, in contrast with this, have tended to understand salvation neither as transparency nor as translucency. Like Christians on spiritual paths which stress transparency, they have focused on individuals in isolation, but their appeal has been mainly to self-preoccupied concerns: God's attitude to *me*, God's rescue of *me*, God's place after death for *me*, and so on. Perhaps the initial appeal of any religious teaching to most human beings has to be to our egoistic self-concerns, whether material or spiritual, for this is our initial perspective. But any individualistic approach to salvation should encourage a movement toward selfless transparency. And this movement should be linked with, though subordinated to, a communal and cosmic approach to salvation, open to others to learn what it means to be human. Then it is possible for a Christian to be open, even intimately open, to other faiths, while remaining loyal to Jesus Christ and while remaining convinced that eventually a relation to God through Jesus Christ will be necessary for everyone.

XI ✳ ✳ ✳ *Spiritual Reality, Academic Skepticism, and Transfiguration*[1]

A few years ago at a theological conference I heard a paper in which a scholar said something like this: "And St. Paul, following the traditional metaphor already used by Jeremiah and Ezekiel, spoke of a spirit of love dwelling in the heart." As I heard these words I wanted to jump to my feet and protest: "Surely it's possible that St. Paul spoke of a spirit of love dwelling in the heart because that's where he *experienced* it—as countless others have in many different religious traditions, and as I have myself, especially during meditation, and as people have in secular psychotherapies such as bioenergetics. It's no metaphor. It's a literal truth."

It is increasingly obvious to me that spiritual reality—and by this I do not mean God—has an objective structure which human beings can discern, just as they can discern the colors of the rainbow. This objective structure has shaped our human language and concepts, though these in turn have developed independent of that structure in varying degrees, shaping our awareness of spiritual reality in ways which may clarify or distort.

Imagine a blind scholar in a blind community saying, "And Paul, following the tradition established by Jeremiah and Ezekiel, located the color orange between red and yellow." Such an explanation of the location is unnecessary if Paul could actually see colors. But if a linguistic tradition, unlike other traditions, included no word for the color orange, or if it included a dozen species of orange colors, such variations would of course be open to various explanations—cultural, historical, geographical, and so forth. It is not the case, however, that we can *never* justify and explain our linguistic distinctions by reference to nonlinguistic experience.[2]

The speaker at the theological conference exemplified an epistemological perspective evident in nearly every paper that I heard at the conference and pervading academic thought in general. This perspective excludes the possibility of any direct awareness of spiritual reality. Accordingly it is sheer superstition, supposedly, for me to claim to experience myself as spirit, to discern loving life energy around my heart, to detect harmful or helpful spiritual influences at work between people at a distance, to see auras or feel vibrations around other people, to contact discarnate spirits of the dead to help them or be helped by them, or to become aware of angels and archangels and all the company of heaven. Why are all such spiritual claims so obviously false and fantastic for most contemporary intellectuals, including theologians? Because their perspective combines what I will call a perspectivalist neo-Kantianism and a common sense empiricism. Let us consider each of these briefly in turn.

Kant's agnosticism concerning reality, including spiritual reality, is well known. All we can know, according to Kant, is how the human mind *must* shape sense experience: the forms of space and time and the very general concepts or categories such as cause and substance we humans impose on sense experience, giving it an intelligible structure. What is really out there we cannot know. We only know reality on our terms, and what these terms are we can deduce in a "transcendental" way. As I pointed out in Chapter IV, many diverse thinkers have followed Kant in emphasizing what the human mind brings *to* our awareness of the world, but differing from him in focusing, not on what we must bring to this awareness, but on what we do bring. What we do bring varies from person to person and group to group, so our alleged knowing is relative to this. The variations in what we bring to our awareness of the world depend on a variety of factors, any one of which can be selected for emphasis. Some epistemologies stress sociological influences, others select psychological influences or cultural-historical influences. And some epistemologies following Wittgenstein depict our knowing as shaped by linguistic practices within a social "form of life." What all these approaches have in common is perspectivalism: the rejection of any allegedly direct way of knowing reality.

Insofar as contemporary *theology* is governed by this neo-Kantian perspectivalism we have a variety of approaches to epistemological questions, but they all agree in assuming that we can only study the human conceptual or linguistic framework that is brought *to* an alleged reality, not the reality itself, for it can only be discerned *through* the framework. This relativism may be either skeptical, fideistic, or conservative. The skeptical version, a "hermeneutics of suspicion," exposes ideology by means of insights drawn from Freud or Marx or sociology of knowledge. Knowledge claims are thus radically undermined. If the stance is fideistic, the theologian makes an explicit leap of faith, trusting in a particular conceptual framework or "language game" as the authoritative vehicle through which to know and by which to live. To be a Christian means to opt for Christian words and symbols. Where the stance is an unreflective conservatism, there is no sense of choice in the matter. Being a Christian means thinking as a member of a reliable historical-traditional community: "If Jeremiah and Ezekiel and then Paul spoke of a spirit of love dwelling in the heart, that is what I will think too." But whether one is skeptical, fideistic, or conservative the common assumption is that I cannot directly know reality—especially spiritual reality. The issue is whether to trust any conceptual or symbolic framework that includes spiritual *terms*. The skeptic refuses to do so, the fideist opts for a framework, and the conservative does not question his or her framework.

In relation to spiritual reality, perspectivalist neo-Kantianism is often accompanied by a commonsense empiricism, which is a species of what in Chapter IV I called *impersonalism*. What I mean by commonsense empiricism is simply the assumption that experience is limited to sense experience and that sense experience of any alleged objective reality is limited to the publicly observable world—which is accessible to anyone who can see, hear, touch, and so on. Concerning this publicly observable world, commonsense empiricism is sometimes qualified by some Kantian caution concerning claims to know what is really there. Usually, however, empiricism and neo-Kantianism are in conflict concerning knowledge of physical reality. But concerning spiritual reality neo-Kantian and empiricist forget their quarrels and agree in rejecting any possibility that you and I can know directly, by experiencing or discerning what is there. Both tend to reject as sheer superstition any alleged spiritual awareness. To a comonsense empiricist the real world is the publicly observable world, plus perhaps the human mind or center of consciousness inside each human body. The mind sometimes imaginatively creates fantasies of spiritual entities during abnormal states of consciousness such as dreams, reveries, trances, and meditations; but to regard these fantasies as realities is a reversion to a preenlightened, subhuman primitivism and superstition—so the empiricist assumes. Or, less harshly, an empiricist can take up a form of perspectivalism on beliefs and practices pertaining to spirit and spirits. Their origins can be explained sociologically, psychologically, or in terms of historical-cultural influences. In such a very typical combination of perspectivalism concerning the spiritual and commonsense empiricism concerning the physical, Kant's own agnosticism concerning physical reality is forgotten and confined to spiritual reality. Such an empiricist has no resort to perspectivalist explanations when someone claims to see a stone. The explanations are called in when someone claims to see a spook.

If theologians are reluctant to accept any knowledge claims concerning spiritual reality, it is not surprising to find that social scientists are also reluctant. Several years ago I attended a conference in Berkeley, California, on new religious movements. The central issue was why people join these movements and remain in them. A wide variety of psychological and sociological explanations were proposed, but one kind of explanation that seems to me at least equally relevant were almost totally overlooked: a spiritual explanation. In my association with some of these groups I have often observed people becoming aware of themselves and others as *spirit*, perhaps for the first time in their lives. This is an exciting and momentous discovery for most post-

Enlightenment Westerners. It may even be mistakenly identified as an experience of God. Often people continue in the
new religious movement mainly because they know they
can continue this awareness of spirit in the movement,
whereas outside—they assume or are taught—it is unavail-
able. Being naive in such matters, they do not realize that
similar experiences can occur in many other groups, with
different leaders, belief structures, and communal practices.
(And they do not realize that elementary spiritual awareness
can occur even though a leader is immoral or crazy, a belief
structure is fanatical or irrational, and a communal practice
is manipulative or dangerous—as is the case in some, but
not all, new religious movements.)

Whether or not a group, in its overall character, is positive
or negative, individuals who join and remain usually have
both nonspiritual motives and spiritual motives. The former
are open to investigation by secular psychology and sociology, but the latter are not. To say, "John and Mary sought and
found an awareness, however minimal or distorted, of spiritual reality" is alien to social science. Such a spiritual explanation presupposes that there really is a spiritual realm
which people sometimes discover. The most that a typical
social scientist can assume here is that one important
motive may be a person's *conviction* that he or she has
found spiritual reality. The conviction itself must be
explained by reference to nonspiritual factors. For example,
a person might believe that he felt a spirit of love in his
heart because that is what the religious tradition taught, or
because he was deprived of love in infancy and needed to
believe this. What I would insist, however, is that there *is* a
spiritual realm and that some forms of meditation enable a
person to begin to be aware of this realm. And if a social scientist will not test my claim by taking up meditation himself, he should be more genuinely agnostic concerning such
claims, never assuming that nonspiritual explanations are
adequate in accounting for people's convictions concerning
spiritual reality.

Thus far we have looked at theological and social scientific assumptions concerning the question, "What can I know

about spiritual reality?" A typical philosophical approach can be seen in a recent book by the distinguished philosopher Susanne Langer. In volume three of her trilogy on the origins of the human mind,[3] she explains the evolutionary origins of human belief in a spirit world: gods and goddesses, devils and angels, souls of dead people and animals, spirits inhabiting not only persons but also animals and trees. She is amazed that human beings who are intelligent enough to carry on the practical affairs of life can possibly have imagined such absurdities and asserted them as facts. Since for her, as for most academics today, such beliefs are false, their explanation must be sought in how the human mind works. Langer's account of the human mind resembles Kant's in that at its core it is a claim concerning how the human mind must work. Since her claims arise from reflections on biology and evolution, we could call it an *evolutionary-transcendental* deduction. In her view our mind must work as a feeling response to our environment. This feeling response is such as to be expressed in symbolism, and the symbolism is a way of understanding whatever is experienced in nature as having a lifelike form.

To this fundamental claim concerning mind as feeling Langer adds several ingenious and insightful theories concerning why human beings have had beliefs and practices concerning spiritual reality. Her explanations are very illuminating in accounting for why the spirit world alleged by various individuals and communities differ and in understanding some of the motivations of people both past and present who have come to believe in spirits and life after death. But for Langer the spirit world is always and entirely a human creation, a fantastic delusion.

What if she is mistaken in this? What if human *discoveries* of supersensible realities are mixed in with the imaginative projections that she astutely describes? Then, although her explanations are still relevant, they are inadequate. What the human mind brings to spiritual reality is not the whole story, for the human mind sometimes discerns spiritual reality, especially during meditation. The whole investigation becomes much more complex. It requires investigators who practice the relevant forms of meditation or who are at least open to study testimonial material from those who do. I readily concede that various nonspiritual explanations are still relevant. Kant and Marx and Freud and Langer and Wittgenstein cannot be ignored. But we also cannot ignore the testimony concerning spirit from most human beings in human history prior to the so-called enlightenment in the West.

Thus far I have questioned a theologian's nonspiritual account of why St. Paul located a spirit of love in the heart, a group of social scientists' nonspiritual account of why people join new religious movements, and a philosopher's nonspiritual account of why most human beings in the past have believed in spirits. Now I am going to question some accounts provided by nonfundamentalist biblical scholars and theologians concerning the Transfiguration of Jesus. In general, the story is not interpreted literally, that is, in terms of an objective spiritual reality which people can sometimes discern. My own first impulse to interpret it literally was evoked thirty years ago when I first saw a fresco of the Transfiguration by the great Florentine artist Fra Angelico. In depicting the change in the appearance of Jesus' face and clothing, he painted a literal oval-shaped aura which is analogous to those which I now realize are discerned by people whom we today call *psychics*. But liberal New Testament scholars today typically do not believe in auras. Nor are they at ease in interpreting what happened when Moses and Elijah allegedly appeared as two discarnate spirits communicating with Jesus on the mount of Transfiguration. Such an event would be entirely intelligible and unsurprising to modern spiritualists and to participants in various non-Christian meditative paths. But most nonfundamentalist biblical scholars seem to be skeptical not only concerning the Transfiguration story but concerning spiritual reality in general. Or if they are not skeptical, they are puzzled and confused.

One notable exception was George Caird. Concerning the various spiritual "principalities and powers," both good and evil, which St. Paul saw as being subjugated by Christ, Caird wrote, "Paul is using mythological language but his language has a rational content of thought; he is working with ideas which have had a long history, but he is describing *spiritual realities* with whom he and his fellow Christians have *personal* acquaintance."[4] and in his commentary on the Transfiguration story, he wrote:

> The transfiguration cannot be understood simply as a stage in the education of the disciples; it must also have been a crisis in the religious life of Jesus. Luke draws our attention to this point in his usual manner: Jesus, he tells us, was praying; and his comment is borne out by the researches of Evelyn Underhill and others, who have shown that the intense devotions of saint and mystic are often accompanied by physical transformation and luminous glow. . . . Many scholars, past and present, have treated the transfiguration story with suspicion, regarding it either as a misplaced resurrection story or as a legendary product of later Christian piety. But the account may be accepted as literal truth.[5]

It would be a monumental task to show that, in contrast with Caird, most nonfundamentalist scholars seem to be skeptical or cautiously agnostic or confused in their comments concerning the Transfiguration story. But I can at least invite readers to consider as a representative example a book entitled *Transfiguration*[6] by a relatively conservative Anglican theologian, J. W. C. Wand. In this study, published in 1967, he draws on many biblical scholars, comparing and appraising their accounts. He himself suggests that probably Jesus' facial appearance did change as he prayed.[7] After all, a person's face can "light up," as we say, on seeing his beloved. How much more so for Jesus in prayer to God. But perhaps the disciples' report of this was amplified by them or by others so as to include talk about a change in Jesus' clothing.[8] Why? Partly because hints of the miraculous tend to be exaggerated as a story is passed along; partly because there was a prevalent traditional notion that such a change can affect the clothing; partly because the Hebrew concept of "glory" linked with the Transfiguration by Luke,[9] includes the notion of a shining garment-like substance.

Wand also notes that early Christian apologists arguing with the Jews could have been moved to depict Jesus as a new Moses being transfigured on a mountain top and as a fulfillment of the Law and the Prophets who conversed there with Moses and Elijah.

Wand is not entirely skeptical. He is convinced that the Transfiguration narrative has a core of historicity and that something significant happened. He notes that St. Matthew refers to the event as a "vision" so probably the event was not physical but only mental.[10] But for Wand this mental status does not make the event unreal. Indeed he ends by calling the Transfiguration a "veridical vision" which Jesus somehow shared with his disciples.[11] But how a veridical vision differs from a private fantasy he does not indicate.

What Wand lacks is a metaphysical and epistemological framework in which one can distinguish between (i) publicly observable physical events, (ii) private fantasies, and (iii) objective spiritual events that are partly discerned through what we today often call *psychic* awareness. Wand does briefly consider an approach that might have led him in this direction, viewing the Transfiguration as a "mystical phenomenon" alongside other alleged paranormal events in the lives of both Christian and non-Christian holy persons: clairvoyance, levitation, telepathy, and so on. I quote:

> Such alleged incidents are generally viewed with dislike by minds trained only in the exact sciences. So far from regarding them as helps to faith we drape them 'in the decent vestments of symbol and myth'. Losing the humble sense of wonder, we only find queerness in the phenomena which our conceptual systems refuse to accommodate. The difficulty about these alleged experiences is that they are individually so difficult to prove, and that, even when accepted as proven, they are almost always capable of a naturalistic explanation.[12]

Wand goes to on to say that it is by no means impossible some such unusual experience may lie behind the narrative of the Transfiguration, but his comment about "naturalistic explanation" remains. What does he mean by this expression? If he means an explanation which requires no reference to special divine intervention, I would agree with him. The spiritual realm has its own "natural" structure and characteristics. But I suspect that what he means by a "naturalistic explanation" is a nonspiritual explanation, for example, one in physical or psychological terms. If so, I would simply assert that he is mistaken. No such explanations are available and adequate with reference to telepathy, clairvoyance, spiritual healing, spiritualistic phenomena, or transfiguration. Instead, we have "naturalistic" assumptions which rule out various paranormal events. It is these assumptions which dictate the conclusions, not only for secular thinkers but also for many Christian theologians. And often the assumptions are unacknowledged. It just seems obvious that some nonspiritual explanation must be possible and that the onus of proof is entirely on the person who makes a claim concerning spiritual reality to show that every possible nonspiritual explanation has been ruled out.

My own personal conviction is that the Transfiguration of Jesus did take place and that it involved both what we now call "paranormal" changes discernible to "psychics" and also, more important, a total surrender and translucency of a human being in body, passions, mind, and spirit to the divine Spirit. Nobody can discern such surrender and translucency unless they are at least beginning *both* spiritual awareness and personal surrender to the divine Spirit. I do concede the remote historical possibility that the Transfiguration of Jesus may not have happened at all, or that we may have only a simple story about a happy face in prayer that was amplified into a fantastic piece of religious propaganda. But although I concede that is possible, for me the onus of proof is on those who hold that the story is not true as it stands.[13] Here I resemble a fundamentalist, but not because I believe in the literal inerrancy of scripture. Rather I have no initial reason to disbelieve the story because of the assumption that such things cannot or do not happen. There may be other reasons to disbelieve the story, or to see it as a composite, a kernel of truth plus a subsequent elaboration. Maybe, for example, a story about a resurrection-appearance was somehow transferred back into the earthly life of Jesus.

But that is a different kind of issue. The main issue for me is whether a transfiguration can occur, as an objective spiritual event which also involves surrender to the divine Spirit, not only for Jesus but also for us.[14] Similarly problems of spiritual exegesis raised by biblical stories of allegedly objective spiritual healing raise issues concerning the possible reality of such healing for us. Is it all superstition, or at best a kind of "faith healing" in which our beliefs can somehow help us to get well—the placebo effect? Even more radically, when St. Paul tells us in Romans 8:16: "The Spirit itself bears witness with our spirit that we are the children of God," is he assuming that we are aware of our spirit? Is such awareness possible? My own view is that such awareness is not only possible but necessary for an adequate awareness of the divine Spirit.

Few Christians today are clearly aware of themselves as spirit. There are various reasons for this. I have stressed the intellectual climate of our age, with its combination of Kantian agnosticism and commonsense empiricism. I should also note, briefly, two other features of the intellectual climate that have deeply influenced Christian theology and that also impede awareness of oneself as spirit. I am thinking of existentialist theology and liberation theology. Both of these have deep biblical roots and emphasize important truths, which must be retained in spite of anything I say here. But existentialist theology tends to exclude, or at best blur, spiritual awareness, because it proposes only two metaphysical and epistemological pigeonholes: scientific investigation and personal discovery or creation of meaning. Discernment of objective spiritual reality fits neither of these. And liberation theology, although rightly recalling Christian thought and practice to the communal justice commitment of the Hebrew prophets, sometimes rejects all concern with the spiritual as a escapist sanctioning of the oppressive status quo: "You may be enslaved and hungry now, but there is pie in the sky by and by." But what if there is such pie in the sky, spiritual consolation in both this life and the next? Does the political misuse of a truth make it false?

Both existentialist theology and liberation theology are post-Enlightenment developments. They share with neo-Kantian relativism and commonsense empiricism a rejection of pre-Enlightenment spiritual awareness as "superstition." Charismatic Christianity, too, is partly post-enlightenment—not concerning God, but concerning spirit, and in a different way. It tends to attribute all positive paranormal phenomena directly to God, provided that the "correct" doctrinal beliefs accompany them, and the rest to the Devil. Hence many experiences of human spirit are misinterpreted as divine or diabolical intrusions. One's new and exhilarating experience of oneself as spirit is often mistakenly assumed to be a visitation by the Holy Spirit, and an eruption from the emotional unconscious or a psychic invasion from another human being is mistakenly seen as a visitation by the Devil. And a genuine surrender of the whole self to God, amply evidenced not only by positive paranormal phenomena but also by an abundance of the fruits of the Spirit, is dismissed or—the ultimate blasphemy—it is attributed to Beelzebub, because the correct Christian beliefs are absent.

Thus in various ways the intellectual climate of our age imposes severe intellectual constrictions on any Christian exploration of spirit. But there is a specifically Christian constriction as well, which emerged long before the Enlightenment. This constriction is, in my view, a distortion of a legitimate pastoral caution which goes back to St. Paul, whom I hear saying something like this: "Do not be egoistically preoccupied with spiritual phenomena such as visions or tongues or prophecies or ascents to the third heaven. What matters is your openness to the Holy Spirit of love, your being lived by God in Christ as you surrender your old self-centered self." I totally agree with this, but a distorted outcome of this has been that there is little practical or theoretical teaching concerning the human spirit and the spiritual realm in Western Christianity. When I asked a Benedictine monk and scholar why this is so, in contrast with, say, the tantric traditions of the East, his reply was that there has been a fear that Christians would become attached to the consolations of God at the expense of their focus on the God of consolations. This caution arises from a realistic sense of the subtlety and strength and pervasiveness of human narcissism, which can pervert all advances in spiritual awareness. Even Jesus was tempted in the wilderness after the splendors of his baptismal experience, which could have been twisted into an egoistic power-trip and even a pact with the Devil. Today, however, most Christians avoid spiritual pride in the same way that a pauper avoids material pride, by having little to be proud about. For St. Paul's caution against a sinful stance toward spiritual phenomena has become, in practice, an effective caution against the phenomena themselves. This is a tragic error. If Christians are to learn how to surrender the whole self to God, to be lived by God, they must have an awareness of self as spirit or spiritual body in complex interdependence with self as physical body, emotions, and mind. We should realize, of course, that spiritual awareness, especially at the lowest or purely psychic level, is no more intrinsically religious than awareness of physical body or emotions or mind. And we should also realize that there are many levels of spiritual awareness, from the psychic, which is merely sensational and fascinating, to the sublimely loving, which is transforming. But a transfiguring surrender of the whole self can occur only if we are aware of our whole self, which includes our self as spiritual body. And spiritual self-awareness has a special importance in all this because a minimal element of it seems to be necessary if we are to *experience* what surrender means in any of our aspects, not only the spiritual but also the physical, emotional, and mental. Spiritual self-awareness is an essential part of the process by which eventually a person surrenders the whole self to the divine Source, so that he or she becomes a transparent channel for the divine Spirit, a luminous human being outshone by the divine Light. For Christians, this transfiguration happens through contemplative identification with Christ: "All of us, gazing on the Lord's glory with unveiled faces, are being transformed from glory to glory into his very image by the Lord who is the Spirit. . . . For God, who said 'Let light shine out of darkness' has shone in our hearts, that we in turn might

make known the glory of God shining on the face of
Christ."[15]

But these words of St. Paul can be read as little more than
a pious inspirational pep talk unless, at the very least, we are
aware of ourselves as spirit in a spiritual realm. How can we
begin to have such an awareness? Concerning this, contemporary Christianity provides little counsel. Yet if Christians
draw on some of the largely lost resources within the Christian tradition and if they have the humility to sit at the feet
of teachers from other traditions who do provide wise counsel, they can readily come to know in their own experience a
great deal concerning spiritual reality. Indeed for many people the initial process is relatively easy: becoming aware of
the various energy centers of the physical body, beginning to
see or to feel other people's energy fields or spiritual bodies,
learning how to channel healing energies to others, getting
into contact with discarnate spirits who can help us or
whom we can help, discovering the blurred boundaries
between self and others in the spiritual realm plus the
blurred agencies ("I yet not I"). None of this by itself leads to
God, and all of this, like any human endeavor, can be perverted into a mere ego trip. Yet it provides the necessary
though elemental basis for what can follow: the arduous process of radical transformation or transfiguration in which we
gradually uncover and surrender whatever prevents our
being lived by God, resonating and channeling the divine
love.

Postscript

   Perhaps the most controversial feature of this book has
been my claim that human beings have a spiritual dimension that links us with trees and animals, with each other,
with spiritual energies, with discarnate spirits and angels,
and with God. Most mainline Christian thinkers, although
believing in God, do not acknowledge the reality of the spiritual. In Chapter XI we saw how they tend to remove all
"supernatural" elements from the story of Jesus' transfiguration. Such skepticism breeds ignorance, so few mainline
Christians can help us understand what is going on if we
begin to have spiritualistic experiences. Thus when, during
the decade in which I was writing this book, I began to
become aware of a variety of spiritual energies and spiritual
presences I turned mostly to teachers outside the Christian
tradition for help as I explored and interpreted this new
realm. The best help that even Christian contemplatives
could offer was a Christian-mantra meditation that tends to
bypass both our emotional unconscious and our spiritual
unconscious and tries to drop directly into the divine
Source. This discipline clearly "works" to some extent for
some people, but it did not speak to my condition.
   Rich resources concerning the spiritual realm were readily
available in Toronto, so I perhaps gave up too soon in my
search for Christian counsel there. Eventually I did have a
brief contact in New York City with the remarkable Mother
Serena, a deeply Christian healer who drew on a vast range
of nonincarnate spirits in her work. And early in the process
I "chanced" to meet an eminent World Council of Churches
figure who counseled me concerning how to deal with inva-
sive evil energies and entities by avoiding both fear and fascination and by calling on the presence of Christ. He joked

about not having revealed at the council that he had any experience in such matters! (Perhaps there are also other distinguished theologians who feel they have to hide their light under a bushel basket of Enlightenment thought.)

One book could have helped me immensely in understanding the eruption of spiritual awareness which was occurring had I known of its existence: *Meditations on the Tarot*.[1] This anonymous work had been available in French since 1967, and by 1985 it appeared in English, but I did not hear about it until after I had finished this book. I know of no Christian thinker who explores the spiritual realm with comparable breadth of scholarly learning and depth of experiential insight. Although the title might suggest a book on how to predict the future by drawing cards from a tarot deck, the book is remote from any such interests. Rather, as indicated in the subtitle "A Journey into Christian Hermeticism," the book is an exploration of the spiritual realm by a Christian mystic. It is a series of profound reflections—and for the reader, spiritual exercises—concerning the hidden sacred symbolism of the twenty-two most important tarot cards. The reader is invited to ponder, in relation to his or her own past or possible spiritual experiences, the significance of the detailed imagery of such cards as The Chariot, The Hermit, The Lover, The Devil, or Death. In this monumental work the anonymous author draws on decades of research not only into Christian scripture and tradition but also into other sources, especially the Western esoteric tradition from its origins in Hermes, as well as Eastern mystical traditions, the Cabbala, much of Western philosophy and science, and even Carl Jung.

The author draws not only on his research but also on his first-hand experiences of spiritual reality. This is obvious, for example, in his description of what happens when one intuits the presence of a non-incarnate being:

> You venerate (i.e. you love and respect) a non-incarnated being—a departed person, a saint, or a hierarchical being—in a disinterested manner. Your veneration—which includes love, respect, gratitude, the desire to conform etc.—cannot fail to create an invisible link of sympathy with its object. It

may be in a subtle and dramatic way, or rather in a slow, gradual and almost imperceptible way—this does not matter—the day will come when you will experience the *presence* . . . not a fluidic, semi-electrical presence close to you in space—as in the apparition of a phantom or ghost—but a breath of radiant serenity, of which you know with certain knowledge that the source from which it emanates is not all in you. It influences you and fills you but it does not take its origin in you; it comes from outside of you. Just as you know, in drawing near to a fireplace, that the warmth that you feel does not arise from you, but rather from the fireplace, so also do you feel that the breath of serenity in question is due to an objective presence. Here, therefore, a relationship of sympathy is established. After this it is up to you to remain silently concentrated so that the relationship is subsequently developed, i.e. that it gains in intensity and clarity—that it becomes a *meeting* in full consciousness.[2]

If I had read this passage fifteen years ago I would have realized that what I was experiencing could be articulated by a Christian thinker who had known similar states of awareness. And by reading his *Meditations* I would also have learned much from his "mapping" of the spiritual realm in relation to a framework that is fundamentally Christian, though open to a great deal outside the Christian tradition. I now find that I disagree with some of Anonymous's teachings, especially concerning the origins of good and evil, the significance of human history, and the allegedly hierarchical structure of reality, but I still revere him as a great spiritual teacher. Anyone whose spiritual journey involves ventures into the territory of the spiritual can learn much from him. And although I still think that Christians can and should learn much from other guides on such a journey, I retract any implicit or explicit suggestion that Christian resources for such a journey are meager. Anonymous is now available.

A Postscript is a useful occasion not only for making retractions, but also for noting unfinished business. Further reflection, sometimes in response to criticisms from readers of *Spirituality and Human Nature*, has made me aware of four issues that arise in it and need to be explored in a more thorough way in another book, a sequel. I will now sketch these issues, partly to assure the reader that I am aware of them, partly to encourage the reader to begin to investigate them, and partly to advertise the sequel, entitled *On Being Completely Human.*

1. *The House of the Self Has Many Dimensions.* In this book I have focused on the spiritual dimension of human beings in relation to several other dimensions: the depth psychological or emotional (Section 1), the intellectual and scientific (Section 2), the moral (Section 3) and the religious (Section 4). There are, however, many other important dimensions: our spontaneous *artistic* urge to be imaginately and playfully creative; our inner *ecological* connection with the earth and with all living beings; our *existential* responsibility for freely choosing our basic direction in life; our longing for fulfilment in intimately *loving* "I-Thou" relations; our unavoidable *vulnerability* to death, suffering (physical pain, separation grief, and unfulfilled hopes) and tragedy; our participation in historical communities whose *traditions* have shaped us with their language, morality, religion, art, and institutions.

   In Chapter III I said, "We need to move toward completeness as human beings, excluding no significant dimension of human life from the self-understanding out of which we live. We need to ask, 'Who am I?' and to answer this question in as all-inclusive a way as we can."[3] If the whole self is to be surrendered into God to be lived by God, we need to become aware of that whole self. In most of us, however, many of these dimensions are repressed and many are in conflict. And derepression has its dangers. When a dimension is derepressed—for example, in a "conversion" to psychotherapy, radical politics, or spiritualism—our newly found perspective on life leads us to a one-dimensional understanding of life which imperialistically subordinates or represses all the other human dimensions, reducing them to its own terms. Such a conversion can bring a false unity which hides a continuing inner conflict and permits only a fraction of the self to be surrendered into God.

Is a true and all-inclusive unity possible? If it is possible, how can we begin, as individuals in relation to humankind, to move toward this End? Does the spiritual dimension have a contribution to make in this process, providing both an inner dynamism and an awareness of our interdependence with the earth and with each other? Even if the spiritual dimension is especially important, can a spiritualistic perspective avoid becoming one-dimensional and imperialistic, reducing all other dimensions to its own terms? If each dimension gives rise to its own perspective, and these perspectives are not only complementary but also conflicting, can truth concerning human nature emerge creatively within a dialogue between perspectives? These are some of the questions that eventually emerge if we persist in pursuit of an all-inclusive answer to the question, "Who am I?"

2. *On the Origin of Evil.* Throughout this book I have pointed to narcissism as the main source of evil in human beings. This claim still seems to me to be true, but at the end of Chapter VIII I noted the possibility that narcissism arises from features of the human condition which cannot be eliminated. This possibility must be investigated. Indeed, there are four reasons for believing that being human involves being prone to narcissism. The four reasons can be distinguished as psychological, historical, existential, and metaphysical. The *psychological* reason[4] points to inescapable features of our birth and early infancy. As newly born infants we are acutely aware of being torn between an elemental desire to continue in undifferentiated union with mother and a fearful, angry passion to differentiate ourselves as a "god" like the all-powerful being from whom we are separating ourselves. The *historical* reason[5] focuses on the self-separation of the "heroic," self-conscious individual from the tribe and nature, in a

quest for independence and supremacy which culminates in tragic hubris. Only through this "fall" from an innocent quasi-animal fusion with each other and with nature did human beings as such emerge on earth. The *existential* reason[6] emphasizes the unlimited scope of our imaginings concerning what might be or what might have been. On the one hand, this involves a sense of individual freedom so unboundaried that we both feel like gods and yet anxiously, idolatrously cling to ourselves (that is, to whatever we find ourselves to be at the moment). On the other hand, the awareness that "I might not have been at all," combined with the awareness that "At any moment I might cease to be," moves us to endless preoccupation with being confirmed as powerful and important in our own eyes and in the eyes of others. The *metaphysical* reason[7] is that when I, as a spiritual being lived by the Source, undergo the crisis of becoming embodied as a human being, the fearful shock of this sudden contraction moves me to contract my self-awareness, so that I now actively identify myself as a fundamentally separate individual whose source of life is myself.

Our "fall" into narcissism is not merely a straying from an ideal, paradisal state to which we can and must return. Our human task is not merely a matter of rediscovering what we previously were (as Anonymous claims) or realizing what we already eternally are (as some Eastern mysticism holds). Rather, our human task is to deal so creatively with our narcissism that we are transformed into a reality which has *not previously existed.* An exploration into the origins of narcissism not only reveals that such a transformation process is immensely arduous and difficult. It also reveals that the process is possible, for our End is not to eliminate the tendency to narcissism but to transform it. To eliminate it would be either to return to a prehuman state or to dissolve into the Source. To transform it would be to let go of the whole self into the Source so that this *whole self* can be lived by the Source. This whole self includes our prehuman, relatively undifferentiated way of being in the womb and in the tribe, which continues to reverberate in us from our personal history and the history of humankind; but this way of being conscious is transformed within a clearly differentiated individual. And the letting go into the Source involves a kind of dissolution or death, but only as a prelude to a reconstitution as a differentiated individual united with the Source. In the End the Source will live as and in each of us in our uniqueness, unimpeded by any narcissistic self-separation or self-preoccupation. Insofar as the tendency to narcissism can become a tendency toward (non-self-separating) individuation, narcissism is not to be eliminated but to be transformed. When I wrote *Spirituality and Human Nature* I did not see this with sufficient clarity.

3. *On Being Female and Male.* Although in Chapter III I explored the emotional and spiritual dimensions of sexuality, I did not focus on the significance of gender or on the need for reconciliation between the sexes. One obvious and very basic answer to the question "Who am I?" is "I am a woman" or "I am a man." Our gendered sexuality is a very important human dimension. And the feminist movement has not only made many of us aware of the need for reconciliation in contrast with the oppression of women by men. The movement has also made it possible, for the first time in human history, to begin to envisage an eventual reconciliation between the sexes in a context where there is genuine equality of power. Only insofar as institutionalized domination of women by men in the power structures of society is reduced can men and women undergo the deep emotional-spiritual-mental changes which are required and which must be lived-out in their everyday life together.

It seems clear to me that the most fundamental cause of war is the unresolved conflict between the sexes and the distortions of humanity that this conflict has reproduced, especially in men. If there were not only justice but peace between men and women, there would probably be peace on earth. and until there is justice and peace between men and women, there will not be peace on earth. My reasons for saying this are too complex to be set forth here and are not likely to persuade everyone, but if there is any truth at all in my contention, the whole issue deserves very substantial scrutiny. We need to examine both the origins of the conflict between the sexes and the ways by which it can be reduced and eventually ended. If the origins are not only institutional (legal, educational, economic, political, religious, etc.) but also deeply psychological and spiritual, the remedies will involve not only institutional changes but profoundly personal changes. Since 1985 I have participated in a weekly men's group that is based on an openness to whatever emotional and spiritual changes are necessary in this process. In my next book I will include some of the findings of this group. We have discovered, for example, the crucial significance of "shamanic" meditation in which one experiences one's inner links with nature. There are both masculine and feminine energies in the cosmos, and a man can gradually learn to live in a steady openness to both of these, thereby beginning to learn how to encounter women in a sexual-emotional-spiritual way which neither threatens them nor feels threatening to him.

Another theme I will need to consider is the possibility that in this book I have viewed human nature from the perspective of a man and that my perspective needs to be not only complemented but also corrected by women. In particular, a male bias may have intensified my emphasis on narcissism and distorted my understanding of narcissism. It now seems likely to me that the remedies for narcissism proposed by mystical teachers 2500 years or so ago were partly a response to the hubris-temptations of the "heroic" man. Perhaps evil arises in women in a somewhat different way. It is clear that women may be more strongly tempted to play the part of the self-deflating Echo than the part of the self-inflating Narcissus, but I suspect there are further differences that go beyond my proposed analysis of narcissism in terms of self-deflation and self-inflation. I should be open to this possibility.

4. *For What End Can We Realistically Hope?* In Chapter X I said, "Christian tradition includes a vision of the End in which humankind as a whole will have been transformed, not as individuals in isolation, but as an intimate, interdependent community. Using the analogy of the physical body as an organism, Christians have envisaged a universal "body politic" that will completely incarnate and fully reveal the indwelling Spirit of God as Love. Because of the intimate involvement between all persons at the End, *each person will somehow participate in the transformed humanity of everyone else* (though in varying degrees). But each individual and each group will contribute a distinctive way of being human, a distinctive way of incarnating and revealing God. . . .

Such a Christian eschatology implies that we do not yet fully understand human nature, for this will emerge communally as individuals and groups contribute their distinctive ways of being human, and as these ways are surrendered into the indwelling God to be lived by God.[8]"

Humankind needs a vision of the End, a vision that provides a sense of direction and a basis of hope, a vision of a completed humanity. This vision should not be exclusively Christian, though it could be compatible with Christian faith. Indeed, what is required is an *inclusive* understanding of our common humanity. This is urgently needed, for if during the next few decades we do not discover much more of our common humanity and begin to live it, a nuclear holocaust or the cumulative misuse of our energy resources could bring an end to all life on this planet.

It is pointless and self-deceptive, however, to live with a visionary hope that is unrealistic. So we must be realistic concerning the origin and nature of evil in human nature and we must be open to whatever resources of good are available. This book has contributed something to the foundations for a realistic hope, but I will try to contribute much more in the sequel, *On Being Completely Human.*

Notes

Introduction

1. See Walter Principe, "Toward Defining Spirituality," *Studies in Religion* 12, no. 2 (1983): 127–141.

I. On Being Open and Closed

1. Donald Evans, *Struggle and Fulfillment: The Inner Dynamics of Religion and Morality* (Toronto: Collins, 1979; Philadelphia: Fortress, 1981).

2. The turning point for Albert Camus's anti hero in *The Fall* comes at a time of complacent self-inflation when he hears a laugh (New York; Vintage Books, 1956, pp. 38–39). After a few days, he hears it within himself (p. 42). Camus goes on to provide a portrait of closedness or narcissism in a brilliantly insightful way.

3. Maggie, the Marilyn Monroe character in Arthur Miller's *After the Fall*, says she can never remember a fake name so she uses "Miss None," for "I just have to think of nothing and that's me!" (New York: Penguin Books, 1964, p. 77). Her precarious sense of her own reality leads her first to idolize her lover as a god (pp. 72, 64–65) and then to demand that people idolize her (pp. 92–96).

4. Fyodor Dostoievsky's description of the father in *The Brothers Karamzov* (New York: Bantam Books, 1970) is a vivid example: "Whenever he appeared among people, he always felt they considered him the most despicable of men and . . . his usual reaction at those moments was to say to himself, 'Well, if that's so, I'll act like the fool they think I am and show them that in reality they are stupider and more despicable than I am.' . . . Since it was not in his power to regain their respect,

why shouldn't he go on and disgrace himself altogether, to show them that he could not care less what they thought of him?" (p. 101).

5. Heinz Kohut, *The Analysis of the Self: A Systematic Approach to the Psychoanalytic Treatment of Narcissistic Personality Disorders* (New York: International Universities Press, 1971).

6. Long before the 1960s Martin Buber had contrasted both objectivizing and subjectivizing "I-It" attitudes with an "I-Thou" attitude that is open to others. See his *I and Thou* (New York: Scribner's, 1970), end of Part II and end of Part III. My own explorations of objectivism and subjectivism began with these passages.

II. On Loving Oneself Well

1. Ovid, *Metamorphoses*, trans. Mary M. Innes (New York: Penguin Books, 1955), pp. 83–87.

2. *Ibid.*, p. 84.

3. *Ibid.*, p. 86.

4. Edmund Bergler, *The Basic Neurosis: Oral Regression and Psychic Masochism* (New York: Grune and Stratton, 1949).

5. Soren Kierkegaard, *The Sickness unto Death*, trans. Walter Lowrie (New York: Doubleday Books, 1954), p. 207.

6. Two very different but perhaps complementary psychotherapies both stress the need for a strong individual-human "container" in which grandiosity can be brought down to earth without losing its creative, visionary resources. Heinz Kohut (*The Analysis of the Self*) is a neo-Freudian who focuses on infantile grandiosity and proposed a gentle and gradual development of inner structures and inner strengths to channel and transform this grandiosity so that it becomes a creatively realistic appreciation of self and others. Marion Woodman is a Jungian who focuses on the grandiosity of archetypal divine symbols by which the ego is in danger of being possessed unless it has or is a container which can receive and integrate the creative energies of the archetype; see, for example, *The Pregnant Virgin* (Toronto: Inner City Books, 1985), pp. 75, 83, 113, 166. Both Kohut and Woodman are important if, as I will suggest in

the Postscript, I have underestimated in this book the extent to which narcissism needs to be transformed rather than eliminated. If the Source is to live as and in each of us in our *uniqueness,* a transformed narcissism can mean a clearly differentiated individual who has shed self-separation and self-preoccupation while sharing in divine creativity.

7. Donald Evans, *Struggle and Fulfillment.*

8. Martin Buber, *The Knowledge of Man* (London: Allen and Unwin, 1965), p. 79.

9. Meister Eckhart, *Breakthrough,* ed. Matthew Fox (Garden City, N.Y.: Doubleday Books, 1980), p. 214.

10. *Ibid.,* p. 216.

11. *Ibid.,* p. 180.

III. Sexuality, Spirituality, and the Art of Therapy

1. "The functioning of living Life is all around us, within us, in our senses, before our noses, clearly visible in every single animal or tree or flower. We feel it in our bodies and in our blood. . . . Outside the trap, right close by, is living Life, all around one, in everything the eye can see and the ear can hear and the nose can smell. To the victims within the trap it is eternal agony, a temptation as for Tantalus. You see it, you feel it, you eternally long for it, yet you can never, never get through the exit out of the trap. . . . Every move is restricted on all sides. This has, in the long run of time, had the effect of crippling the very organs of living Life. . . . Still, a deep longing for happiness in life and a memory of a happy Life long past, before the entrapment, has remained. But longing and memory cannot be lived in real life. Therefore, *hatred of Life* has grown from this tightness." Wilhelm Reich, *The Murder of Christ* (New York: Noonday Press, 1970), pp. 4–5. For Reich, repression of sex is not remedied by promiscuity, for what is repressed is our awareness of, and openness to, sexual life energies.

2. "For thousands of years, rites of initiation have been teaching spiritual rebirth; yet, strangely enough, man forgets again and again the meaning of divine procreation. This is surely no evi-

dence of a strong life of the spirit; and yet the penalty of mis-understanding is heavy, for it is nothing less than neurotic decay, embitterment, atrophy and sterility." Carl G. Jung, *Modern Man in Search of a Soul* (New York: Harcourt, Brace, 1933), p. 142.

3. Donald Evans, *Struggle and Fulfillment.*

4. See, for example, Alan Fromme, *The Ability to Love* (New York: Pocket Books, 1966). This is an excellent nontechnical introduction to this Freudian perspective. It was recently republished by Wilshire Book Company, Hollywood, California.

5. Wilhelm Reich, *The Murder of Christ.* Reich defines the orgasm as follows: "a unitary convulsion of one single energy unit which long before the merger was two units and which after the merger will divide again into two individual exis-tences. Bio-energetically, the orgasm amounts to a true loss of one's individuality into an entirely different state of being" (p. 30).

6. Bernard Gunther, *New-Tantra* (New York: Harper Books, 1983).

7. Alexander Lowen, *Depression and the Body: The Biological Basis of Faith and Reality* (Baltimore: Penguin Books, 1973).

8. For a thorough description of the chakras, see Swami Sivanan-da Radha, *Kundalini Yoga for the West* (Boulder, Colo., and London: Shambhala, 1981).

9. Reich equates God with Life and Life with life energies experi-enced sexually and he says, "Knowing God as Love would con-firm God's existence, would make Him accessible. But No! you must not ever know God or Life as bodily Love. . . . There is but one single approach to knowing God, and living Life accordingly: the Genital Embrace" (*The Murder of Christ*, p. 39). Reich insists that Jesus Christ could not have been so radi-ant and loving if he had been celibate rather than knowing God through the genital embrace (see ibid., pp. 32. 93.)

10. Martin Buber, *I and Thou*, pp. 134–135.

11. Soren Kierkegaard, the father of existentialism, calls the syn-drome of megalomania and masochism *despair*. See *The Sick-ness unto Death*, Part I, section B (b) (2) pp. 200–207. Jean-Paul

Sartre says, "The best way to conceive of the fundamental project of human reality is to say that man is the being whose project is to be God"; see *Being and Nothingness*, trans. H. E. Barnes, (New York: Washington Square Press, 1966), p. 724, cf. pp. 713–734, 784. Sartre's feeling of *revulsion* in his consciousness of objective-factual existence and his feeling of *shame* in his consciousness of being objectivized by another free locus of consciousness are both ways of realizing that I am *not God*. Concerning revulsion see ibid., pp. 765–784 and *Nausea*, tr. Alexander, (New York: New Directions, 1964). Concerning shame see *Being and Nothingness*, pp. 340–406.

12. See Edmund Bergler, *The Basic Neurosis* (New York: Grune and Stratton, 1949). Although Bergler probes human motivation as a Freudian psychoanalyst, his account of fundamentals is very similar: megalomania and masochism.

13. For Da Free John, a contemporary contemplative, narcissism is the fundamental pattern in human motivation. See *The Knee of Listening* (Clearlake Highlands, Calif.: Dawn Horse Press, 1972) pp. 16–28, 103, 116–121; also *Compulsory Dancing* (Clearlake Highlands, Calif.: Dawn Horse Press, 1978) pp. 7–29. What he primarily associates with narcissism, however, is not a resentment at not-being-god but rather a *fear* of surrendering into God to be lived by God: "Fear is simply our inability to relax, to be surrendered, to feel and breathe fully into the Living Principle, the Great Accomplishing Power in Which we are inhering and Which is now alive as us. . . . Surrender as the physical body into the Living Principle" (*Easy Death*, (Clearlake Highlands, Calif.: Dawn Horse Press, 1983, pp. 117, 179). I find Da Free John more profound than Kierkegaard, who does not adequately challenge the basic fear of surrender into Life that underlies the megalomania and the masochism. As Master Da points out, existentialists make philosophy out of fear or anxiety, as if it were an insightful and authentic state, whereas in reality it is the main self-deceptive obstacle to Love: "Fear is just an ordinary mechanism that you must master, an attitude of the body. It is something that you are doing. It has no ultimate philosophical significance. You can breathe and feel and relax beyond it. . . . Convert the energy that is fear and to which you have been devoting your life. Convert it, since fear no longer has any purpose, to the will to Radiance. . . . Just radiate the feeling. Feel

it so intensely that you shine with it. . . . What you identify as fear is the Life-Energy of the being contracting upon itself and causing an explosive and unpleasant pressure" (pp. 111–112, 116).

14. "It is probable that this *narcissism* is the universal original condition, out of which *object-love* develops later without thereby necessarily effecting a disappearance of the narcissism," Sigmund Freud, *Introductory Lectures on Psychoanalysis,*" tr. J. Riviere, (London: George Allen & Unwin, 1922), p. 347. Compare Sharon MacIsaac, expounding Freud: "The infant is born in a state which Freud described as primary narcissism. In a healthy situation, that self-interest develops to include others in what is essentially the same dynamic" (*Freud and Original Sin,* New York: Paulist Press, 1974, p. 73). For an influential book which insists that narcissism is inescapable, see Ernest Becker, *The Denial of Death* (New York: Free Press, 1973). I criticize Becker's argument in "Ernest Becker's Denial of Life," *Religious Studies Review* 5, no. 1 (January 1979).

15. Surrender *begins* in the heart chakra, but according to Da Free John the physical location of a surrender of the *whole* self, including all its chakras, is slightly to the right of the center of the chest. See *The Knee of Listening,* p. 138, and pp. 134–144, 116–120, 149–150.

16. This is a basic insight in Da Free John, *Compulsory Dancing,* pp. 57–89.

17. It is also remote from most religion today. For example, although some Christian writers have a vision of sexual intercourse as a divine-human sacrament uniting two lovers with each other and God, there is very little recognition of the radical human transformation that this requires, or of the disciplines—psychological, spiritual, and contemplative—that can be utilized. See my "Can Christianity be Good News about Sex?" in *Concilium* (June 1982).

18. Erich Fromm, *Psychoanalysis and Religion* (London: Rutledge and Kegan Paul, 1983), p. 87.

IV. Two Dogmas of Skepticism Concerning Spiritual Reality

1. By *pure reason* I do not mean to imply rationalism as contrasted with empiricism. What I mean by pure or impersonal rea-

son is quite compatible with an emphasis on evidence acquired through experience, provided that the experience is open to *anyone,* regardless of personal differences in character, values, and so on.

2. Although Jean-Paul Sartre's account of existentialist freedom goes beyond, in questionable ways, what I have set forth here, he does provide a very powerful challenge to our self-deceptive evasions of freedom and responsibility. See the essay "Existentialism" in *Existentialism and Human Emotions* (New York: Philosophical Library, Citadel Press, 1957); in other editions the essay is entitled, "Existentialism and Humanism" or "Existentialism Is a Humanism." See also Part One, Chapter Two, "Bad Faith" in *Being and Nothingness.*

3. In Chapter IX I will be exploring this further. See also Gregory Baum, *Religion and Alienation* (New York: Paulist, 1975) and Donald Evans's discussion of Baum in *Faith, Authenticity and Morality* (Toronto: University of Toronto Press, 1980).

4. Not all skepticism is based on references to *actual* errors. Some skepticism is based on the *logical possibility* of error. Such skepticism, however, is based on the arbitrary assumption that only what is logically necessary can be known.

5. If the consequences of believing that *p* is true are regarded only as my own impressions as seen from my perspective, then there is no point to any pragmatic testing of the belief that *p* is true, for I can already appeal to my impressions concerning *p* as seen from my perspective; but then one has not avoided total relativism.

6. Some philosophers have denied that this is possible. For an attempt to refute such a denial, see Donald Evans, "Can Philosophers Limit What Mystics Can Do? A Critique of Steven Katz," *Religious Studies* 25 (Summer 1989) 53–60.

7. For Evelyn Underhill, contemplative awareness means that we would "escape from the terrible museum-like world of daily life, where everything is classified and labeled, and all the graded fluid facts which have no label are ignored. . . . It would mean that we should receive from every flower, not merely a beautiful image to which the label 'flower' has been affixed, but the full impact of its unimaginable beauty and wonder, the direct sensation of life having communion with life." See

Practical Mysticism (Columbus, Ohio: Ariel Press; originally E. P. Dutton, 1914), p. 44.

8. For Martin Buber's contrast between "I-Thou" and "I-It" see his *I and Thou*. For the same basic contrast expressed in other language, see "Elements of the Interhuman," in Martin Buber, *The Knowledge of Man*. Although Buber is very clear concerning the possibility of combining "I-Thou" and "I-It" when contemplating a tree (*I and Thou*, pp. 57–59), he is not as clear concerning this possibility when contemplating a person.

V. Positivism and the Paranormal

1. When I use the term *positivism* I do not restrict this to what in this century has been called *logical positivism*, a distinctive species of positivism which claims that any statement which is unverifiable has no meaning. It is possible to reject this claim while nevertheless insisting that scientific method is the only way to knowledge of reality.

2. For a roughly similar account see E. L. Dellow *Methods of Science: An Introduction to Measuring and Testing for Laymen and Students*, (New York: Universe Books, 1970). The principles I list are not a recipe for making scientific discoveries, but they do reflect the testing procedures used by ordinary scientists in, for example, behavioral psychology, the testing of new drugs, and parapsychology. It is important to realize, however, that many philosophers of science are skeptical concerning attempts to define scientific method. See, for example, Ian Barbour: "At the outset it should be stated that there is no '*scientific method*', no formula with five easy steps guaranteed to lead to discoveries. There are many methods, used at different stages of inquiry, in widely varying circumstances. The clear, systematic schemes of the logicians or of the science teacher's lectures may be far removed from the *ad hoc* procedures and circuitous adventures of the man on the frontier of research" (*Issues in Science and Religion*, Englewood Cliffs, N.J.: Prentice-Hall, 1966, p. 138).

3. The classic treatment of the view that there is no more to causality than "constant conjunction" is, of course, in David Hume, *A Treatise of Human Nature* (Oxford: Clarendon, 1888), p. 87. This view is endorsed by H. Reichenbach, *The Rise of Scientif-*

ic Philosophy (Berkeley: University of California Press, 1963) and by B. Van Fraassen, *The Scientific Image* (Oxford: Clarendon, 1980). Recently Nancy Cartwright has opposed this view in *How the Laws of Physics Lie* (Oxford: Clarendon, 1983).

4. For a discussion of this contrast between two kinds of causality, see Richard Taylor, *Action and Purpose* (Englewood Cliffs, N.J.: Prentice-Hall, 1966), p. 111: "If it is really and unmetaphorically true, as I believe it to be, that I sometimes cause something to happen, this would seem to entail that it is *false* that any event, process or state not identical with myself should be the real cause of it."

5. Darwin's theory of evolution is generally conceded to be scientific, but it is not, strictly speaking, quantifiable. E. L. Dellow, however, says, "Measurement is of the essence of the scientific method. This is not always immediately obvious, and indeed as recently as fifty years ago, it was still possible to do important and original work in some branches of science—mainly in the biological sciences—without making a single measurement. The situation has changed drastically today, and it is now quite clear to all scientists, as it had long been to all physical scientists, that quantitative work is by far the most important aspect of the scientific method" (*Methods of Science*, p. 27).

6. See Bernard R. Grad, "The Biological Effects of the 'Laying on of Hands' on Animals and Plants: Implications for Biology," in Gertrude R. Schmeidler, ed. *Parapsychology, Its Relation to Physics, Biology, Psychology and Psychiatry* (Metuchen, N.J.: Scarecrow Press, 1976), pp. 76–90. In the experiments on mice, Grad did not have other hands as his first control group, but rather used heated electrothermal tapes delivering heat similar to that from the healer's hands. In the experiments on plants, other hands were used.

7. The extent to which concepts used by scientists are theory laden is a matter of debate. In general, the more pervasive scientific theory is alleged to be in shaping our experience, the less stress there is on "scientific method" and the less willingness to grant metaphysical reality to theoretical entities. Influential advocates of a theory-laden approach were N. R. Hanson, *Patterns of Discovery* (Cambridge: Cambridge University Press, 1965) and T. Kuhn, *The Structure of Scientific Revolutions* (Chicago, University of Chicago Press, 1970), Cautions concerning this can be found in Ian

Hacking, *Representing and Intervening* (Cambridge: Cambridge University Press, 1983). It seems to me that contemporary scientific investigations of the paranormal appropriately invoke minimal theory in the concepts used. Eventually, however, if and when sufficient data are accumulated, what Kuhn would call a scientific *revolution* may occur, with new scientific theories functioning as paradigms in explaining both paranormal and normal phenomena.

8. For a painstaking analysis of ascriptions of causation to human agents in court, see H. L. A. Hart and A. M. Honore, *Causation in the Law* (Oxford: University Press, 1959).

9. I am using the word *clairvoyant* in a loose sense here, where it can include some telepathic elements; that is, where someone else's experience may contribute to one's having the paranormal awareness of the event.

10. The example given is made up by me. For a selection of several actual cases drawn from the Proceedings of the Society for Psychical Research, see C. D. Broad, *Lectures on Psychical Research* (London: Routledge and Kegan Paul, 1962) pp. 118–129.

11. C. D. Broad argues that impressive cases involving others are also relevant in increasing the rationality of belief: "In the sporadic cases the odds against chance-coincidence cannot be stated numerically. One can judge only that, in some cases, they are very great; that they are very much greater in this case than in that; and so on. Nevertheless, the ordinary rules of probability hold. In judging the evidence for paranormal agency or for paranormal cognition, we must not, e.g. confine ourselves to this, that, or the other case, taken *severally*. What we have in the end to consider is the probability that *at least one* (no matter which) of all the numerous well attested sporadic cases really *did* happen as reported (and) was *not* a chance-coincidence" (ibid., p. 115). Note that Broad is not arguing that if there are 1000 impressive cases this makes *all* of them more plausible than if there are only 100; rather, this makes it more plausible that at least 1 of the 1000 is genuinely telepathic.

12. Positivism as reliance on scientific method is often accompanied by a conviction that reality is fundamentally *material* and that consciousness has only a derivative reality. Thus the consciousness associated with the arrangements of matter which we call *human beings* is dependent of changes in matter for its contents.

That is, for every change in consciousness there is allegedly a brain change which not only accompanies it but actually causes it. We should note that such materialism is not an intrinsic part of scientific method as such. Rather, it is a metaphysical belief held by many scientists, a belief that has spread into the general public.

13. The insistence that scientific tests must be repeatable *at will* if causal connections are to be shown involves scientists in a contradiction unless willed human behavior is assumed to be outside deterministic causal connections. On the one hand, there is a sense of oneself as an independent will, as the origin of one's own decisions and actions, as an agent who causes events. When I move my arm voluntarily, *I* cause it to move. When I repeat an experiment, *I* cause the initial event(s) in the experiment. On the other hand, there is the scientific view of oneself as a material body conditioned by physical stimuli in a deterministic way. When I move my arm some external stimulus causes a brain change which in turn causes the arm movement. When I initiate the experiment it is not really I, but some material stimulus. Since our culture's commonsense view includes both liberalism's *agent* causality and science's *mechanical* causality, and since science itself presupposes agent causality in its methodology, a serious problem arises. Usually we deal with it by not facing it. Instead, we alternate the perspectives. When I am pondering a choice between alternatives and then choose one and enact it, I cannot at the same time be viewing myself as totally determined; so I forget about science then. But on other occasions I ignore the fact that I am making decisions and acting on them—for example while I am doing a scientific experiment—and I focus on the causes at work. This is much easier when the focus is outside myself, that is, on something else or someone else. To view *myself* deterministically I have to be considering my past or future actions, not what I am doing right now.

14. For an outline of some scientific studies of both remote viewing and psychokinesis, see Russell Targ and Harold E. Puthoff, *Mind-Reach: Scientists Look at Psychic Ability* (New York: Dell, 1977).

15. Henri Bergson, in his 1913 presidential address to the Society for Psychical Research, London, argued that all one needs is one impressive case for it to be rational to believe that telepathy has occurred. The case under discussion was one where the wife of an officer allegedly had a clear vision of her husband's death in battle

at the time when it occurred. Bergson says that even if the woman had had thousands of false visions he would be convinced concerning telepathy "if I could be sure that even the countenance of one soldier unknown to her, present at the scene, had appeared to her such as it was in reality." See his *Mind-Energy* (Westport, Conn.: Greenwood Press; reprint from New York: Henry Holt and Co., 1975), p. 85. In stark contrast with this, William D. Gray says, "It is very clear what would prove that ESP *does* exist. If a person consistently scored 99 percent on carefully controlled ESP tests for several years under conditions precluding the possibility of cheating and could perform for skeptics as well as believers, this would be convincing evidence of ESP" (*Thinking Critically About New Age Ideas*, Belmont, Calif.: Wadsworth, 1991, pp. 87–88). He goes on to say, "It is a fundamental principle of science that if a phenomenon occurs once, it will occur again, if the conditions are the same. Thus it is possible for one scientist to test the claim of another scientist by copying the procedure to see whether the result is the same. This is called a *replication study*. Replication studies are required in science" (p. 121). It is true that replication studies are required in science, but the issue is whether science is the only way to knowledge of reality. On this score Gray's position seems to be positivist, for all that he excludes from the range of science are private, subjective states and ascriptions of meaning or value (see pp. 90, 139). For Gray, statements about God, the soul, life after death, and spirits are "empirically meaningless" (p. 40).

16. "In analyzing an experiment that purports to prove ESP, it is wise to adopt initially the assumption that ESP is impossible, *just as it is assumed that the conjuror cannot saw the same girl in half twice each evening.*" "If the result *could* have arisen through a trick, the experiment must be considered unsatisfactory proof of ESP, *whether or not it is finally decided that such a trick was in fact used.* C. E. M. Hansel, *ESP and Parapsychology: A Scientific Reevaluation* (New York: Prometheus Books, 1980), pp. 19, 18, my italics). According to Hansel, "If their [parapsychologists'] claims are justified, a complete revision in contemporary scientific thought is required at least comparable to that made necessary in biology by Darwin and in physics by Einstein" (pp. 7–8). Fortunately the critics of Darwin and Einstein did not successfully put the onus on Darwin or Einstein to disprove charges of fraud! For a further discussion of issues concerning the requirement that parapsychologists disprove fraud, see Jan Ludwig, ed., *Philosophy and*

Parapsychology (New York: Prometheus Books, 1979), section II, pp. 145–204.

17. Thus far the case as reported is an actual one, reported by Ian Currie in *You Cannot Die* (New York: Methuen, 1978), pp. 218–220. Currie cites Jeffrey Iverson, *More Lives Than One? The Evidence of the Remarkable Bloxham Tapes* (New York: Warner Books, 1977) pp. 66–67. I do not know whether the reporter described how the crypt looks now, rather than how it did in 1189, or indeed whether there is any such describable difference; but in a hypothetical case there might be, so that clairvoyance could be ruled out.

VI. Positivism and the Genuinely Spiritual

1. This has come to be my own hunch concerning Martin Buber when he attacks mysticism (*I and Thou*, pp. 131–143). More plausible, but still questionable, is Abhishiktananda, who reports having gone through an empty-mind or nondualistic state and then "beyond" this to a state of participation in the Holy Trinity. See his *Saccindananda, A Christian Approach to Advaitic Experience* (Delhi: I.S.P.C.K., 1974).

2. For an excellent outline and discussion of such theorists (e.g., Sheldrake, Bohm, and Prigogine), see David Toolan, *Facing West from California's Shores; A Jesuit's Journey into New Age Consciousness* (New York: Crossroad, 1987), pp. 179–253.

3. My own antirealist philosophy of natural science developed in the 1950s and 1960s, when I was influenced by such thinkers as P. W. Bridgman, *The Logic of Modern Physics* (New York: Macmillan, 1960) and Stephen Toulmin, *The Philosophy of Science* (London: Hutchinson, 1953). For Bridgman, "the concept of length involves as much as and nothing more than the set of operations by which length is determined" (ibid., p. 5). For Toulmin the question, "Do electrons exist?" is analogous to the question, "Do contours exist?" and his answer to the latter question can be summarized as follows: contours do not exist in the sense that there are visible marks corresponding to them on the ground for us to point to; they are cartographical fictions. Yet they do "exist" in the sense that talk about contours should not be discredited or discarded, like talk about unicorns, for "contour" is a useful explanatory concept (see

ibid., pp. 135–137.) During the last decade or so, although antirealism has continued in such distinguished philosophers of science as Bas Van Fraassen (*The Scientific Image*), realism concerning theoretical entities had been strongly endorsed by Ian Hacking (*Representing and Intervening*) and Nancy Cartwright (*How the Laws of Physics Lie*). The controversy is explored from both sides in a symposium edited by J. Leplin, *Scientific Realism* (Berkeley: University of California Press, 1984). I am grateful to Valerie Schweitzer for bringing me more up to date concerning the controversy in the 1980s.

VII. Mystical Humanism and Morality

1. This chapter was originally published in H. A. Meynell, ed., *Religion and Irreligion* (Calgary: University of Calgary Press, 1985). I have shortened or deleted many of the philosophical notes that appeared in the original. Readers who wish to study my position, or Nielsen's, in greater detail, should consult the Meynell volume, which also contains Nielsen's reply. The exchange took place at a conference on Religion and Irreligion at the University of Calgary in 1983.

2. A list of the articles from the late 1970s and early 1980s follows, with the abbreviations that will be used in subsequent notes:

CJA: "Considered Judgments Again," *Human Studies* 5 (1982): 109–18.

DML: "Death and the Meaning of Life," *Proceedings of the International Conference on the Unity of the Sciences* (New York: International Cultural Foundation Press, 1977).

GBM: "God and the Basis of Morality," *Journal of Religious Ethics* 10, no. 2 (Fall 1982): 335–350.

GR: "Grounding Rights and a Method of Reflective Equilibrium," *Inquiry* 25: 277–306.

NMT: "On Needing a Moral Theory: Rationality, Considered Judgments and the Grounding of Morality," *Metaphilosophy* 13, no. 2 (April 1982): 97–116.

PT: "Politics and Theology: Do We Need a Political Theology?" in Benjamin G. Smillie, ed., *Political Theology in the Canadian Context* (Waterloo: Wilfred Laurier University Press, 1982), pp. 61–98.

RGB: "On the Rationality of Groundless Believing," *Idealistic Studies* 11, no. 3 (September 1980): 215–229.

RR: "Religion and Rationality," in Mostafa Faghfoury, ed., *Analytic Philosophy of Religion in Canada* (Ottawa: University of Ottawa Press, 1982), pp. 71–124.

SB: "Skepticism and Belief: A Reply to Benoit Garceau," *Dialogue* 22, no. 3 (September 1983): 391–403.

3. My conception of morality includes much more than what many philosophers envisage; that is, much more than action guides concerning behavior that impinges, directly and dramatically, on others' "welfare." I include not only action guides concerning welfare but also *being* guides, that is; answers to "What ought or ought not I to *be*? I should note that my conception of morality involves both (a) universal *rules* whose violation is appropriately condemned and in some cases appropriately *punished* by law and (b) universal ideals whose nonrealization is appropriately *regretted* rather than condemned and is never appropriately punished by law. I agree with modern liberal moralists that when additions are made to the universal rules of a minimal moral code on the basis of religious claims these additions should usually be understood not as additional rules in the code but rather as proposed universal ideals. Also, such universal ideals can be realized in a great variety of individual ways. Nevertheless such additions should sometimes be understood as universal rules, and then there may be a serious conflict between secular morality and religious morality.

4. Kai Nielsen, *SB*, p. 399.

5. The notion of an overdetermining set of reasons may seem initially puzzling, but it is a commonplace in everyday moral and empirical reflection, for example, "I always ought to try to rescue a child in danger, and when it was my own daughter there was even more reason to do so" or "Either the testimony of a reliable eyewitness or a freely signed confession would provide an adequate reason for establishing that Jones killed Brown but in this case we have both reasons."

6. I agree with Nielsen when he says, "God or no God, some actions can be appreciated to be desirable and some as through

and through evil and despicable" (*GBM*, p. 336). He goes on to say, however, "If there is no reason that torturing little children could cease to be bad in a godless world, we have no reason to believe that, in any important sense, morality is dependent on religion" (*GBM*, p. 344). By a similar mode of reasoning, someone would have to claim that, if there is no reason to believe that torturing little children would cease to be bad in a society where humans are merely sentient animals, we have no reason to believe that, in any important sense, morality is dependent on a secular understanding of human beings as being fulfilled in love (loving and being loved). If only a minimal moral code is regarded as "important'," then both claims are plausible.

7. My formal conception of religion in this chapter differs from my formal conception of morality in that, whereas the latter does, I think, correspond to what many people in various cultures think of as "morality," the former is a conception of religion that arises from an *esoteric* perspective on what most people in various cultures think of as religion, namely, exoteric religion.

8. Nielsen, *SB*, p. 402.

9. Ibid., pp. 394–396.

10. Nielsen queries the very intelligibility of most of Garceau's talk about human freedom in relation to God. For Garceau, the possibility of becoming a person is "the possibility of being liberated from all things, including the thing that he is, this being actualized only in as much as he gives himself to a Presence that is in him the source of freedom" (quoted in Nielsen, *SB*, p. 400). The opaqueness of Garceau for Nielsen arises not only because Garceau is talking about God but also because Garceau's conception of freedom is different even in *non*religious contexts. For Nielsen, freedom seems to be a freedom to do what I choose, whatever that may be, a freedom from external and internal compulsions or impediments (see ibid., p. 400). Another agent could "liberate" him by removing such constraints, but Nielsen seems to see any influence on his *choice* as a reduction of his freedom (cf. Kant and early Sartre). For Garceau, as for Buber and Marcel, another agent can increase my freedom where freedom is my ability to "become what I am"; that is, my ability to realize my inherent capaci-

ties and inclinations. I must freely consent to the other's influence if it is to do its work; hence the change in me is wrought by both of us. In such a view, God as pervasive spiritual agent can by analogy liberate me when I encounter Him, enabling me to be most genuinely free, enabling me to recognize and choose and become that which genuinely fulfils me as a human being. This goes beyond merely being free from obstacles to doing whatever I choose. What genuinely fulfills us? In Garceau's contemplative view, we are fulfilled in a life freed from attachment to all things and freed from the self-preoccupied mode of existence which is otherwise our self-imposed bondage. It is arguable that most esoteric and some exoteric religion in both East and West pertains to liberation from a mode of existence by a spiritual power or in a spiritual process. Liberation is experienced as *enabling* one to realize what one truly is: a child of God, Brahman-Atman, Nirvana-Samsarsa.

11. Basil Mitchell, *Morality: Religious and Secular* (Oxford: Clarendon Press, 1980) p. 148.

12. Quoted by Mitchell, ibid., p. 148.

13. "The falsity lies in making God into an infinite false self, an infinite ego that jealously guards his life against all who would approach.' Thus James Finley, drawing on Merton's *The New Man*, expounds a central theme in Merton. See *Merton's Palace of Nowhere* (Notre Dame, Ind.: Ave Maria Press, 1978), p. 75.

14. Nielsen, *SB*, pp. 397–398.

15. Nielsen, *GBM*, 337–339.

16. Concerning the distinction between submission to external agents and surrender into God, see Donald Evans, "Faith versus Sin" in *Analytic Philosophy of Religion in Canada*, pp. 261–268.

17. Nielsen, *PT*, p. 64; *GBM*, pp. 337–339.

18. Nielsen, *PT*, 70.

19. I should note, however, that where Nielsen might dismiss childish forms of Western theism, I am more tolerant of some of them. In particular, as I have indicated in my book *Struggle and Fulfillment*, I see *stages* through which people grow psy-

chologically, with corresponding changes in their idea of God. The earlier stages are not to be despised, for everyone, whether explicitly religious or not, has to go through them in the process of maturation, and virtually everyone retains them partially and reverts to them at times. For example, if a person's pervasive trust comes to predominate over his or her pervasive distrust, this is progress—even if the person is still, like most people, radically narcissistic, preoccupied with whether or not he or she is loved rather than opened up to loving. If in our distrust we feel unloved, we are incapable of loving; hence a trustful acceptance of love is a significant step. and it is one to which we need to return again and again, as the crises of life tilt us back into our childish preoccupations. In relation to God, as in relation to one's spouse, a denial of the infant inside us is inappropriate. The self-preoccupation of, say, the 23rd Psalm has its legitimate though subordinate place alongside the lofty love of Corinthians 13. Moreover, I am convinced on the basis of personal experience that there is a vast and complex spiritual realm in which the creative and loving energies of God are experienced with varied degrees of distortion and transparency, corresponding to the various stages of human maturation and transformation. So I do not dismiss relatively primitive forms of Christian faith and of other religious faith if they are part of this process of development. But I agree with Nielsen that these are not based on experiences of *God* as such. I disagree, of course, in that I hold that they are experiences of the revelatory energies of God.

20. For me the "ledger" of good and harm as appraised solely in secular terms emerges somewhat on the debit side. But even if we consider good and harm as recognized from a humanistic mystical perspective (which includes secular values but goes beyond them), the ledger is difficult to balance. This is partly, or course, because the notion of a "ledger" here is especially dubious. How does one measure the life of St. Francis or the Passion of Jesus against, say, the sack of Constantinople or Christian persecution of the Jews?

21. *SB*, pp. 398–399; cf. *DML*, 346.

22. Nielsen asks, "Can we not . . . live in accordance with the . . . hope that we humans *can attain a certain rationality and come to see things whole* and in time make real, through our struggles, a truly human society without exploitation and

degradation, in which all human beings will flourish?" (*DML*, p. 346, my italics).

23. Nielsen, *GR*, p. 283.

24. Only when technical reason is temporarily set aside do we become deeply aware of what it is in ourselves and others that warrants the respect and concern that is independent of ordinary public observation and that is ordinarily mostly repressed: passions, spirit, and soul.

25. See Nielsen, *NMT*. p. 99; *DML*, pp. 341, 343; *PT*, p. 75; *GBM*, p. 344.

26. See Nielsen, *PT*, p. 70; *GR*, p. 284.

27. See Nielsen, *PT*, p. 72.

28. See *GR*, especially p. 290, and *NMT*, especially pp. 107–110; also *CJA*.

29. See Nielsen, *GR*, pp. 289–290; *NMT*, pp. 107–108.

30. See Nielsen, *CJA*, pp. 110–111, 114; *NMT*, p. 113.

31. Nielsen, *GR*, p. 301.

32. See Nielsen, *NMT*, p. 109.

33. See Nielsen, *GR*, p. 284, my italics.

34. See Nielsen, *NMT*, p. 116.

35. Nielsen himself holds (*NMT*, p. 115) that only if WRE were so wide as to "cover agreement in world-views" would it bring moral agreement.

36. For example, *GR*, p. 287, and *SB*, p. 399.

37. See Nielsen, *DML*, p. 344; *PT*, p. 77; *GBM*, p. 346. My own view is that even on a secular perspective we can *discover* (though we doubtless also create) meaning and purpose in that we discover inherent needs and interests that human beings share and that provide a rational basis for moral action which tries to fulfil these needs and interests.

38. See Nielsen *GR*, p. 279, and *SB*, pp. 398–399.

39. I have conflated two versions (Vlastos's and Dworkin's) cited by Nielsen in *GR*, p. 279.

40. See, for example, Nielsen, *GR*, p. 303.

41. See Nielsen, *SB*, p. 399.

42. See Nielsen, *GR*, p. 303.

43. Ibid., p. 287.

44. See ibid., pp. 293–300

45. Perhaps Nielsen's acknowledgment of how difficult it is for us to answer this question leads him, in his defense of egalitarianism, to focus on secondary issues concerning the possibility of less qualitative differences among people. Here is his acknowledgment: "When we say all human beings have a right to an equality of concern and respect because they all share some common characteristic, we are likely to find that this is, on the one hand, false, or, on the other, that the characteristic in question is of doubtful relevance, or (like capacities to experience pain or to be just) people have it in various ways and to various degrees, which appear, at least on the surface, to be morally relevant" (ibid., p. 286).

46. This is the esoteric theme of the otherwise very exoteric religious movie, *Return of the Jedi*.

47. For a discussion of this distinction, see Donald Evans, *Faith, Authenticity and Morality* (Toronto: University of Toronto Press, 1980), pp. 247–253. Nielsen claims (*SB*, p. 393) that Evans-Pritchard "understood Azande witchcraft practices very well indeed, but his mind was firmly shut concerning the very possibility of there really being witches." But if there really are witches, that is, people who know how to influence others psychicially for good or ill— and I am completely convinced that there are—then Evans-Pritchard's "understanding" of their practices is a paradigm of linguistic-behavioral understanding accompanied by minimal experiential understanding—like a totally deaf sociologist at a rock concert. Perhaps there will be in the future competent anthropologists who also share some of the mediumistic or shamanistic or witchcraft abilities of the people they are studying, being able, for example, to discern the spirit which is possessing an individual to see whether it departs when the witch brings discernable counterenergies to bear on it. Perhaps such anthropologists already exist, but cannot openly admit their talents in an academic setting.

48. For example, Nielsen, *SB*, p. 393.

49. Ibid., pp. 395–396, 398, 401. Nielsen is considering alleged experiential bases for claiming that a (nonmystical) God exists. But his position seems to be the same concerning any spiritual claims, for example, concerning the soul.

VIII. On the Nature and Origin of Good and Evil in Human Beings

1. This chapter is a revised version of an essay presented at a conference in honor of Paul Ricoeur at the University of Ottawa. The proceedings were edited by Theodore Geraets and published in the *University of Ottawa Quarterly* (December 1985.

2. David Frum, "Crime and Punishment," *Saturday Night* [Toronto] (October 1983), pp. 11–13.

3. Soren Kierkegaard, *The Sickness unto Death.*

4. Gabriel Marcel, *The Mystery of Being*, (Chicago: Henry Regnery, 1960), vol. 1, chs. 5, 6.

5. Louis Lavelle, *The Dilemma of Narcissus* (London: George Allen and Unwin, 1973).

6. Da Free John (Franklin Jones), *The Knee of Listening; The Paradox of Instruction* (Clearlake Highlands, Calif.: Dawn Horse Press, 1978).

7. Chogyam Trungpa, *Cutting Through Spiritual Materialism* (Boulder, Colo., and London: Shambhala, 1973).

8. Martin Buber, *Good and Evil* (New York: Scribners, 1952).

9. Kierkegaard, *The Sickness unto Death.*

10. Soren Kierkegaard, *The Concept of Dread*, trans. Walter Lowrie (Princeton; N.J.: Princeton University Press, 1957).

11. For an example of what I call the *cynical* view, see Ernest Becker, *The Denial of Death.* For an exposition and criticism of Becker, see Donald Evans, "Ernest Becker's Denial of Life." Becker claims that narcissism is inescapable, for it has a biological basis in human nature. Each person as an organism has an inbuilt tendency to incorporate and expand and protect himself or herself against the world. As a conscious, symbol-

making organism one expresses this tendency in narcissism. That is, in one's imagination one inflates oneself to cosmic proportions so as to include the whole world within oneself, becoming *the* center of power and reality and value in the universe. Instead of being dependent on anything or anyone else for one's existence and significance one tries to be one's own parent, "the creator and sustainer of his own life." One's project is to be one's own god—glorious, self-sufficient, and omnipotent. Like a god one would be *causa sui* (cause of oneself) and like a god one would "recreate the whole world" out of oneself. According to Becker this megalomaniac fantasy of divinity, though repressed, is at work in all of us. It is manifested in the many diverse "heroic" projects of humankind, all of which are ways of pretending that we are gods. Each person is moved by a narcissistic desire to stand out from others, showing one's superiority, making a special imprint on the universe, proving oneself in an alien world, running first in the race of life.

12. Erik Erikson's developmental psychology sees in human beings a succession of tendencies to *relate* to other human beings mutually and creatively. These tendencies begin to emerge in early infancy and continue through various stages in human life. Their actualization requires appropriate responses from others, especially in early infancy, but in each case the predisposition to become positively involved with other people is inherent in us as human beings. In early infancy the initiatives come more from others than from us, but there is some mutuality. In adult life there can be intimate mutual love between husband and wife and a deep parental concern for the next generation. If the natural inclination to become involved with others is frustrated in childhood, it is repressed. Narcissistic self-sufficiency than becomes dominant over the natural yearning to relate. See *Childhood and Society*, 2d ed. (New York: W. W. Norton, 1963), chs. 2, 7.

13. See Wilhelm Reich, *The Murder of Christ*, especially, ch. 3.

14. Gabriel Marcel, *Homo Viator* (New York: Harper, 1962), especially pp. 13–28.

15. Paul Ricoeur, *Fallible Man* (Chicago: Henry Regnery, 1967).

16. Paul Ricoeur, *The Symbolism of Evil* (New York: Harper and Row, 1967).

17. Ricoeur, *Fallible Man*, pp. 156, 129.

18. Ricoeur, *The Symbolism of Evil*, pp. 3, 15, 19, 25–29, 33.

IX. Spirituality and Social Action

1. This chapter is a revised version of a paper presented at a Buddhist-Christian conference on spirituality and social action at York University, Toronto, in June 1984. The paper was published in Stanley Fefferman, ed., *Awakened Heart: Buddhist-Christian Dialogue in Canada* (Toronto: United Church House, 1985).

2. Eckhart uses the metaphor of the "virgin" to depict the first kind of contemplative awareness, with its total detachment from images and from self: "The word *virgin* means a person who is free of all false images and who is detached as if he or she did not yet exist" (p. 273). Eckhart uses the metaphor of the fruitful "wife" to depict the subsequent stage: "It is good for a person to receive God into herself, and in this receptivity she is a virgin. But it is better for God to become fruitful within the person. . . . A virgin who is also a wife, and who is free and liberated and without ego attachment is always equally close to God and herself. She bears much fruit, and the fruit is of good size. It is no less nor more than God himself (pp. 274–275). For Eckhart this unity of the divine and the human, the eternal and the temporal, somehow takes place in the soul: "The soul, as it were, was created at that point which divides time from eternity; it touches both of these points. With its highest faculties the soul touches both of these points. With its highest faculties the soul touches eternity, with its lowest, however, it is in touch with time. That is why the soul acts in time,not according to time, but in accordance with eternity" (p. 116). When Eckhart disappears into the imageless divine eternity what then emerges is divine creativity, like a womb constantly giving birth. And not only is the Son of the heavenly Father born there, but "*you* also are born there as a child of the same heavenly Father" (p. 301). And then one is reborn into the world, for "It would mean little to me that the 'Word was made flesh' for man in Christ, granting that the latter is distinct from me, unless he also was made flesh in me person-

ally, so that I too would become the Son of God" (p. 311). All quotations are from *Breakthrough, ed. Matthew Fox.*

X. Spirituality and Christian Openness to Other Faiths

1. This chapter is a revised version of an essay published in Wesley Cragg, ed., *Challenging the Conventional: Essays in Honour of Ed Newbery* (Berlington, Ont.: Trinity Press, 1989). The chapter includes brief explorations of many complex and controversial issues that I investigate more thoroughly not only in previous chapters of the book but also in three published essays: "Mysticism and Morality," *Dialogue* 24 (1985); "Relativism and Religious Tolerance," *Toronto Journal of Theology* (Fall 1987) "Conflicting Paradigms of Conversion," in *Being and Truth* A. Kee and Eugene Long, Eds., London: SCM Press, 1986).

2. I first saw this analogy in a doctoral thesis for the Department of Philosophy, University of Toronto: Robert Gibbs, "Responsibility in Community" (1985) ch. 5.

XI. Spiritual Reality, Academic Skepticism, and Transfiguration

1. This chapter was published in L. D. Hurst and N. T. Wright, eds. *The Glory of Christ in the New Testament* (Oxford: Clarendon Press, 1987).

2. As J. L. Austin pointed out in a lecture at Oxford during the 1950s, psychological experiments show that people can distinguish colors even when they have no words to mark the distinction, philosophers should qualify their claim that we only experience reality *through* language and thus can never justify our linguistic distinctions by reference to nonlinguistic experience.

3. Susanne K. Langer, *Mind: an Essay on Human Feeling*, vol. 3 (Baltimore; John Hopkins Press, 1982). My remarks concerning Langer are selected from a lengthy review in *Commonweal* (July 15, 1983).

4. George B. Caird, *Principalities and Powers* (Oxford; Clarendon Press 1956), p. x. Caird's nonfundamentalism is evident in

many parts of the book, for example his commentary on 1 Cor. 11:10f. (pp. 17–21) where he criticizes St. Paul's "faulty logic and equally faulty exegesis" and his "spurious arguments."

5. George B. Caird, *Saint Luke*, (Harmondsworth, Middlesex: Penguin Books 1963), p. 132. Caird, "The Transfiguration," *Expository Times* vol. 67 (1955–1956): p. 291.

6. J. W. C. Wand, *Transfiguration* (London: 1967).

7. Ibid., p. 24, cf. p. 26.

8. Ibid., pp. 27–28.

9. Cf. Caird's early work "The New Testament Conception of Doxa" (unpublished Ph.D. thesis, Oxford University, 1944).

10. Wand, *Transfiguration*, pp. 40, 31–32.

11. Ibid., p. 62.

12. Ibid., p. 51.

13. Some form critics take the opposite view. For them the story is so obviously false that they see the authors of the Gospels as here writing a legend to *create* an aura or halo around Christ! For an outline and rejection of this perspective see Eugène Dabrowski, *La Transfiguration de Jésus* (Rome; Institute Biblique Pontifical 1939), pp. 36–42.

14. W. R. F. Browning allows that some saints may have been transfigured: "It cannot be irrelevant that a similar radiance, transforming the whole bodily appearance is recorded of some of the saints and other persons of sanctity. . . . If the Transfiguration of Jesus had no natural cause, it is credible that a similar radiance should be experienced by the saints, for 'the glory which thou hast given me I have given unto them' (John 17:22)." *The Gospel According to St. Mark, Introduction and Commentary* (London: SCM Press, 1960), pp. 100–101. For Browning such phenomena are either supernatural or paranormal. The latter may seem to resemble the former but they are "imitative and merely universal." Indeed, he implies that paranormal phenomena are "explicable *psychologically* without recourse to the supernatural" (p. 101, my italics). Browning has only two pigeonholes: supernatural versus natural-paranormal-psychological. He has no intermediate category, that is no place for a natural event which is not merely psychological

because it is objectively *spiritual.* Such an event may, or may not, involve a supernatural surrender to, and transfiguration *by the divine Source.*

15. 2 Cor. 3:18–24: 6, New American bible translation. Concerning a luminous human being *outshone* by the divine Light, see the non-Christian spiritual teacher, Da Free John: "I surrender body and mind and all self-attention to the Living God. . . . Who Shines above the head of those who are Awake, Transforming every part of them with Heart-Light, Who is the Transcendental Heart, the Eternal Mystery, the Wonderful Truth, the Unyielding Paradox that finally Outshines the souls of all beings, every part of the body-mind of Man and all the possible places in the worlds of experience" (*Compulsory Dancing,* p. 141).

Postscript

1. New York: Amity House, 1985.

2. Ibid., pp. 529–530.

3. See p. 90 in this book.

4. See Dorothy Dinnerstein, *The Mermaid and the Minotaur* (New York: Harper and Row, 1977). She combines insights from psychoanalysis and evolutionary anthropology and stresses the typically different strategies of response by male infants and female infants.

5. See David Toolan, *Facing West from California's Shores,* especially ch. 4.

6. See Soren Kierkegaard, *The Concept of Anxiety* (Princeton, N.J.: Princeton University Press, 1980) especially pp. 35–61.

7. See Da Free John, *The Paradox of Instruction* (Clearlake Highlands, Calif.: Dawn Horse Press, 1977), especially ch. 1.

8. See p. 240 in this book.

Index

✳